KEY ISSUES IN SPECIAL EDUCATIONAL NEEDS, DISABILITY & INCLUSION

Education Studies: Key Issues Series

In the last two decades Education Studies has developed rapidly as a distinctive subject in its own right. Beginning initially at undergraduate level, this has grown at Master's level and is characterised by an increasingly analytical approach to the study of education. As education studies programmes have developed there have emerged a number of discrete study areas that require in-depth texts to support student learning.

The central book in the series is *Introduction to Education Studies*, Fourth Edition (Spring 2016) which gives students an important grounding in the study of education. The 'Key Issues in Education Studies' texts have evolved from this and use the same critical approach. Each volume outlines a significant area of study and all of the books have been written by experts in their area to provide the detail and depth required by students as they progress further in the subject.

Taken as a whole, this series provides a comprehensive set of texts for the student of education. Whilst of particular value to students of Education Studies, the series will also be instructive for those studying related areas such as Childhood Studies and Special Needs, as well as being of interest to students on initial teacher training courses and practitioners working in education.

We hope that this series provides you, the reader, with plentiful opportunities to explore further this exciting and significant area of study and we wish you well in your endeavours.

Steve Bartlett and Diana Burton

Series Editors

Books in the series

Steve Bartlett and Diana Burton: *Introduction to Education Studies, Fourth Edition* (2016)
Diana Burton and Steve Bartlett: *Key Issues for Education Researchers* (2009)
Alan Hodkinson: *Key Issues in Special Educational Needs and Inclusion, Second Edition* (2016)
Emma Smith: *Key Issues in Education and Social Justice* (2012)
Stephen Ward and Christine Eden: *Key Issues in Education Policy* (2009)

KEY ISSUES IN SPECIAL EDUCATIONAL NEEDS, DISABILITY & INCLUSION

3RD EDITION

ALAN HODKINSON

Los Angeles | London | New Delhi
Singapore | Washington DC | Melbourne

Los Angeles | London | New Delhi
Singapore | Washington DC | Melbourne

SAGE Publications Ltd
1 Oliver's Yard
55 City Road
London EC1Y 1SP

SAGE Publications Inc.
2455 Teller Road
Thousand Oaks, California 91320

SAGE Publications India Pvt Ltd
B 1/I 1 Mohan Cooperative Industrial Area
Mathura Road
New Delhi 110 044

SAGE Publications Asia-Pacific Pte Ltd
3 Church Street
#10-04 Samsung Hub
Singapore 049483

Editor: Delayna Spencer
Assistant editor: Orsod Malik
Production editor: Imogen Roome
Copyeditor: Aud Scriven
Indexer: Adam Pozner
Marketing manager: Lorna Patkai
Cover design: Wendy Scott
Typeset by: C&M Digitals (P) Ltd, Chennai, India
Printed in the UK

Library of Congress Control Number: 2019933550

British Library Cataloguing in Publication data

A catalogue record for this book is available from
the British Library

ISBN 978-1-5264-8397-3
ISBN 978-1-5264-8396-6 (pbk)

Despite working in this area for three decades, I continue to be inspired by the children, young people, parents and professionals who inhabit the world of SEND. This book is dedicated to all those who seek to work together to provide a world where children and young people with SEND are valued and respected.

To Fin, Zac and Helen: a day never passes where I do not think of the light you have brought into my life. Thank you for walking this journey with me and 'putting up' with my selfishness as I worked to bring this third edition to completion.

To Professors Steve Bartlett and Diana Burton: I have you to thank for this book. I remember with fond memory how you encouraged me to write the first edition. I never believed I was capable of such an undertaking but you always did. Thank you for the faith you placed in me, and the support you have offered me throughout my career. I shall be forever grateful.

And finally, to all the students and staff, past and present, in the Department of Disability and Education at Liverpool Hope University. You are an inspiration – your passion and dedication to your studies and work provide the energy that keeps me going.

Alan Hodkinson

CONTENTS

LIST OF FIGURES AND TABLES

FIGURES

TABLES

ABOUT THE AUTHOR

Alan Hodkinson was for many years a special educational needs co-ordinator and senior manager in the primary school sector. Currently, he is an Associate Professor for Learning Support in Schools, in the Department of Disability and Education at Liverpool Hope University.

PREFACE TO THIRD EDITION

The first edition of *Key Issues in Special Educational Needs and Inclusion* provided a starting point for students to engage in informed debate about the complexity of SEND and inclusion that existed within the first decade of the 21st century. The second edition updated the text by examining and exemplifying the 'radical overhaul' of SEND and inclusion that has taken place since 2010. This edition took a more critical stance to inclusion and how its conceptual underpinning was defined through policy and the manner in which it was operationalised in schools. A student review of the book emplaced on a well-known shopping website stated that the book was:

> Most useful for an essay on SEND as background. The writing isn't too dry and academic, so I managed to stay awake for more than 4 pages, which must be a record when it comes to academic studies of education. Pleased I got it ...

I have found in conversations with my students that they too like the book as it is easy to read and enabled them to understand the sometimes-difficult concepts that underpin the study of SEND.

INCLUSION – MOVING FORWARD BUT STANDING STILL?

It is now forty years since the publication of the Warnock Report and twenty years since the Salamanca Statement and we again stand at a crossroads in relation to SEND policy and practice. It is unclear, at this time, whether current government interventions will pay dividends in relation to the quality and consistency of the SEND practice that children and young people experience in early years settings, primary and secondary schools and tertiary education. This third edition specifically updates the text in relation to the operationalisation of the 2014 Children and Families Act, and how professionals, parents, young people and children have responded to its Code of Practice. In addition, responding to the constructive criticisms provided by the anonymous reviewers, this edition has introduced more materials that relate to mental health and how SEND might be considered from early years through to further education settings. It is hoped that these revisions will enable students to find continued value in this text as an introduction to special educational needs and inclusion.

CONTEXT OF THE BOOK

SEND and inclusion provide an area which is both complex and multifaceted. This is a world where professionals, families and administrators co-exist with each other, and despite their sometimes competing agendas have to ensure that through their 'best endeavours' children and young people's needs are met. This world though has another side – that of government departments, educational and health policies, civil servants and the public at large. This 'underworld' provides the political will which confirms, conforms and constrains the systems and processes of SEND and inclusive provision that children and young people experience in their educational journeys through our schooling system. This world has in recent times been subject to change as in 2014 the government radically overhauled policies relating to SEND. In creating its policy, government articulated that it was responding to the frustrations of children and families to the landmark educational policy of the last Labour government, namely that of inclusion.

The study of such policy and practice transformation, within the context of SEND and inclusion, necessitates students' recognition of the complex interplay between these two worlds (Norwich, 2000). SEND exist upon a continuum of abilities and impairments and sometimes there is no clear-cut distinction between those who have SEND and those who have not (Terzi, 2005). Conceptualising differences such as disability, impairment and the SEND of children and young people upon this continuum is complicated and often fraught with difficulties, not least in that we are dealing with an individual's life, hopes and aspirations. There are many competing views as to the definition of SEND and impairment and how these affect children and young people in early years settings, schools and colleges. Perhaps most contentious of all, certainly in light of the government's 'radical overhaul' of SEND policies, is how and indeed where educational provision for these children and young people should be organised.

USES OF THE BOOK

This volume explores and critically examines the world of SEND and inclusion. It will raise students' awareness of the key issues and concepts that dominate this world by providing a perspective of the ideological and political debates that have shaped its historical and current development. Whilst catalogues of publishing houses (Nind, 2005) and journals are bursting with titles which relate to SEND and inclusion, a closer examination of such material reveals that many texts assume a level of knowledge, understanding and sometimes practical experience that many students may not possess. The aim of this book, therefore, is to provide a starting point to enable students to develop a basic knowledge and understanding so that they might be better able to engage in a meaningful, informed and critical discussion of the issues that dominate SEND and inclusion. Whilst this text is not intended for teacher trainees or early years students, many such students have found previous editions of this text a useful supplement to their studies. However, in the space allowed in a text such as this, one cannot hope to provide in-depth information or detail teaching strategies, which relate to the plethora of 'conditions and syndromes' that exist. Nor can this text offer a detailed guide of how to operate the policy of SEND and inclusion in the complex world of practice. There are many excellent texts that provide such detail and, where appropriate, such texts will be specified in the reading sections offered at the end of each chapter. The intention of this book is to provide the student with an overview and a critical analysis of the history, practice, policies, ideologies and ideas that have led to the system of SEND that we have in the United Kingdom and other parts of the world today.

A text such as this, then, directed as it is towards the novice student, can only provide an overview of the complexity of the issues. As such, some concepts are necessarily subject to simplification and it is accepted that this may, perhaps, cause a distortion of the facts. However, throughout the book the student is directed towards materials that will help them to develop a more complete grasp of this area. I therefore want to emphasise from the outset that this text is only the beginning of a student journey into this complex world, as it offers only a basic introduction to provide a point of departure to a deeper exploration and critical examination of SEND and inclusion.

FORMAT OF THE BOOK

This book is organised into three distinct sections. Section I defines the concepts of SEND and examines how provision for such is maintained in England, Northern Ireland, Wales and Scotland. In addition, it analyses how the development of the concept of disability has been defined through ideological models that have developed over time. Furthermore, it considers how the attitudes of teachers, parents and non-disabled people have affected the inclusion of disabled children and young people within schools. Section II considers the historical development of the world of SEND and the emergence of inclusive education within England during the latter part of the 20th century. Section III examines the legislation governing SEND and inclusive education in England. It also offers an outline of how the SEN Code of Practice operates and examines the responsibilities of the various education, health and social care professionals involved in the delivery of SEND and inclusive educational provision. The last major chapter of the book offers a comparative analysis of the legislation and practices that govern the delivery of SEND and inclusion within the English education system and that of a number of other countries.

Throughout this edition the term SEND will be employed, as opposed to the term special educational needs (SEN) – unless that is, a point of legal definition needs to be made. Whilst SEN has a legal determination and SEND does not, it is clear in early years settings, schools and colleges that it is an acronym which dominates the language of practice. The difference between SEN and SEND is explained more fully in Chapter 1.

SECTION I

CONTEXTUALISING SPECIAL EDUCATIONAL NEEDS AND DISABILITIES (SEND)

1

INTRODUCTION

The major questions this chapter addresses are:

- What are SEND and what is the scale of the issue in England?
- What are the differences between SEN, special needs and SEND?
- What is the SEND legislation that is employed in England, Scotland, Wales and Northern Ireland and how is it similar or different in each country?

This chapter introduces you to the concept of SEND. It includes definitions of SEND and outlines the scale of the issue in England. It also provides a brief overview of how processes of SEND are operationalised in Wales, Scotland and Northern Ireland. In addition, it will provide you with a number of case studies which will help you develop a better understanding of these key concepts. The final section of the chapter suggests 'Taking it further', student activities, reflective questions and further reading that will broaden your knowledge and understanding of SEND and inclusion.

DEFINING SEN IN ENGLAND (DfE, 2014)

Clause 20 of the Children and Families Act 2014 denotes that a child or young person has a SEN when he or she has a learning difficulty or disability which calls for special educational provision to be made for him or her.

According to the Act a child or young person has a learning difficulty if he or she (a) has a significantly greater difficulty in learning than the majority of others of the same age, or (b) has a disability which prevents or hinders him or her from making use of facilities of a kind generally provided for others of the same age in mainstream schools.

Following a formal assessment under section 37 of the Children and Families Act 2014, a local authority may issue an Education, Health and Care Plan (EHCP). This is a legal document specifying the child's needs, the special educational provision required and the outcomes that will be sought for that child.

(DES, 1978)

The term SEN was coined by the Warnock Report of the late 1970s. Previously, children were labelled by the employment of ten categories of 'handicap' set out in the regulations of the 1944 Education Act (see Chapter 3).

The ten categories of 'handicap' defined by the 1944 Education Act were:

- blind
- partially sighted
- deaf

- delicate
- diabetic
- educationally sub-normal
- epileptic
- maladjusted
- physically handicapped
- speech defect.

The Warnock Report in 1978, followed by the 1981 Education Act (DES, 1981), altered the conceptualisation of special education by emphasising that an educational need should be prioritised first and not an individual learning disability or impairment. Today, in the context of educational provision, the term SEN has a legal definition which refers to children and young people who have learning difficulties and/or disabilities that make it more difficult for them to learn or access education than most pupils of the same age. We will discuss the differences between SEN, SEND and special needs later in the chapter.

The Children and Families Act (DfE, 2014a) (see Chapter 7 for further detail) offers guidance that helps teachers and other professionals make decisions upon whether a child or young person has a SEND that will require special educational provision. For example, it states that:

> A child or young person does not have a learning difficulty or disability solely because the language (or form of language) in which he or she is or will be taught is different from a language (or form of language) which is or has been spoken at home. (Section 20[4])

(SEND code of Practice: 0-25 years (DfE & DoH, 2015)

Furthermore clause 77 of the Act creates a Code of Practice (henceforth referred to as the Code) which relates to children from 0 to 25 years of age. The Code provides advice to local authorities, maintained schools, early years educational settings and colleges on how to identify, assess and make provision for children and young people's SEND. This Code ensures that 'all children achieve their best, become confident individuals living fulfilling lives; and that they make a

The Code indicates that a child or young person's needs may fall into at least one of four broad categories:

→ SLCN
→ Autism

- Communication and interaction → SpLD
- Cognition and learning ——→ Learning difficulties
- Social, mental and emotional health ——→ ADD, ADHD
- Sensory and/or physical. ——→ VI
  ——→ HI
  PD →MSI

5

successful transition into adulthood' (DfE, 2014b: 58). Teachers and professionals must have regard for the Code in all the work they do with children and young people with SEND.

The Code also details that behavioural difficulties or a disability do not necessarily mean that a child has a SEN (DfE, 2014b). The Code does make clear though that when behaviour is consistently disruptive or a child has become withdrawn, this can be a sign of an unmet SEND.

The four categories are sub-divided into:

1. Communication and interaction

- **Speech, language and communication needs** (SLCN). These pupils find it more difficult to communicate with others and may have difficulties in taking part in conversations. (Further resources are available at: www.thecommunicationtrust.org.uk/policy-and-practice/send-reforms/)

- **Autistic spectrum disorder** (ASD), including Asperger's syndrome and autism. These pupils have difficulty in communication, social interaction and imagination. In addition, they may be easily distracted or upset by certain stimuli, have problems with changes to familiar routines or have difficulties with co-ordination and fine-motor skills. (Further resources are available at: www.nice.org.uk/guidance/CG128)

2. Cognition and learning

- Pupils with learning difficulties will learn at a slower pace and may have greater difficulty in acquiring basic literacy or numeracy skills or in understanding concepts. They may also have speech and language delay, low self-esteem, low levels of concentration and underdeveloped social skills.

- Children and young people with a learning difficulty are at increased risk of developing a mental health problem and may need additional support with social development, self-esteem and emotional well-being.

- **Severe learning difficulties** (SLD). Pupils may have significant intellectual and cognitive impairments. They may have difficulties in mobility and co-ordination, communication and perception, and the acquisition of self-help skills.

- **Profound and multiple learning difficulties** (PMLD). These pupils have severe and complex difficulties as well as significant other difficulties such as a physical or a sensory impairment.

- **Specific learning difficulty** (SPLD). A pupil may have difficulty with one or more aspects of learning including a range of conditions such as dyslexia (reading and spelling), dyscalculia (maths), dyspraxia (co-ordination) and dysgraphia (writing).
- Further information is available at:
  - www.bdadyslexia.org.uk/educator/what-are-specific-learning-difficulties
  - www.challengingbehaviour.org.uk/learning-disability-assets/valuingtheviews ofchildrenwithalearningdisability.pdf

3. Social, mental and emotional health

- Pupils who have difficulties with their emotional and social development may have immature social skills and find it difficult to make and sustain healthy relationships. These may be displayed through them becoming withdrawn or isolated, as well as through challenging, disruptive or disturbing behaviour.
- Some pupils may have a recognised disorder, for example attention deficit disorder (ADD), attention deficit hyperactivity disorder (ADHD), attachment disorder, autism or pervasive developmental disorder. (Further resources which address mental health are available at www.minded.org.uk/)

4. Sensory and/or physical needs

- There are a wide variety of sensory and physical difficulties that affect pupils, and some of these may require special educational provision. It is this group that should be identified as having a SEN.
- Visual impairment (VI) or hearing impairment (HI) may require specialist support and equipment for access to learning.
- Multi-Sensory impairment (MSI) is a combination of visual and hearing difficulties, which makes it much more difficult for pupils to access the curriculum.
- Physical disability (PD) requires ongoing support and equipment for access to all the opportunities available to peers.
- Further information is available:
  - www.rnib.org.uk/information-everyday-living-education-and-learning-young-childrens-education/special-educational
  - https://councilfordisabledchildren.org.uk/sites/default/files/uploads/documents/import/ChildrenAndFamiliesActBrief.pdf

(Source: DfE, 2014b: 97–98)

DEFINING SPECIAL EDUCATIONAL NEEDS AND DISABILITIES

The four categories of SEND as defined in the Code are explained more fully in the case studies below.

CASE STUDY 1.1
SPECIFIC LEARNING DIFFICULTIES

Akriti is an eight-year-old pupil in a small rural primary school in the South of England. She is normally a very well-behaved pupil who excels at art and drama. Akriti has a satisfactory aptitude for mathematical activities and loves reciting her basic times-table number facts. However, she has difficulty in learning her weekly spelling words and is failing to make any progress with her reading. Despite her class teacher employing differentiated learning activities she has made no progress in her basic literacy work. In the past few months, she has displayed irritation and periods of aggression towards staff and other pupils during her literacy lessons. Her parents and staff have become increasingly concerned about her performance and behaviour in school. In light of these difficulties, Akriti was referred to an educational psychologist for an assessment of her needs. The psychologist detailed that she was 30 months behind in her ability to recognise basic words, phonological abilities and short-term working memory compared to that expected for a child of her age.

In terms of the legislation it may be observed that Akriti will require SEND provision because she has a 'discrepancy between achievement and her general intellectual ability'. If we examine the categories box above we will observe that she would be considered under Section 2 (those of cognition and learning), and that her SEND would be described as a specific learning difficulty, i.e. dyslexia.

CASE STUDY 1.2
SOCIAL, MENTAL AND EMOTIONAL HEALTH

Ben is eight years old and a member of class in an urban primary school. He has difficulty making and keeping friends both at school and in his home environment. In addition, over the past six months he has become isolated and withdrawn. His class teacher reports that Ben is failing to achieve and often disrupts the class with outbursts of very challenging behaviour. She has also noticed that he has intense difficulty in sitting still and an inability to concentrate on even simple activities. Ben's mother has said that he has also had difficulties at home with simple tasks such as dressing and feeding himself. She is very concerned about her son's progress at school as well as his impulsive and challenging behaviour at home.

Ben is presenting with significant difficulties which are providing a barrier to his learning. In terms of the legislation his behaviour is so severe that he would be classified as having a SEND that fell into the category of social, mental and emotional health. After several assessments by the educational psychologist and paediatric team he was assessed as having the recognised impairment of ADHD.

CASE STUDY 1.3
SENSORY AND/OR PHYSICAL NEEDS

Julie is a very happy, polite and well-motivated four-year-old pupil who loves attending her local nursery school. She is often found at the centre of any games and has a wide circle of friends. She likes nothing better than reading her favourite fairy stories to her friends and engaging in digging large holes during sand play sessions. However, recently Julie has become increasingly slower at navigating her way to the different areas of the classroom. Her teachers have also noticed that she has been finding it more and more difficult to move around the outdoor play area and she has fallen over several times. She has stopped reading out loud to her friends too. The SENCo referred her to the school nurse service and at a recent hospital assessment, Julie was found to have a deteriorating eye condition. With this knowledge, the nursery has begun to make adaptations both to Julie's play areas and to her curriculum. The teachers have made sure that large-print books are available and that support is on hand to ensure that she is able to engage fully in the life of the early years setting, especially sand play.

TAKING IT FURTHER

For more information regarding how to support children and young people with mental health issues you could read the Department for Education Report (2017) *Supporting Mental Health in Schools and Colleges*. This is available at https://assets.publishing.service. gov.uk/government/uploads/system/uploads/attachment_data/file/634728/Supporting_ Mental-health_Case_study_report.pdf

SEND IN SCOTLAND, NORTHERN IRELAND AND WALES

Within the United Kingdom, the educational provision for children and young people with learning difficulties broadly operates under similar legislative systems. It is important to remember, however, that aspects of the Scottish, Northern Irish and Welsh system can still differ substantially from those observed within English schools.

For more detailed information that relates to the organisation of SEND support in Scotland, Northern Ireland and Wales, you will need to access the following links:

Scottish Executive

www.gov.scot

Enter the search term 'additional support needs' to find the latest information.

Northern Ireland Department of Education

www.deni.gov.uk/index/support-and-development 2/special_educational_ needs_pg.htm

Enter the search term 'special educational needs' to access the latest information.

Welsh Assembly

http://wales.gov.uk/?lang=en

Enter the search term 'additional needs' to find the latest information.

SCOTLAND

Until 2004, special education in Scotland was organised in a broadly similar manner to that in England. However, the legal framework in Scotland changed in 2005 with the implementation of the Education (Additional Support for Learning) (Scotland) Act 2004. This Act, amended in 2009, abolished the term SEN and replaced it with a much broader definition – that of 'additional support need'. In 2016 the Act was further amended by the 'Keeling Schedule' which gave more rights to children aged 12 to 15. Later in 2017, a major consultation exercise resulted in a new Code of Practice for additional support needs coming into force across Scotland.

Additional support needs, as defined by the Act, refer to any child or young person who would benefit from extra help in order to overcome barriers to their learning. A child with additional support needs may also require a learning plan which is referred to in the Act as a 'co-ordinated support plan'.

The Act stipulates that some children and young people may require additional support for a variety of reasons, such as those who:

- have motor or sensory impairments;
- are being bullied;
- are particularly able or talented;

- have experienced a bereavement;
- are looked after in social care surroundings;
- have a learning difficulty;
- are living with parents who are abusing substances;
- are living with parents who have mental health problems;
- have English as an additional language;
- are not attending school regularly;
- have emotional or social difficulties;
- are on the child protection register;
- are young carers.

For the most up-to-date edition of the Scottish Code of Practice see:

https://www.gov.scot/Publications/2017/12/9598/2

WALES

In 2014, the system of educational provision in Wales was subject to a comprehensive review. This review proposed a new legislative framework for supporting children and young people with additional learning needs (ALN), SEN and learning difficulties and/or disabilities (LDD). The legislation named as the Additional Learning Needs and Education Tribunal Act (2018) aims to be the cornerstone of the Welsh government's approach to supporting children and young people with additional needs. The legislation, which is expected to come into full force in September 2020, provides uniformed provision for learners aged 0 to 25 and will replace the terminology of SEND with additional learning needs. Furthermore, the legislation also intends to replace Statements with a new Individual Development Plan.

The Additional Learning Needs Code for Wales 2021

According to the Welsh Government, the transformed system will:

- ensure all learners with ALN are supported to overcome barriers to learning so they can achieve their full potential;
- improve the planning and delivery of support for learners from 0 to 25 with ALN, placing learners' needs, views, wishes and feelings at the heart of the process;
- focus on the importance of identifying needs early and putting in place timely and effective interventions to ensure they deliver the desired outcomes.

NORTHERN IRELAND

Special education in Northern Ireland is governed by the legal framework established within the Education (Northern Ireland) Order 1996, as amended by the SEN and Disability (Northern Ireland) Order 2005 (DoE, 2005) and the Special Educational Needs and Disability Act (Northern Ireland) 2016. The Department of Education in Northern Ireland also provides guidance to schools about SEND through a Code of Practice which came into force in 2005. These orders and the Code place a duty for the provision for children and young people with SEND upon the education and library boards and the boards of governors within mainstream schools. These Orders increased the rights of children and young people with SEND to attend mainstream schools and they also introduced disability discrimination laws for the whole of the education system in Northern Ireland. Similar to Scotland, Wales and England, the Department for Employment and Learning in Northern Ireland offers advice and guidance on how to operate a system for identifying and assessing children with learning difficulties. Currently, further regulations are being considered which will, according to the Northern Ireland education department, strengthen the legislation so that a more responsive and effective SEND framework may be delivered for children and young people.

SEND – THE SCALE OF THE ISSUE

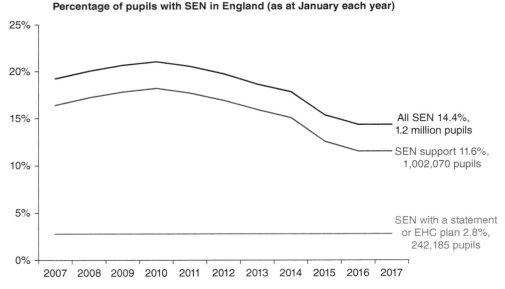

Percentage of pupils with SEN in England (as at January each year)

All SEN 14.4%, 1.2 million pupils

SEN support 11.6%, 1,002,070 pupils

SEN with a statement or EHC plan 2.8%, 242,185 pupils

Figure 1.1 Prevalence and characteristics of SEN in England 2007–2017

(Source: DfE, 2008: 6)

TAKING IT FURTHER

Consider the graph shown in Figure 1.1, which apparently shows that SEND is reducing. Do you think, given these data, that government policy is working in relation to the education of children and young people with SEND?

Now read the article by Eleanor Busby, 'Thousands of children with special needs do not have school places amid crisis in education funding, union warns', on the *Independent* newspaper's website (https://www.independent.co.uk/news/education/education-news/special-educational-needs-school-funding-cuts-national-education-union-neu-a8282816.html), or the piece 'Cash shortage for special educational needs' support' by the BBC News education reporter, Katherine Sellgren (https://www.bbc.co.uk/news/education-36425290).

How does this evidence change the picture of SEND provision in our early years settings, schools and colleges? Do you think that government policy has been wholly successful?

You may wish to add to your knowledge and understanding of the current issues in SEND by reading the latest NASUWT survey report (https://www.nasuwt.org.uk/advice/in-the-classroom/special-educational-needs.html).

From 2014 onwards, a child must have an EHCP to receive the highest levels of special educational provision. The EHCP replaced the Statement of Special Educational Need.

In 1978 the Warnock Report (DES, 1978) initially estimated that 20% of children, during their time at school, might experience a SEND that would necessitate additional educational provision to be made. The report also estimated that around 2% of all children and young people of school age may have an educational need so severe that they would require a Statement of Educational Need. Forty years later, data from the Department for Education (DfE, 2018a) revealed that in January 2018 some 285,722 pupils in England had an Education, Health and Care plan (EHCP) or equivalent. Those data (see Figure 1.1) also revealed that the figure of 2%, provided by the Warnock Report in relation to children who would require a Statement (now an EHCP), had underestimated the numbers of children and young people who would need the highest level of special educational provision. The percentage of pupils requiring a statement or EHCP has remained steady at 2.8% since 2007 (see Figure 1.1). However, the number of pupils requiring the provision of a new EHCP rose during 2017 to 11.3% (see Figures 1.2 and 1.3).

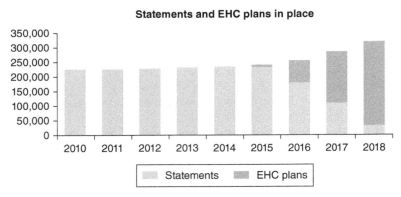

Figure 1.2 Number of pupils with Statements or EHCP

(Source: DfE, 2018a: 4)

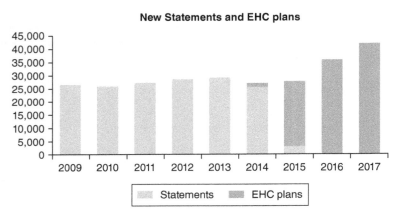

Figure 1.3 New Statements and EHCP

(Source: DfE, 2018a: 6)

During the period 2010 to 2017, the overall proportion of pupils with SEND has decreased to 14.4%. The number of pupils who require SEND support but do not require an EHCP has also fallen, so that in 2017 it was 11.6% (DfE, 2018b) (see Figure 1.1). In 2017 government data (DfE, 2018a: 7) denoted that the highest need identified among pupils in state-funded schools was a 'moderate learning difficulty' followed by 'speech, language and communication needs' (see Figure 1.4). For those pupils with an EHCP the commonest form of need was that of 'austic spectrum disorder'.

In 2017 government data also revealed that SEND remains more prevalent in males than females, with 14.6% of males requiring support as opposed to 8.1% of females. In relation to the provision of an EHCP, 4% of males require the highest form of educational provision compared to 1.6% of females. Pupils who were entitled to free school meals and pupils from a Black Caribbean heritage were also more likely to have an EHCP.

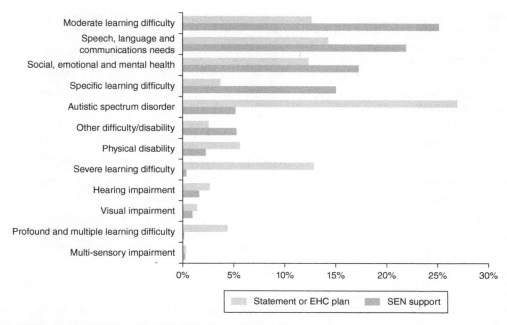

Figure 1.4 Percentage of pupils, by need of provision

(Source: DfE, 2018a: 7)

EARLY YEARS

During 2017, the number of two-year-olds who entered early years education rose, as did the proportion of children designated as having SEND, which now stands at 3.2% of the population. Whilst the number of three- and four-year-olds in early years education has fallen, the number of children designated as having SEND has risen to 6.1% of the population. The government figures reveal that 3.9% of pupils under five years of age now require an EHCP (DfE, 2018b: 4).

Table 1.1 Number and percentage of children and young people with Statements or EHCP, by age group

Age group	Statements	%	EHC plans	%	Total	%
Under 5 years	14	0.0	12,502	4.4	12,516	3.9
Aged 5–10	13,566	39.8	92,123	32.2	105,689	33.0
Aged 11–15	15,954	46.8	101,400	35.5	117,354	36.7
Aged 16–19	4,563	13.4	65,521	22.9	70,084	21.9
Aged 20–25			14,176	5.0	14,176	4.4
Total	**34,097**		**285,722**		**319,819**	

(Source: DfE, 2018b: 4)

Table 1.2 Number and percentage of children and young people with Statements or EHCP on roll, by establishment type

Establishment type (grouped)	Statements	%	EHC plans	%	Total	%
Non-maintained early years settings in the private and voluntary sector	6	0.0	1,470	0.5	1,476	0.5
Mainstream school	14,747	46.1	113,367	41.4	128,114	41.9
Special school	17,031	53.2	109,929	40.2	126,960	41.5
Alternative Provision (AP) / Pupil Referral Unit (PRU)	221	0.7	2,109	0.8	2,330	0.8
Further Education			46,854	17.1	46,854	15.3
Total	**32,005**		**273,729**		**305,734**	

(Source: DfE, 2018b: 5)

Overall, that data denote that children and young people aged 11–15 account for the highest proportion of those requiring an EHCP (see Table 1.1), and that the majority of children with SEND are educated within mainstream schools, although it is still the case that the majority of pupils who have an EHCP are educated in special schools and alternative settings (see Table 1.2).

- A mainstream school is one that provides an education for all pupils, including those with SEND.
- A special school is normally one that provides an education for children who have an EHC plan.

SEND – A CONTESTED CONCEPT

In relation to an individual and the implementation of government legislation deciding what is or is not a learning difficulty, and what counts or does not count as a SEND, or at what age support for a SEND should or should not be withdrawn, this can be difficult (Palikara et al., 2018). For example, Terzi (2005) argues that the concept of SEND itself is difficult to specify and in practice unworkable. Others have argued that a label of SEND necessarily leads to children and young people being placed within a system of education that sorts, categorises and segregates (Hodkinson and Burch, 2018). Ironically, the current Code employs SEND to categorise pupils into four main areas of need (see page 6) despite it stating that 'the purpose of identification is to work out what action the school needs to take, not to fit a pupil into a category' (see Allan and Youdell, 2017). Of interest is that Ofsted in its review of special educational provision, in 2010, found wide variations both within local authorities and within schools themselves in the numbers of pupils specified as having a SEND. It is of further interest to note that their investigations revealed an inconsistency as to how SEND were defined within schools in England. Moreover, Ofsted expressed a concern that some schools were employing the term SEND to refer to those pupils who simply needed better teaching or pastoral support. It seems apparent that SEND is not defined solely in relation to pupils who have a learning difficulty.

In recent times, it has become even more apparent that educational professionals have been subject to difficulties and confusion in establishing the differences between disability/special needs and the legal definition of SEN itself (Curran et al., 2017). This confusion, it seems, is exacerbated by the employment of the new terminology of SEND brought into being by the Children and Families Act 2014. A pupil, for example, may have a special need and so be labelled as SEND, but might not actually have a SEN in terms of the legal definitions that have continued to be employed in the Children and Families Act 2014. Special needs in the UK, like SEND, does not have a legal basis in terms of the legislation governing this area of education. Many people do confuse SEN, SEND and special needs and this can result in serious consequences. For example, this form of confusion may lead to low expectations of achievement for all pupils whose first language is not English. In addition, difficulties in defining special needs and SEN may lead to confusion in planning support, for example, expecting the same staff to have an expertise in teaching English as a second language as well as teaching children with reading difficulties (Frederickson and Cline, 2015).

SPECIAL NEEDS, SEND OR SPECIAL EDUCATIONAL NEEDS?

A child or young person has a special need if they 'come from a social group whose circumstances or background are different from most of the school population' (Frederickson and Cline, 2002: 36). A special need may relate to any pupil, at any time, during their school career. So, for example, a pupil could have a special need if they have emotional or physical challenges not normally experienced by their peers; or if they have a history of physical abuse; or if they are a member of a religious or cultural group. The difference between this concept and that of SEN is that a special need does not necessarily manifest itself as a barrier to learning. As such, a pupil with a special need would not normally need access to SEND provision as detailed within the Children and Families Act 2014.

Using the information given in each of the case studies below, and the detail offered above in relation to special provision, decide if each child has a SEN, a special need or both.

READER REFLECTION

CASE STUDY 1.4
JOSEPHINE'S STORY

Josephine (aged 10) employs a wheelchair to aid her mobility around her school. She really enjoys history and swimming but does not like having to learn her times-table for the numeracy test she has to take on a weekly basis.

CASE STUDY 1.5
PAULO'S STORY

Paulo (aged 8) migrated to England with his family three month ago. He has a hearing impairment and has had difficulty in learning English in the time he has been in school.

In examining the cases studies above, you may have found that defining special needs and SEN can be a difficult thing to do. In the first case study, Josephine might be considered as having a special need because of her reduced mobility. Yet whilst she might not enjoy having to learn her 'spellings', this would not be classified as a barrier to her ability to learn. In the second case study, Paulo presents quite a different and rather interesting case, as he perhaps could have a special need as a result of being from a minority cultural group. In terms of the Children and Families Act 2014 though, Paulo's employment of English as a second language would not constitute a SEN. What is interesting here is that his inability to learn English is being complicated by his hearing impairment. If you examine the categories box on page 6, it is clear that a hearing impairment would indeed be considered as a SEN.

A further issue with the employment of the term SEN is that the definition itself is negatively linked with a medical view of disability. In addition, Frederickson and Cline (2015) believe that SEN is a problematic term because it is associated with negative conceptualisations and difficulties in decision making such as those denoted in the case studies above. Terzi (2005) suggests that the term SEN, rather than moving away from the notion of categorising children as Warnock (DES, 1978) envisaged, in reality does nothing more than introduce a new category – that of SEN! As such, any difficulty a pupil may have with learning may be seen by the professionals involved as resulting from a personal deficit and difference, and not from the barriers created by such things as inaccessible buildings, inflexible curricula, inappropriate teaching and learning approaches and school organisation and policies (we will discuss these ideas more fully in Chapter 2). This form of labelling not only is disrespectful and hurtful to the individual pupil but also has repercussions for the manner in which their learning is supported

(CSIE, 2005). To some academics and practitioners these issues have led them to believe that the term SEN has outlived its usefulness (Norwich, 2010). Despite these beliefs and arguments, we must remember that SEN has, within the context of the English educational system, a legal status, and is a term commonly employed alongside the new term of SEND in the vast majority of early years, schools and colleges.

CONCLUSION

In this chapter, you gained knowledge and understanding of:

- the scale of SEND in England;
- the differences between SEN, Special Needs and SEND; and,
- how the SEND legislation employed in England, Scotland, Wales and Northern Ireland is similar and also different.

Within this chapter the definition of SEND and associated terms of additional support needs were considered in terms of the legislation that governs England, Scotland, Northern Ireland and Wales. Recent data were detailed that determined how many children in England were considered to have a SEND and how these figures showed that males have a greater prevalence of SEND than do females. The final section of this chapter demonstrated the difficulties professionals sometimes have in deciding whether a child has a special need or a SEN or SEND.

The 'Taking it further' box in the chapter, along with the student activities, reflective questions and further reading detailed below, will help you develop a much deeper understanding of the terminology and operation of SEND in our schools. These are also designed to make you question whether SEND is still a term that is useful for pupils being educated in the 21st century.

STUDENT ACTIVITIES

1. With another student, discuss the definition of SEND as outlined in this chapter. Use the internet to contrast the definition of SEND in England with the definition of additional needs employed in Scotland.

2. Read Ofsted (2010) *The special educational needs and disability review – A statement is not enough* (www.ofsted.gov.uk/resources/special-educational-needs-and-disability-review) and then make a list of the problems that this review found with employment of the term SEN.

3. Download the Nasen Policy Option Paper – *Special Educational Needs Has Outlived its Usefulness: A Debate* (www.nasen.org.uk/policy-option-papers/). With other students, consider what the benefits and drawbacks are of the continued employment of the term SEND within an educational system. You may wish to use your reading and discussion to plan for a debate in one of your seminar sessions.

REFLECTIVE QUESTIONS

Given your reading of this chapter do you think that 'additional support needs' is a better definition than that of SEN develop by the Warnock Report of 1978?

What is your position on employment of the terms SEN, SEND or additional support needs? Do such terms help or hinder the education and socialisation of all of our children and young people?

FURTHER READING

Bates, B. (2017) *A Quick Guide to Special Needs and Disabilities*. London: Sage. This text will provide the reader with an overview of the 'conditions and syndromes' a practitioner might experience within the applied educational setting.

Frederickson, N. and Cline, T. (2015) *Special Educational Needs, Inclusion and Diversity* (3rd edn). Maidenhead: OUP. Chapter 1 provides an expansive overview of the principles of SEND.

Shakespeare, T. (2018) *Disability: The Basics*. London: Routledge. Chapter 1 of this book will enable you to gain a conceptualisation of how we might understand disability outside of that presented by cold statistics and categorisation.

Warnock, M. and Norwich, B. (2010) *Special Educational Needs: A New Look* (edited by L. Terzi). London: Continuum. This text offers a critical examination of the principles and practices of SEND. The interest in this text lies in the fact that one of its main contributors is Baroness Warnock, who was a key architect of the SEND system we can observe in operation in schools today.

2

PRINCIPLES OF SEND: THEORETICAL PERSPECTIVES

The major questions this chapter addresses are:

- What are the models of disability?
- How do models assist in the examination of the complex concepts that surround SEND?

INTRODUCTION

This chapter examines how ideological frameworks contained within the models of disability shape our perceptions, experiences and conceptualisations of SEND and inclusion. The chapter will provide you with a theoretical toolbox to critically examine, interpret and gain an understanding of the difficult and complex concepts employed within the field of SEND.

SEND provision is governed in England by the Code of Practice (DfE, 2014b); similar Codes operate in Scotland, Northern Ireland and Wales. The Code, which came into force in September 2014, details the principles for the management of SEND provision.

The Code differs from the previous one in that:

- it covers children and young people in the 0–25 age range;
- it has a clearer focus on the views of pupils in the decision-making process;
- for children with complex needs a co-ordinated EHCP replaced Statements and Learning Difficulty Assessments;
- there is guidance on the support pupils should receive in education settings.

(DfE, 2014b)

Clause 19 of the Children and Families Act (DfE, 2014a) sets out the principles underpinning the Code. These principles support:

- the involvement of children, parents and young people in decision making;
- the identification of children and young people's needs;
- collaboration between education, health and social care services;
- high-quality provision to meet the needs of children and young people with SEND;
- greater choice and control for young people and parents over their support;
- successful preparation for adulthood, including independent living and employment.

The Code also operates alongside the statement of inclusion that exists in the National Curriculum, which came into force on the 1st of September 2014. Parts of this statement relate directly to SEND.

This inclusion statement maintains that teachers should:

1. Set suitable challenges:

    - Teachers should set high expectations for every pupil. They have an even greater obligation to plan lessons for pupils who have low levels of prior attainment or come from disadvantaged backgrounds. Teachers should use appropriate assessment to set targets which are deliberately ambitious.

2. Respond to pupils' needs and overcome potential barriers for individuals and groups of children:

    - Teachers should take account of their duties under equal opportunities legislation that covers race, disability, sex, religion or belief, sexual orientation, pregnancy and maternity, and gender reassignment.
    - A wide range of pupils have SEND, many of whom also have disabilities. Lessons should be planned to ensure that there are no barriers to every pupil achieving. In many cases, such planning will mean that these pupils will be able to study the full National Curriculum. A minority of pupils will need access to specialist equipment and different approaches.
    - With the right teaching, which recognises their individual needs, many disabled pupils may have little need for additional resources beyond the aids which they use as part of their daily life. Teachers must plan lessons so that these pupils can study every National Curriculum subject. Potential areas of difficulty should be identified and addressed at the outset of work.

(Source: DfE, 2014a: 4.1–4.6)

Reading the Code together with the National Curriculum inclusion statement reveals that, in part, the documents conflict with each other. For example, whilst the Code makes plain how factors internal to the child should be considered as the prime focus, the national curriculum places external factors such as the learning environment and teachers' ability to be able to set suitable learning targets as the prime importance. What is made clear by reading these two documents together with the statements made by the prime minister of the day David Cameron (see Chapter 3) is that the provision of SEND education is an area which is subject to differing ideologies as to how, and indeed where, pupils with SEND should be educated. In the following chapters, we will trace the history of these competing ideologies in detail. However, for the moment we will concentrate on determining what these differing ideologies are and how these lead to different forms of educational practice and provision.

THE INFLUENCE OF IDEOLOGICAL FRAMEWORKS

Special and inclusive education are viewed by society from differing perspectives. Those perspectives are contained in the numerous models of disability detailed within the literature. However, four major ideological frameworks may be distinguished (see Figure 2.1):

- **The psycho-medical model** locates disabilities within an individual's impairment or the restrictions in activity caused by that impairment. In essence, it focuses upon the 'person with disability as the problem and looks for cures' (Harpur, 2012: 2). This model is also called the individual tragedy, deficit or medical model.

- **The biopsychosocial model** reflects disability through the interaction of biological, psychological and social factors (Wade and Halligan, 2017).

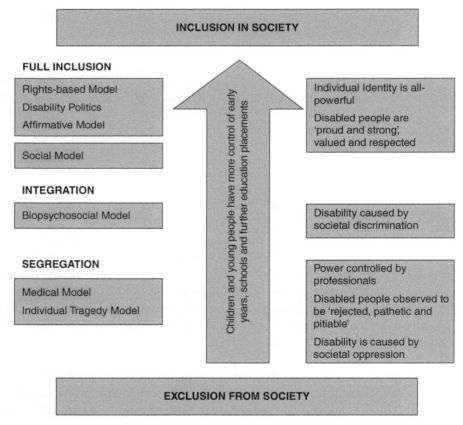

Figure 2.1 From segregation to inclusion: a continuum of models

add neurodiversity paradigm

- The **social model** rejects the categorisation of disabled people on the basis of their impairment (Goodley, 2014) and presents SEND as being the result of society's actions, values and beliefs (Slee, 1998).

- The **disability movement perspectives** – by which disabled people have sought to assert their human rights to be included within society through the employment of politics, the legal system and the disability arts movement.

Each of these theoretical frameworks operates using different theories of:

- focus
- causation
- intervention methods
- education.

THE PSYCHO-MEDICAL MODEL

Focus: Individual child's difficulties

Causation: Individual pathology, impairments and disability

Intervention: Medical, health and educational professionals

Education: Segregation – special schools or units

This model has had a long and influential history (see Chapter 3). It is the traditional ideology through which western society has conceptualised SEND. These conceptualisations are embedded within the society and reveal themselves through the media, school textbooks, internet images, children's story books, language, beliefs, research, policy and the operation of professional practice. Within this model, SEND are understood to arise from the psychological, neurological or physiological limitations displayed by an individual (Durham and Ramcharan, 2018). The model employs practices borrowed from the medical profession to judge children and young people's limitations against so-called developmental and functional norms.

Developmental and functional norms are employed as a process of developmental screening and assessment of a pupil suspected of having an SEND. By comparing a pupil's performance with the typical performance of other pupils of a similar age across a range of areas, such as cognition, speech and language, fine and gross motor skills, and social and emotional functioning, the scope and severity of a pupil's SEND might be determined.

The premise of this model is that a child or young person's limitations will equate to a deficit in functioning that will need to be treated or cured by professionals (Goering, 2015). Through a process of screening, assessment and identification, a pupil's limitations are labelled and described using clinical terminology, such as the 'aetiology of the syndrome' or 'the pathology of impairment' (Skidmore, 1996). In keeping with this model, the 'symptoms' displayed by a pupil are diagnosed and treatments are employed in an attempt to cure or remediate the condition (Goering, 2015).

The psycho-medical model:

- assesses the symptoms a pupil presents with;
- diagnoses and labels the condition or syndrome;
- attempts to fix the pupil's disability or syndrome (Harpur, 2012).

This model's preoccupation with the need to diagnose and label, as well as the consequences of doing so, is highlighted in the case studies below.

CASE STUDY 2.1
SARA'S STORY

Sara was born in 1999 in what was a difficult birth. When she was one-year-old the doctors told me that her mental functions were delayed and that she would not achieve much in life. When she was two the health care worker told me that she had special needs and that she had a significant learning difficulty which meant that mainstream schooling would be impossible. At four, Sara was deemed to have a mental impairment and I was told that she would never be able to speak. When she went to school I was informed that she had a SEND and she would need special teaching in a special school. By the age of six, she was diagnosed with asthma and autism, along with complex and multiple learning difficulties. When she should have gone to secondary school she went into special care as she had multiple, severe and complex learning difficulties and significant mental health issues. When Sara was twelve we removed her from the special school system and once again she became a person with a name and not a syndrome or an issue. She was Sara – a beautiful girl with a mischievous laugh and a smile that lights up the room.

CASE STUDY 2.2
PETER'S STORY

I always knew from the first day I went to school that I was different. The other children constantly informed me of this. Other children were so hurtful they labelled me as a nutcase and a geek and laughed at me when I twitched my head. One teacher said that I was an emotional cripple and that I was badly behaved. Another just used to call me vulgar and foul because I did swear a lot. To be honest I prefer the label the doctors eventually gave me of Tourette's. Some people do now understand that I cannot help what I do: it's just who I am.

CASE STUDY 2.3
ASHAN'S STORY

Ashan was a happy student who attended his local community college. He was described by his teachers as a likable student who enjoyed going to college. He was studying for his O-levels in mathematics and English and had been making good progress. However, after the death of his friend in a car crash his parents and his teachers had become concerned as to his irritable behaviour and other difficulties which were affecting his college and social life. In recent weeks, Ashan had been involved in confrontations with his teachers and other students. His parents also reported that he had difficulty sleeping and was lethargic at home. Given this situation, he was referred to both the college's Wellbeing Centre and his local doctor. He was diagnosed as having depression. In time, Ashan was treated by a therapist and given medication. After a few months, his sleeping and behaviour had improved and his studies were back on track. Although he subsequently had to have his medication increased, he is now making good progress especially in his English work. The diagnosis of depression helped Ashan, his friends, family and teachers to understand what was happening in his life.

After reading Sara's, Peter's and Ashan's stories, reflect on what the benefits and drawbacks are of having a system of SEND that relies so heavily on diagnoses and labels.

READER REFLECTION

THE PSYCHO-MEDICAL MODEL AND EDUCATION

Since the earliest days, there has been a link between educational provision for children and young people with SEND and the medical profession. The employment of medical ideas has formed a significant part of the identification and placement of pupils within the schooling system. This has resulted in the perpetuation of educational goals within the confines of remediation, diagnosis and prescription. Therefore, pupils who do not conform are labelled and often removed from mainstream classrooms. Indeed, when provision for special education was formulated in the 19th century, medical officers identified and placed children with SEND within a segregated system (see Chapter 3). Carrier (1986) contends that special education has employed the medical model to cloak itself in an aura of respectability in order to justify the interventions made by doctors, paediatricians and psychologists in the teaching of children and young people with SEND. In reality, many people question this model's accuracy and its links to medicine, science and health (Elkins, 2009).

SENCo – stands for Special Educational Needs Coordinator. The SENCo manages the day-to-day working of the Code of Practice and the SEND policy within an educational setting.

CASE STUDY 2.4
GARY'S STORY

Gary is ten and has a history of 'behaviour problems' which have resulted in him being suspended from lessons and excluded from the school. He is aggressive towards other pupils and displays defiant behaviour to staff. In class he is easily distracted and often leaves his seat and runs around the classroom and school. Gary's SENCo estimates that his literacy and numeracy are two years behind those of other class members. As a result of the SENCo's assessments he was referred to an educational psychologist and also the paediatric department of his local hospital for assessment. The psychologist saw Gary in school and administered the Wechsler intelligence test. She also gave his teachers and parents a rating scale questionnaire to assess his behaviour both at home and at school. Additionally a paediatrician saw Gary in clinic and conducted a number of observations of his behaviour. As a result of these assessments his parents were told that their son had attention deficit hyperactivity disorder (ADHD). Gary's paediatrician prescribed a drug called methylphenidate (Ritalin) which he now takes twice a day.

TAKING IT FURTHER

Gary's story shows how the application of the medical model seeks to assess, diagnose and cure the child. Having read his story reflect upon what other methods could have been employed rather than medication to help Gary progress with his learning, and consider if

Ritalin is the best answer to his learning difficulties. To help you further with your reflections on this issue you may wish to read and watch:

Does medication turn me into a different person? This is part of the 'ADHD and Me' film (http://www.youtube.com/watch?v=ovfL_cceBuk).

'Ritalin Gone Wrong', the *New York Times* (http://www.nytimes.com/2012/01/29/opinion/sunday/childrens-add-drugs-dont-work-long-term.html).

'Lily's Story – Mental Health in Schools', the *Guardian* (https://www.theguardian.com/education/2016/may/31/mental-health-schools-child-exams-abuse).

What do you feel would be the problems in applying the medical model to this case? What is missed when examining Lily's story if only the medical model is applied to her treatment and schooling? (To help you in your examination of this case it would be useful to read the information available at https://www.mentalhealth.org.uk/a-to-z/c/children-and-young-people)

CRITICISMS OF THE PSYCHO-MEDICAL MODEL

One of the criticisms of the psycho-medical model is that it is theoretically weak. This is because it locates the causation of disability with the individual and their 'medical' problems. In this model there is professional power over children and young people and little co-ordination or collaboration between the professionals themselves. Indeed, for many writers in Disability Studies this model is a 'patchwork quilt' approach 'whereby different and sometimes contrasting information is integrated' into a care plan 'but not necessarily with a unified outcome' that benefits the child (Gargiulo and Kilgo, 2014: 132). The model's application of pseudo-medical taxonomies and treatments, which aim to cure disability, is undermined because such treatments invariably fail to take into account the society in which disabled people live. Many writers believe not viewing disability holistically means that this model denies disabled people their human rights and fails to take into account their experiences of living in a disabling society (Swain and French, 2000). As it centres on the employment of scientific positivist methods of measurement, disabled people's lives are controlled by professionals and not by themselves. It is this, many would argue, that leads disabled people to be objectified and dehumanised by medical and educational professionals. The negative aspects of the medical model are clearly highlighted by Linda's personal account in the case study below.

CASE STUDY 2.5
LINDA'S STORY

Hello, I'm Linda – A sixty-year-old artist living in London. I know I am supposed to say at this point what my condition is and then tell you the words that the doctors use to label me, but I am a person not a number, and you can save your labels for your jam

(Continued)

jars! My life has been dominated by doctors who have told me that I had a problem that they just had to fix. When I went to school I was told that I had to change, I had to fit in and that I should thank the doctors and teachers who controlled my life. Note, here, that it's me that should change not **them**, the professionals or society. I was not prepared to change so they shut me away in an institution: 'out of sight and so out of mind'. The medical model teaches people to see me as different, not normal – to have suffered a tragedy. Through this model I am stereotyped; I become the pathetic victim and people should either fear me or, worse, pity me and my plight. From the time I was born doctors and their assessments have been used to say where I should live, where I should go to school and what type of education I should be allowed. Nobody listened to me and what I wanted. In my late thirties I broke away from all of this and became *me* again – Linda – a woman who just loves to paint!

It has also been suggested that these so-called scientific assessments are based upon symptoms which professionals artificially construct into unitary medical conditions (Lewis, 1991). Many hold the view that disabled people cannot be seen to be a single homogeneous group. Therefore, as they do not conform to particular types or behaviours, how can they be labelled using specific unitary taxonomies of sickness and illness (see Johnstone, 2001)?

The premise that there is one homogeneous group of disabled people is undermined by this personal account:

> Well I must admit that I have difficulties interacting with people with autism or worse, those who have Down's. I might use a wheelchair but I am not weird like some of those people who have mental handicaps. I just cannot stand to be near those people. But there is the problem; I am always campaigning to stop people looking down on me, treating me as different, but I do it to other people with disabilities.

As Johnstone (2001: 17) states: 'the creation of taxonomy of categories does little to adequately represent the sheer diversity and range that makes up the population of people with disabilities.' Furthermore, when this model is applied to SEND it becomes a mechanistic process whereby pupils' symptoms are identified and diagnosed and the condition is treated within a specialised and segregated system of education. As Skidmore (1996: 35) accounts, learners within this system arrive 'at one end of a conveyor belt and are issued from the other end neatly allocated to their appropriate track in a smooth uninterrupted stream'. During the 1970s this mechanistic process, amongst other things, led to the medical model falling out of favour. However, in recent years – because of an 'explosion' of diagnosed cases of mental health, dyslexia and ADHD – it has experienced a renaissance. For many disabled people the application of this model to education is wrong, because it leads to professionals focusing solely on what the child or young person cannot do rather than on what they can learn (Corbett and Norwich, 2005). Many disabled people point out that to employ the medical model to learning and behavioural difficulties effectively lets educational institutions 'off the hook', because the causation of a pupil's 'problem' firmly resides with the pupil and not with the learning context (Lewis, 1991).

Rieser (2014) discusses how the medical model observes the disabled person as the problem that needs to be fixed. He believes that within this model the person has to adapt to fit into the world of normal people, and that if this is not possible then disabled people are segregated in specialised institutions or isolated at home. Rieser also believes this model puts power in the hands of the medical profession who seek to change the bodies in which disabled people live.

Read the account above based upon the work of Richard Rieser, a campaigner on disability issues. Do you agree with the medical model's central tenet that it is the child's fault that they are unable to learn and not the teacher or the doctor? Is it possible or desirable to 'fix' all impairments, and what does this say about society's view of disabilities?

READER REFLECTION

THE BIOPSYCHOSOCIAL MODEL

Focus:	Illness and health result from a complex interaction of factors
Causation:	Individual pathology, impairments and disability combined with psychological factors – for example mood and social factors such as those derived from culture, family, economics and medical
Intervention:	Medical, health and educational professionals
Education:	Segregation – special schools or units and for some integrative education in mainstream schools

The biopsychosocial model developed by George Engel, in 1977, attempts to integrate the factors that often underpin illness and health. Engel proposed that biological factors, encompassed by the medical model, were also affected by psychological and social factors. He believed that only by assessing all of these factors together could illness be understood. He felt that the medical model was reductionist and failed to consider the realities of modern life. The biopsychosocial model was adopted by the World Health Organization, and it has become fundamental to the assessment principles utilised in the International Classification of Functioning, Disability and Health that is employed to classify disabilities (see Chapter 3 for more detail) (Norwich, 2016).

THE BIOPSYCHOSOCIAL MODEL AND EDUCATION

During the last two decades or so, educational psychologists and others have begun to realise that SEND do not always stem from the individual impairments that children and young people experience. Indeed, many professionals are aware that the medical model does not address factors such as low socio-economic backgrounds, or the larger social climate that surrounds a person labelled with SEND. This has been evident where SEND has been conceptualised in syndromes such as ADHD and Asperger's syndrome. Within mental health for example, there is an awareness of sociological research which demonstrates that socio-environmental factors are often implicated in many areas of SEND. At the practitioner level such understandings have led to the development of community psychology, which seeks to address the social aspects of mental health. Within education itself, some school psychologists and Disability Studies scholars have been at the forefront of these developments. Indeed, in Malta educational psychologists have, for over twenty years, been utilising approaches that bring in the sociological aspects of disability. It is clear that whilst the medical model holds ascendency in health care and education, especially in terms of the assessment of needs, it is the case that many professionals and practitioners have a much wider view of SEND than was the case at the start of the 21st century (Bartolo, 2010).

CRITICISMS OF THE BIOPSYCHOSOCIAL MODEL

Although many professionals now accept that illness and health are formed in an interplay of biological, psychological and social factors, the biopsychosocial model has not had a great impact upon health care (Wade and Halligan, 2017) or education. Others have argued that the model lacks coherence, is unscientific and does not respond fully to people's daily living experiences (Benning, 2015). In 2011 Gregg Henriques set out the limitations of the biopsychosocial model.

1. It is based on a narrow concept of biology.
2. It is inconsistent about the relationship between mind and the body.
3. It is no more beneficial than other models.
4. Some professionals believe that some areas of the model are more important than others.
5. It can be too simply applied in practice-based settings.

(Source: Henriques, 2011)

CASE STUDY 2.6
THE DIFFERENCES BETWEEN THE MEDICAL MODEL AND THE BIOPSYCHOSOCIAL MODEL: BETHANY'S STORY

Bethany was an overweight mature student who studied drama at college. She rarely if ever exercised – indeed she hated to exercise despite being told by her doctor that she needed to lose weight. After members of her study group verbally abused Bethany because of her weight, she put on her running shoes and jogged around the local park. After 10 minutes of fast running she suffered a heart attack and was taken to the accident and emergency department. A&E diagnosed that Bethany had a blocked artery and during subsequent surgery she had a stent fitted. She made a good recovery and has since returned to college to complete her drama course.

If you analyse the case study above using the medical model the diagnosis is simple: Bethany had a heart attack because one of her arteries become blocked. The intervention was surgery to keep the blocked artery open. However, what the medical model fails to take into account is that the heart attack was a result of her going running. She felt compelled to run because of the psychological effects of her weight and the sociological factors of being verbally abused. It is clear in this case that the medical model provides a simplistic analysis of Bethany's situation – one that was, in reality, a complex interplay of a multitude of factors (see Henriques, 2015). Indeed, if she is to make a full recovery then the psychological and sociological factors that were a precursor to this incident must also be addressed as well as the biological cause of the heart attack.

THE SOCIAL MODEL

Focus:	Societal attitudes, built environment
Causation:	Barriers placed in the way of inclusion by society
Intervention:	Non-disabled and disabled people working co-operatively to overcome the barriers
Education:	Education evolves to make schooling inclusive

This model is built upon a number of guiding principles, these being that:

- It is the attitudes, values and beliefs operating within society that cause disability, not medical impairments.
- It is society that needs to be treated and cured.
- Power over the lives of people with impairments should be held by those individuals, not professionals.
- Society, through its political apparatus, legislation and government, denies people with impairments their civil rights.
- Solutions to these issues cannot be imposed from the outside, but can only be resolved by disabled and non-disabled people working together.

(See Johnstone, 2001; Oliver, 1996.)

This model was born out of the work of the Union of the Physically Impaired Against Segregation and their document 'Fundamental Principles of Disability' (UPIAS, 1976). This document argued that disability was not created by impairments but rather by disabling barriers created by society itself. As Oliver, a key architect of this document stated:

> this was no amazing new insight on my part dreamed up in some ivory tower but was really an attempt to enable me to make sense of the world for my social work students and other professionals whom I taught. (Oliver, 1990a: 2)

So the aim of this model is to undermine the idea that disability is caused by bodily impairment. Within this framework, it is society that disables people because it restricts their movements and their ability to communicate and function as effectively as people without impairments (Morgan, 2012). This model's central tenet is that society actually causes disability by placing barriers to accessibility in the way of people with impairments (Goering, 2010).

After years of experiencing segregation and medicalisation many disabled people found the social model revelatory. For example, Morgan's (2012) work recounts how many people saw the social model as radical and an explanation for the difficulties they had been experiencing for years. Having been told that they were the problem the focus now began to shift away from individuals with disabilities to external factors and the manner in which society created barriers that restricted access. Morgan states that the social model was also important because for the first time the attitudes and values of non-disabled people became subject to examination, and hence for the disabled community it was simply revolutionary.

Most built environments, for example, are designed by non-disabled people who have little understanding of the needs of people with impairments. A person who is a wheelchair user only becomes 'disabled' by the environments they operate within if these are not designed with accessibility in mind. If, for instance, a building lacks lifts, ramps and wide doorways, as well as accessible light switches, door handles, toilets and motorised doors, then some disabled people will be unable to function unaided within that building (Brainhe, 2007). The social model is brought into sharp focus by the case study below of a student who was 'disabled' by the actions of her local council.

CASE STUDY 2.7
THE CREATION OF 'DISABILITY': LYNETTE'S STORY

I had been using my local library, which is located on the corner of my road, since I was five. During the past two years I have been studying for my A-levels and have used the library a lot. I enjoyed going to the library, although it was sometimes difficult to get into the building as it had been designed in the 1900s. The ramps were to say the least difficult to use, and the narrow corridors made it tricky to move about especially when the library was full of people. A few months ago the council informed me that the library was closing down and its resources were to be amalgamated, with others, into a new learning centre which was to be on the site of a secondary school two miles away from where I live. Although this learning centre would not be as handy as the old library, I was so excited and looked forward to using it because it had up-to-date computer equipment and was in a building which had been specifically designed for people with impairments. Last week I decided to go to the new learning centre; I don't drive so I planned my journey and found the best way to get there was by bus. Luckily the 'kneeling' bus service stopped at the end of my street, and I knew that this bus could accommodate wheelchair users because the driver could lower the floor so I could gain access. I waited at the bus stop for about 15 minutes before the bus arrived and the door duly swung open; however, the bus did not 'kneel down' and so I could not get from the pavement onto the bus as the step was just too high up. I asked the driver to lower the step. He just shouted back 'I am sorry, I have not been trained in how to make the bus lower. Only Trevor can do that and he's not on duty till tomorrow.' In that moment I went from being happy and excited about my visit to the learning centre to being a disabled person whose life was limited and controlled by the actions of others.

Think about what could or indeed should have been done when the learning centre was opened to ensure that it was fully accessible to every person.

READER REFLECTION

THE SOCIAL MODEL AND EDUCATION

It is often claimed that disabled people are amongst the poorest and the most disadvantaged in their communities, and that they have been systematically excluded from education (EHRC, 2017; Miles and Singal, 2010). For example, the Equality and Human Rights Commission (EHRC) reported, in 2017, that disabled 16- to 18-year-olds were twice as likely not be in education, employment or training than non-disabled young people. Moreover, their report detailed that 18.4% of disabled people had no qualifications whereas for the non-disabled population it was only 6.4%. A core component of the social model therefore is that education is an important means of overcoming the prejudices shown by society towards people with impairments. Many people argue that our schooling system teaches children to observe disabled people as different from themselves and sadly how to discriminate against them. The social model is clear in its advocacy for school transformation (Norwich, 2014) and how education should evolve to make all schooling inclusive. Indeed, the application of the principles of the social model to current educational systems would engender a major change in provision for children and young people with SEND. A full application of this model would ensure that segregated special schooling would be ended and replaced with local accessible schools for all. Educational institutions which adopted this framework would also review their curriculum approaches, classroom management and organisations, as well as the expectations of teachers, assistants and their general ethos, in order to ensure that the stereotypical and discriminating attitudes that society holds in relation to disability and people with impairments would be broken down. (Chapter 4 provides a further analysis of the move from segregated to inclusive approaches.)

CRITICISMS OF THE SOCIAL MODEL

TAKING IT FURTHER

It would be useful to read the report *Towards a social model of madness and distress?* (https://www.jrf.org.uk/sites/default/files/jrf/migrated/files/mental-health-service-models-full.pdf). It will provide you with information which relates to mental health and how moving to a social model approach can provide benefit for those people who are involved with mental health services; its Chapter 4 would seem especially useful.

The social model is recognised as being central to any debate relating to disability issues and inclusive education (Terzi, 2005). As a framework, it has also become embedded within the consciousness of many elements of British society. Furthermore, this model has helped to shift individuals and the collective understanding of disability (Johnstone, 2001), in addition to transforming the attitudes that disabled people experience on a daily basis (Swain and French, 2000). However, from the outset the model was subject to criticism from disability charities and professional organisations as well as from disabled people themselves (Oliver, 2013).

That criticism, Oliver (2013) argues, has two main foci. The first is that the social model does not account for an individual's impairment. For example, Jenny Morris argued that:

> there is a tendency within the social model of disability to deny the experience of our own bodies, insisting that our physical differences and restrictions are entirely socially created.

> While environmental and social attitudes are a crucial part of our experience of disability – and do indeed disable us – to suggest that this is all there is, is to deny the personal experience of physical and intellectual restrictions, of illness, of the fear of dying. (Morris, 1991: 10)

The second area of critique is that this model fails to account for difference and presents disabled people as one homogeneous group rather than a complex group of individuals who differ in terms of gender, sexuality, race, age and impairment (Oliver, 2013). To some, this model's only achievement is that it has resulted in a re-definition of the 'problem' of impairment and disability, and although it works in theory it fails in practice (Morgan, 2012). For example, Swain and French (2000: 575) argued that this model does not challenge the 'erroneous idea that disabled people cannot be happy or enjoy an adequate quality of life'. As such, they contend that it allows the continuance of the notion that disability is a tragedy which persons with impairments are forced to endure. Morgan (2012) also accounts that there is evidence that many practitioners have struggled with the social model's premise that power and control should be shared with disabled people.

CASE STUDY 2.8
BECKY'S STORY

Becky is a student who has a hearing impairment. She is training to become a playworker. As part of this training, Becky undergoes training in nursery and hospital settings. Her tutors carefully select the nursery and hospital wards that she visits. However, on her present placement the nursery refused to allow Becky to continue her work as they felt that her impairment created a risk. The head teacher of the nursery felt that she would not be able to successfully control the children nor facilitate their learning as she could not hear them talking, and that Becky's speech was sometimes difficult to understand.

For Terzi (2010) whilst the social model has made a fundamental contribution to knowledge it has, by overlooking the concept of normality, presented only a partial view of the relationship between impairment, disability and society. Terzi suggests that although this model provides a corrective to those based upon medical deficit, it still needs to clarify and extend its ideological framework if it is to be employed to understand the important and fundamental issues relating to the development of inclusive education.

TAKING IT FURTHER

1. You might like to read Mike Oliver's chapter, 'Defining Impairment and Disability: Issues at stake', in Emens, E. (2016) *Disability and Equality Law*.

2. What does Oliver feel are the problems in the application of the social model? You will gain valuable information relating to this issue on page 48 of this text.

3. You might find it helpful to also read Jonathan Levitt's (2017) paper, 'Exploring how the social model of disability can be re-invigorated: in response to Mike Oliver', *Disability & Society*, 32(4): 589–94. This paper identifies five major discussion questions on the way forward for the social model.

Table 2.1 Contrasting the medical and social models

Medical model	Social model
Disability is an individual problem	Disability is a societal problem
Disabled people need care	Disabled people have rights
The agent of change is the professional	The agent of change is the individual, advocate or anybody who affects the arrangements between the individual and society
Segregation	Social integration
The remedy for disability and its related issues is a cure for or normalisation of the individual	The remedy for disablism is in the interactions between the individual and society
Disabled people can never be equal to non-disabled people	Disabled people have the same rights to full equality in society and education as all citizens
Personal adjustment	Environmental manipulation

An examination of Table 2.1 should leave you in no doubt that the differences in the ideological standpoints between the medical and social models are substantial. For those who subscribe to the medical model, then, the individual is the problem, and the causation of the problem is limitations in physical or psychological functioning (Oliver, 1990a). However, for those who accept the social model, it is society itself which is the problem, and therefore the causation of disability stems from the barriers that it places in the way of the inclusion for all its citizens. As Oliver (1996: 41–42) famously stated, 'disability is wholly and exclusively social … disablement has nothing to do with the body.' This view is brought to the fore in the following, somewhat whimsical, account of the giraffe and the elephant.

A giraffe and an elephant consider themselves friends, but when the giraffe invited the elephant into his home to join him in a business venture, problems ensued. The house was designed to meet the giraffe's needs, with tall ceilings and narrow doorways, and when the elephant attempted to manoeuvre, doorways buckled, stairs cracked and the walls began to crumble. Analysing the chaos, the giraffe saw that the problem with the door was that it was too narrow. He suggested that the elephant take aerobic classes to get him 'down to size'. The problem with the stairs, he said, was that they were too weak. He suggested the elephant take ballet lessons to get him 'light on his feet'. But the elephant was unconvinced of this approach. To him the house was the problem.

(Source: Glenn Thomas, *Teaching Students with Mental Retardation* (1996). Reprinted by permission of Pearson Education Inc., New York: p.26.)

THE AFFIRMATIVE MODEL OF DISABILITY

Focus: Societal attitudes and individual attitudes

Causation: Impairment isn't the problem, learnt stereotypical attitudes are

Intervention: Disabled people take control over their own bodies

Education: Inclusive education

Within the United Kingdom, the examination of the contradictory explanations of causation of disability has led to the development of a more positive model of disability (Johnstone, 2001). This model emerged during the late 20th century due to the work of the disability arts movement and disabled people's organisations (see Chapter 3). The affirmation model was first introduced by Swain and French in 2000 as a development of those underlying principles of the social model (Cameron, 2013).

The principles of this model according to Swain and French (2000) were that it promoted a non-tragic view of disability and impairment that included positive social identities for disabled people. Swain and French believe that in affirming this positive identity, people with disabilities sought to undermine the systems of normality that dominate society.

READER REFLECTION It is argued that the medical model is based upon negative conceptuali-sations of disabled people. How would the model that Swain and French present lead to the creation of positive identities for disabled people?

The affirmative model developed in opposition to the personal tragedy view of disability that had dominated societal thinking in the 20th century (Seligman and Darling, 2017). The model's significance is that it extends the social model by incorporating the lived experiences of dis-abled people (Johnstone, 2001). Swain and French (2004) identified what the affirmation is and is not about (see Cameron, 2013).

The affirmation model is about:

- being different and thinking differently;
- the affirmation of unique ways of being situated in society;
- disabled people challenging presumptions about themselves and their lives in terms of not only how they differ from what is average or normal;
- ways of being that embrace difference (Swain and French, 2000: 185).

This model challenges the assumption that disabled people want to be cured, as well as encouraging the undermining of societal presumptions of what it means to be normal and what constitutes a happy and fulfilling life (Swain and French, 2000; 2004). Deeply rooted beliefs about what it means to be 'normal' are illustrated in the three case studies detailed below.

CASE STUDY 2.9
WHAT DOES IT MEAN TO BE NORMAL?: PAULA'S STORY

I attended a special school during the 1950s that was miles away from where I lived. One day I became upset because the school nurse told me that I should never give up hope that one day medical science would find a cure for my illness. 'Wouldn't that be great?' she said, if I could run around and play like the other little normal children. Well, I became angry and shouted at the nurse. I told her that I just loved the way I was and did not want to be fixed. My mates fell about laughing when I said this. The nurse though was not pleased, and told me that I did not understand my condition and that I was 'wrong in the head' to believe that my disability was a good thing. She sent me to the head teacher and I was kept in detention for showing a bad attitude to the nurse.

CASE STUDY 2.10
WHAT CAN HAPPEN IF WE STRIVE FOR NORMALITY?
ISMAIL'S STORY

Well I do not have extraordinary hearing; I cannot navigate well in foggy conditions; and no, I would not be good at tuning pianos. These are all things that 'normal' people have said I should be good at. What I am is visually impaired and this means I can only 'see' light and dark and nothing else. It is a condition I have had from birth. Before I was born my parents were advised to have a termination because my impairment also comes with learning difficulties. The doctors told my mum that my life would not be worth living. Since the age of one, through operations and filling me full of tablets they have tried to fix me and remediate what they say is my poor behaviour. I do not want to be fixed. I am happy as I am and I think it is disgraceful that my parents were told to terminate my life. The doctors never ask what I want; if they did I would tell them that I have a happy and fulfilling life and that I just want to be left alone.

CASE STUDY 2.11
WHY DO PEOPLE FEEL THAT CREATING NORMALITY IS IMPORTANT TO ALL DISABLED PEOPLE?
'A PERSONAL BLOG': LYNETTE'S STORY

My name is Lynette. I am 15 and a wheelchair user. I like my wheelchair: it is the latest model. It is powered and I can beat my friends in races because it goes fast. However, despite this wheelchair I still find life difficult. Many buildings are inaccessible and exploring my local area is difficult as all the pavements are full of potholes. This means my wheelchair constantly gets broken, or worse it sometimes tips over. When I travel about, I am often told that I get in the way. On buses I often cannot get on because the accessible space is taken up with people's bags or pushchairs. In the social model, my impairment is recognised but it states that the disability I face on a daily basis comes from people's attitudes and the barriers that society places in my way. In my view, all buses and buildings should be accessible and people would be taught in school to have a better attitude towards people with impairments. No medical operation or new tablet will cure an inaccessible building or a bad attitude. We need to move away from this simple notion that a medical cure can fix.

Swain and French (2004) argue that it is the premise of normality created by the medical model that causes stereotypical attitudes towards disability. They argue that it is these attitudes which act as a catalyst to the continuance of disability and the view that disabled people endure a tragic and pathetic state. This model, therefore, is built upon the premise that disabled people should have control of their lives and not medical or educational professionals. It is based firstly upon identifying how society excludes people, and secondly on developing an image of disabled people which is 'strong, angry and proud'.

DISABILITY POLITICS AND THE RIGHTS-BASED MODEL OF DISABILITY – 'NOTHING ABOUT US WITHOUT US'

Focus:	Political/full inclusion
Causation:	Societal structures, values and beliefs
Intervention:	Radical interventions, use of the law to end discrimination
Education:	Fully inclusive, with no tolerance being given to a separate segregated system of education

Within the rights-based approach people with disabilities would have the same rights and access to employment, health care and education. This approach is about removing physical, attitudinal and social barriers that blight the lives of disabled people. The rights-based model takes on employers, educational and health care professionals as well as policy makers to ensure our rights as people are upheld. This means that people would employ universal building designs, co-ordinated public services and accessible technology, and that government would ensure that these are well resourced through the services we use. It also means though that those who do not do so would face the penalties that are enshrined in the laws that govern our land.

> **'Nothing about us without us'** was the slogan promoted in 1981 by Disabled Peoples' International. This slogan's power derives from its opposition to oppression and resonates with the philosophy and history of the disability rights movement (Charlton, 2000).

According to Johnstone (2001: 22) both the social and the affirmative models are based upon 'liberal rather than radical conceptions of equal opportunities'. Critics of these models suggest what is actually required is a framework where the politicisation of disabled people (Johnstone, 2001) challenges the 'hegemony of disabilism' (Allan, 2003: 31). This framework, then, should challenge the exclusion of disabled people from governance structures of businesses and education, and challenge the general perception of disabled people as helpless and defined by impairment (Vanhala, 2010). Disability politics seeks, therefore, by the employment of the political and the social arena, to confront the non-disabled 'oppressors who perpetuate the exclusion of disabled people' (Allan, 2003: 31). Disability politics as a movement aims to liberate the silent voices of disabled people in an attempt to undermine societal values, beliefs and conventions, which are based upon the ideology of the medical model of disability (Allan, 2003). Proponents of this model argue that through direct action new affiliations and identifications for disabled people can be constructed. They maintain that it is through such new identities that people with impairments will emerge into mainstream politics to campaign for better provision for their minority group and for the removal of all barriers to inclusion in society (Shakespeare, 2006). In recent years, the growing impetus of the disability movement has moved the discussion of disability into encompassing legislation that governs human rights (Johnstone, 2001). Through the application of disability politics a more radical ideology has now emerged, one whose core principles follow a rights-based approach to the explanation of the provision received by disabled people.

THE RIGHTS-BASED MODEL AND EDUCATION

The rights-based model's central principle is that all children and young people should attend a mainstream educational setting located within their local community (Kenworthy and Whittaker, 2000). This model of disability challenges the widely held societal belief regarding the legitimacy of segregated education, and the premise that it is simply impossible to include all children and young people in mainstream education (CSIE, 2005). Based upon the principles encompassed by the rights-based model, the Centre for Inclusive Education has outlined ten reasons why inclusive education should become the norm and not the exception within British schools.

HUMAN RIGHTS

1. All children have the right to learn together.
2. Children should not be devalued or discriminated against by being excluded or sent away because of their disability or learning difficulty.
3. Disabled adults, describing themselves as special school survivors, are demanding an end to segregation.
4. There are no legitimate reasons to separate children for their education. Children belong together – with advantages and benefits for everyone. They do not need to be protected from each other.

GOOD EDUCATION

1. Research shows children do better, both academically and socially, in inclusive settings.
2. There is no specific teaching or care in a segregated school which cannot take place in an ordinary school.
3. Given commitment and support, inclusive education is a more efficient use of educational resources.

(Continued)

SOCIAL SENSE

1. Segregation teaches children to be fearful and ignorant, and it breeds prejudice.

2. All children need an education that will help them develop relationships and prepare them for life in the mainstream.

3. Only inclusion has the potential to reduce fear and build friendship, respect and understanding.

(Source: CSIE, 2005)

CASE STUDY 2.12
MECHANISMS FOR CLAIMING RIGHTS AND HOLDING GOVERNMENTS ACCOUNTABLE

Access to the courts can be an effective means of challenging the failure of the State to make adequate provision for education, achieve equality of opportunity or protect children whose rights are violated in the education system. A successful illustration of the use of legal redress is provided by a small disability organisation in Nepal that took the government to Court to argue that the failure to provide additional time in public examinations for 'blind children' denied them the right to equality of opportunity in education, given that Braille takes longer to read and write. The Court decreed that blind children should be entitled to extra time in examinations to reflect this difference. (UNICEF, 2007: 42)

CONCLUSION

In this chapter you gained knowledge and understanding of:

- models of disability;   Psycho medical   Affirmative   Biopsycho social   Rights based   social
- how these models might be utilised to analyse the issues surrounding the world of SEND.

This chapter introduced you to the major ideological models which affect people's knowledge and understanding of disability, impairment and inclusive schooling. Within the chapter we analysed the different ways in which each model identifies what the causation of disability is, and how their effects might be ameliorated. This analysis revealed huge ideological differences – differences which affect the contemporary values and beliefs about the way schooling for children with SEND should be organised. Analysis of these ideological frameworks highlighted the inherent limitations in each model.

We observed for example how, within the psycho-medical model, pupils can be objectified and dehumanised, whereas within the social model the problem of disablism is placed firmly with society, and pupils' impairments are in some way diminished. For Skidmore (1996), however, the fault of many of the models is how they reduce complex personal and societal issues to single unitary solutions. As such, the medical, biopsychosocial and social models do not provide a complete or satisfactory explanation of the way in which disability and SEND are conceptualised within our society. Oliver (1990a) contends that spending too much time on a consideration of what is meant by the models should be viewed as dangerous. He believes this to be the case because such discussions are based upon nothing more than semantics and as such obscure the real issues of disability – namely those of oppression, discrimination and inequality.

In Chapter 3 and Chapter 4, we will examine how these ideological frameworks have developed over time and critically analyse their effect upon the development of education for children with SEND. Furthermore, in Chapter 5 we will examine how the development of the social model was influential in the emergence and evolution of inclusive education.

The 'Taking it further' boxes in the chapter, as well as the student activities, reflective questions and further reading detailed below, have been designed to provide you with a clearer understanding of the major ideological models of disability considered in Chapter 2.

STUDENT ACTIVITIES

1. You may wish to complete some research in relation to models of disability that are employed throughout the world. What is the major model that dominates thinking about disability? The briefing paper 'Scoping models and theories of disability' may prove useful to your research (https://www.ncbi.nlm.nih.gov/books/NBK378951/#__NBK378951_dtls__).

2. Carefully consider the CSIE inclusion statement; by using internet and journal sources provide the evidence to support their view that fully inclusive education is the only way to organise educational provision for children with SEND.

REFLECTIVE QUESTIONS

Throughout the completion of the above activities, it would be useful to consider the following question: is it possible, or even desirable, to have a system of fully inclusive education?

This chapter has been dominated by the major models that overshadow theory and practice in relation to SEND assessment, provision and practice. A question that you might like to consider and discuss is: do any of these other models hold any usefulness in the daily lives of children and young people labelled with SEND? To help you consider your answer it would be useful to read Beaudry, B. (2016) Beyond models, *Journal of Medicine and Philosophy*, 41(2): 210–28.

FURTHER READING

Cameron, C. (2014) 'The Affirmation Model'. In Cameron, C. (ed.), *Disability Studies: A Student's Guide*. London: Sage. Chapter 2 of this book provides an expansive discussion of the history and development of the affirmative model of disability.

Evans, N.J., Broido, M.E., Brown, K.R. and Wilke, K.A. (2017) *Disability in Higher Education: A Social Justice Approach*. San Francisco, CA: Jossey-Bass. Whilst this is an American text, there is some usefulness in the overview offered in relation to the models in its Chapter 2.

Patton, S. (2011) *Don't Fix Me, I'm Not Broken: Changing Our Minds About Ourselves and Our Children*. Alresford: O Books. In this book Sally Patton brings a rather different perspective to how parents feel about their children with SEND. Rather than trying to 'fix them' she presents a powerful message in relation to how we as a society must move on from labelling our children.

Wearmouth, J. (2017) *Special Educational Needs and Disabilities in Schools: A Critical Introduction*. London: Bloomsbury. Chapter 1 of this text provides a very useful guide to SEND.

3

DISABILITY: EXPLANATORY BEGINNINGS

The major questions this chapter addresses are:

- How have people with disabilities been perceived by society throughout history?
- How has disability been defined in legislation from the 1990s onwards?
- What is the image of disability created by the media and children's books, as well as internet technology?
- How might societal attitudes towards disability influence educational policy?

INTRODUCTION

This chapter provides an introduction to disability by tracing how perceptions have changed over time. It examines how disability in the ancient world and developments in 'scientific thinking' led to the creation of the theoretical frameworks that dominate educational practice today. It also looks at how disability evolved within legislation from the 1990s to the present day. The final section discusses how conceptions of disability are formed through the media and children's books as well as internet technology. The chapter ends by considering how societal attitudes have the propensity to influence the evolution of policies for inclusive education.

READER REFLECTION   Before you begin reading make a note of your understanding of disability. You may also wish to consider what have been the major influences on the development of your knowledge of disability.

From 1997 until 2010, educational policy indicated that the placement of disabled children and young people into mainstream educational settings, so-called inclusive education, coupled with successful learning experiences would lead to non-disabled people's attitudes and conceptions of disability becoming more positive (Hodkinson, 2007). Whilst some argued that this policy initiative was based upon 'idealistic assumptions', as in reality some pupils with impairments were 'socially ostracised' (Spaling, 2002: 91), it did at face value indicate that for the New Labour government a social model of disability was of importance.

Interestingly, David Cameron, who in 2010 became prime minister of a coalition government of Conservatives and Liberal Democrats, stated that:

> We believe [that] the most vulnerable children deserve the very highest quality of care. We will improve diagnostic assessment for schoolchildren, prevent the unnecessary closure of special schools, and remove the bias towards inclusion. (Cabinet Office, 2010)

This statement was important because it advocated the continuation and expansion of a segregated education system. Furthermore, the language contained in Cameron's statement (e.g. phrases such as 'vulnerable children', 'highest quality of care', 'improve diagnostic assessment' and 'remove the bias towards inclusion') suggests that for this government a different model of disability was perhaps dominating policy decisions. Theresa May's government have continued with policies that seemingly do not promote respect for disabled people. Indeed, most recently the prime minister's knowledge of disability was called into question when she confused mental health issues with those for learning disabilities.

TAKING IT FURTHER

Watch the video below and then read the letter sent by Scope to the prime minister. Do her actions in the video or the sentiments contained within the letter enable you to determine which model of disability is dominating government thinking?

The video of Theresa May is available at: www.youtube.com/watch?v=xlxWPd5JO_M

Scope's letter is as follows:

7 December 2017

Dear Prime Minister,

I felt compelled to write to you following oral evidence from the Chancellor yesterday (Wednesday 6 December 2017) at the Treasury Select Committee in respect of the impact of disabled employees on low UK productivity levels.

Statistically and historically, the correlation between increases in productivity and disability employment have gone hand-in-hand. It has never been the case that increasing the number of disabled people in employment has had a harmful effect on productivity levels. In no study, projection or analysis released by the Office for Budget Responsibility, who have looked at the issue of productivity extensively, has disability employment been referenced as key driver of low productivity.

It is therefore entirely unacceptable that the Chancellor decided to attribute productivity challenges to disabled people so publicly in this way.

Last week, you personally committed your government to getting a million disabled people back to work, a move Scope warmly welcomed. We have worked constructively with government ministers and officials to ensure that your strategy, Improving Lives: The Future of Work, Health and Disability, provides a step change in the employment opportunities for disabled people, and we recognise the commitment of your colleagues in the Department of Health and Department for Work and Pensions to getting this strategy right.

I am confident that you will understand the adverse impact yesterday's derogatory comments will have on disabled people's chances of entering and staying in work.

We have called on the Chancellor to apologise and retract his factually inaccurate and incredibly harmful accusation and we hope that you will support the 13.3 million disabled people in the country by doing likewise.

(Continued)

> I would appreciate it if you would clarify if the Chancellor's statement represents a change of policy for your Government and whether this is a view which you share.
>   I look forward to receiving your response.
>
> Yours sincerely
>
> Mark Atkinson
>
> Chief Executive, Scope.

Whatever may be said about the Coalition's or Teresa May's policies it would seem important to gain a knowledge, understanding and appreciation of how society views disability and disablism. This is because 'at the end of the day' governments are influenced by the attitudes which dominate societal thinking.

HISTORICAL CONCEPTIONS OF DISABILITY

Disability, conceptualised in history, is difficult to study, as the terminology employed in ancient texts is often 'slippery' when viewed through the lens of modern times (Goodey and Rose, 2013: 17). However, in many 'western' societies disability is grounded within superstitions and beliefs about people with impairments. These perceptions dominate societal thinking, and that is despite archaeological evidence which suggests Neanderthal peoples incorporated disability and impairment as part of a common good within society (Spikins, 2014). Moreover, in Roman times whilst some impairments were seen as sources of humour, skeletal remains from Gloucester and Dorchester show that during this period some people with severe impairments did survive into adulthood. Indeed, evidence suggests that some individuals with impairments prospered (Wright-Southwell, 2013).

READER REFLECTION Read the statement by Pliny the Younger (61–113AD), a magistrate in ancient Rome. What might this tell us about the attitudes of some ancient Romans towards disability and impairment?

> Crippled and deformed in every limb, he could only enjoy his vast wealth by contemplating it and could not even turn in bed without assistance. He also had to have his teeth cleaned and brushed for him ... Yet he went on living, and kept his will to live, helped chiefly by his wife ... (Wright-Southwell, 2013)

Present-day conceptions of disability, however, have their roots in classical Greek theatre and culture. Here, the 'image of impairment' was linked with people's 'judgements about social acceptance' (Johnstone, 2001: vii), and society was grounded within 'the idealisation of the body shape' (Barnes and Mercer, 2003: 23). Throughout the cultures of ancient Greece and ancient Rome, and in the literature and art of Renaissance Europe, mainly negative conceptions of people with impairments were perpetuated (Borsay, 2005).

TAKING IT FURTHER

For an overview and critique of these issues, it would be useful to read:

Penrose, W.D. (2015) 'The discourse of disability in Ancient Greece', *Classical World,* 108(4): 499–523.

Penrose suggests that as far back as ancient Greece categories of disability existed. This paper also offers a critique of disability theory as it relates to ancient history.

DISABILITY: EARLY RELIGIOUS CONCEPTIONS

Throughout the history of our society, disability has been viewed as a contentious issue where the role of cultural values in the development of attitudes has been crucial. From the distant past, conceptions of impairments and disabilities have been influenced by Judaeo-Christian theology. The Bible contains many examples that reinforce people's dread of impairment, and this fear was further enforced by the Church's determination that people with impairments were afflicted with the soul of Satan as punishment for their ancestral transgressions (Machingura and Museka, 2018).

In Leviticus, Chapter 21, verses 17–20, the Bible calls for people with visual and physical impairments to be excluded from offering bread in the temple. In Deuteronomy, Jones (2003) believes there is a reference that people with mental impairments should be regarded as 'beasts' and should be treated as less than human.

In Leviticus, God instructs Moses to tell Aaron that He will not permit Aaron's disabled descendants to serve as priests:

> No one of your offspring throughout their generations who has a blemish may approach to offer the food of his God. For no one who has a blemish shall draw near, one who is blind or lame, or one who has a mutilated face or

(Continued)

a limb too long, or one who has a broken foot or a broken hand, or a hunch-back, or a dwarf, or a man with a blemish in his eyes or an itching disease or scabs or crushed testicles. (http://www.kingjamesbibleonline.org/)

(See Parry, 2013: 22 for a detailed account of disability and early Christian traditions.)

It is apparent, then, that the development of religious conceptions of impairment and disability was inextricably linked to impurity and sin.

READER REFLECTION

Carefully read these passages from the King James Bible. What message do they offer of how people with impairments should be treated?

John 9: 1–3

Now as Jesus passed by, He saw a man who was blind from birth. And His disciples asked Him, saying, 'Rabbi, who sinned, this man or his parents, that he was born blind?' Jesus answered, 'Neither this man nor his parents sinned, but that the works of God should be revealed in him.'

Samuel 25: 8

Wherefore they said the blind and the lame shall not come into the house.

(http://www.kingjamesbibleonline.org)

Now consider St Augustine's statement (354–430AD), a theologian who was significant in the growth of Western Christianity. What does this statement tell us about early Christian conceptions of disability?

[why did you] ... place in this oh so beautiful world the blind, the one-eyed, the cross-eyed, the deaf, the mute, the lame, the deformed, the distorted, the wormy, the leprous, the paralysed, the epileptic and those who are deficient in various other ways – some even look monstrous to us, because of their extreme ugli-ness and the horrible strangeness of their limbs ... some of slow mind, and others of mind so foolish that a human being, would rather live with cattle than with that sort of human being.

(See Laes et. al., 2013.)

Noteworthy, in this respect, is that the founders of the western church, Luther and Calvin, both 'damned as emissaries of Satan people who today we would label as having mental health impairments' (Manion and Bersani, 1987: 235). Furthermore, Luther proclaimed that he had seen Satan in a visually impaired child (Haffter, 1969). During this period people with visual impairments were labelled as 'changelings' and were offered up by the Church as living proof of Satan's power on earth. In the *Malleus Maleficarum*, a late 15th-century treatise sanctioned by the Pope, children with visual impairments were classified as being born from a liaison between their mother, witches and sorcery (Oliver and Barnes, 1998). These views are of course dated; however, it is perhaps relevant to note the alleged comments of one England football manager and 'television pundit' who seemed to openly subscribe to these religious prejudices (see www. theguardian.com/football/1999/jan/30/newsstory.sport7).

Whatever may be said about such comments, it seems apparent that throughout history society has held that people with impairments 'were possessed by the devil and therefore the common treatment was to beat the devil out of them' (Shakespeare, 1994: 284). Whilst we may argue as to the modern relevance of these theological conceptions, it is perhaps more relevant here to examine how this concept has been transformed within our society with the passage of history.

TRANSFORMATIONS THROUGH TIME

In tracing the historical development of societal attitudes to, and the conceptualisation of, disability it is helpful to employ the organising construct proposed by Finkelstein (1980). Within this construct, there are three periods in the development of the concept of disability. Later in the chapter, we will consider Finkelstein's third period of development, that of the post-industrial society (which will be considered through examination of government legislation and the development of theoretical frameworks of impairment during the 20th century). For now, though, let us turn to Finkelstein's first phase, that of the feudal period.

THE FEUDAL PERIOD

During the pre-industrial phase, which operated during the 17th to the early 19th century in western Europe, most people with impairments were routinely integrated within their villages and local communities. During this period, existence for many people was mainly based within agrarian economies, and for some, small cottage-based industries provided a livelihood (Barnes and Mercer, 2003). Indeed, conceptions of being 'abled-bodied' did not at this time relate to physical attributes per se, rather in an individual's capacity for farm labouring.

As societal relations during this period focused on subsistence rather than wealth accumulation, many people with impairments were able to survive within their local community, albeit with the majority existing on the bottom rung of the economic ladder. So whilst people with impairments might be observed to be individually unfortunate they were not, as a rule, explicitly excluded from society (Oliver, 1990b). On occasion, though, people with impairments did experience a form of segregation which was directly due to economic and familial circumstances. For example, for those rejected by their families or whose economic performance was curtailed by impairment, begging or a reliance on charity alms could become the norm (Barnes and Mercer, 2003). In addition, for those with severe impairments who had managed to survive the high infant mortality rate, their existence might become framed alongside the sick and bedridden in the small religious hospitals (Oliver and Barnes, 1998).

During the feudal period, then, although categories of disability were observable, and this did create a stigma around some individual disabilities (Parry, 2013), people with physical and mental impairments were included although they mainly occupied the lowest echelons of society. It is also important to recognise that throughout this period disability was not solely conceptualised within the realms of bodily impairment, but rather was correlated to economic performance. As Gleeson writes, 'whilst impairment was probably a prosaic feature of feudal England, disablement was not' (1997: 194).

TAKING IT FURTHER

Consider the concept of disability that operated during the feudal period. What did society observe to be the causation of disability during this time?

To further develop your knowledge of disability during this period, please read section one of Simon Jarret's (2012) paper entitled 'Disability in time and place' (https://content.historicengland.org.uk/content/docs/research/disability-in-time-and-place.pdf).

THE INDUSTRIAL CAPITALISM PERIOD

Towards the end of the 18th century Britain, Europe and North America witnessed an 'intensification of the commercialisation of land and agriculture' (Oliver and Barnes, 1998: 29). For Finkelstein, this period of industrial capitalism is important as it transformed society's concept of disability. The rapid spread of market economics led to changes in working and living conditions as 'westernised' countries absorbed the new mechanised systems of production. Increasingly, however, the Industrial Revolution introduced limitations upon the employment of people with impairments. As Ryan with Thomas (1980: 101) explain, 'The speed of factory work, the enforced discipline, the time keeping and production norms – all these were highly unfavourable changes from the slower, more self-determined and flexible methods of work into which many handicapped people had been integrated.'

'Handicapped' may be defined as a physical or mental impairment that renders a person unable to perform certain functions. It is a term that was used extensively in the original World Health Organization Classifications' system of disability, but has now been replaced with the term 'participation'. This reflects the social model of disability which considers what a person 'can do' when given the appropriate resources and support, rather than focusing upon what a person can't do.

Gradually, the new social and economic order, with its expanding cities and towns, forced the decline of local and family-based support systems. Ultimately, this led to some people with impairments becoming disadvantaged and excluded from employment and society. Both Finkelstein (1980) and Oliver (1990b) have argued that it was the spread of this 'liberal utilitarianism' (Oliver and Barnes, 1998: 26) which forced society to consider that 'defective bodies and minds were … dangerous and threatening' (Barnes and Mercer, 2003: 32). These negative conceptions were further reinforced by the spread of Darwinism and its theory of the survival of the fittest. With the passage of time and the development of the principles of eugenics, people with impairments were increasingly identified as being a threat to social progress.

> **Eugenics** was a term employed by Sir Francis Galton (1822–1911) in relation to the study of selective breeding to improve the quality of the human race.

Finkelstein (1980) contends that the birth of industrial capitalism was significant because it established society's modern-day concepts of disability. He suggests that as a direct result of these transformed conceptions, people with impairments became segregated from the rest of society.

Using the knowledge you gained in Chapter 2, consider which model of disability would best fit that which was created during the industrial capitalist phase of history.

READER REFLECTION

The rise of industrial capitalism, then, created a new ideology, one in which 'able-bodied' normality 'became the yardstick' for 'judging people with impairments as less than whole' (Oliver, 1990b: 89). The transformation of society's conception of disability led to the birth of large institutions as a method of controlling these societal 'misfits'. In turn, the individualistic medical approach to disability emerged as the new conceptual orthodoxy. From this time forward, Finkelstein comments, western societies equated disability with 'flawed' minds and bodies. People with impairments were observed to have 'suffered' a 'personal tragedy', and so became a social problem and a burden to society. Therefore, the 19th and 20th centuries witnessed the approaches to dealing with people with impairments becoming dominated by this conception of disability.

THE POST-INDUSTRIAL PERIOD

In his third phase, Finkelstein (1980) proposed that the post-industrial society brought forth more positive opportunities for the inclusion of people with impairments. He suggested that within this period disability will become reconceptualised, moving from the notion of 'individual tragedy' to the premise that disability is nothing more than a form of oppression (see Chapter 2 for a fuller discussion). However, before we proceed in employing this schema to trace the transformation of the concept of disability, it is important to note that Finkelstein's construct has been subject to criticism.

Firstly, it is apparent within the 21st century that the concept of disability as an individual medical tragedy has maintained a powerful influence on societal attitudes. This is because the work of professionals in our society is still very important for the management of some people's medical conditions. Secondly, Finkelstein's analysis assumes a simple correlation between the development of industry and changing conceptions of impairment and disability. For some, this model is subject to a theoretical naïvety in its premise that technological development and professional involvement will bring a new wave of integrative sentiment into society. Thirdly, the model is further criticised because it fails to acknowledge that negative constructs of impairment existed before the advent of the Industrial Revolution. Indeed, as we will observe later, even today they exert a powerful influence over societal conceptions of disability through such enterprises as the media.

Leaving this critique aside, though, it is useful to trace how the concept of disability transformed during the late 20th and early 21st century through the work of the Disabled People's Movement, international organisations and also government legislation.

DISABILITY: A RECONCEPTUALISATION FROM WITHIN

The latter part of the 20th century witnessed societal conceptions of disability slowly transforming and this was in no small part due to the work of people with impairments themselves. The 1970s and 1980s were a period when disabled people collectively emerged from the shadows and moved 'from acquiescence [to government policy] to uncertainty, discontent and finally to outright anger' (Davis, 2000: 124), becoming united in their condemnation of the way society treated them as second-class citizens. Within the next section we will examine how, through the work of disabled people, society's understanding of disability has moved from observing it to be a tragic individual problem to one that observes it as a 'situation of collective institutional discrimination and social oppression' (Oliver and Barnes, 1998: 3).

During the mid to late 1970s, the first political groups of disabled people were founded in the United Kingdom. In 1974 the Disability Alliance group was formed and 1976 saw the emergence of the Union of the Physically Impaired Against Segregation (UPIAS). The latter's aim was to replace segregated institutions for people with impairments with a right for all to be able to engage fully in society and live independent lives (Shakespeare, 2006). These groups re-examined the orthodoxy of the individual tragedy model of disability. In turn, this led to the transformation of the concept of disability into what we know today as the social model. Crucially, the UPIAS drew an important distinction between impairment and disability (Barnes, 1997), namely that people with impairments became disabled not because of their medical pathology, but rather as a result of isolation and being prevented from participating fully in economic, social and political life (Johnstone, 2001).

In the UPIAS's (1976: 3) terms then:

> [D]isability is a situation, caused by social conditions, which requires for its elimination, (a) that no one aspect such as incomes, mobility or institutions is treated in isolation, (b) that disabled people should, with the advice and help of others, assume control over their lives, and (c) that professionals, experts and others who seek to help must be committed to promote such control by disabled people.

The UPIAS (1976: 3) went further and articulated a radically new conception of disability, stating that:

> In our view, it is society which disables physically impaired people. Disability is something imposed on top of our impairments, by the way we are unnecessarily isolated and excluded from full participation in society. Disabled people are therefore an oppressed group in society.

A new era of disability had begun, one that was to be dominated by a reconceptualisation of the nature of society's understanding of the link between impairment and disability. This new social contextualisation led directly to the birth of the social model in which radical new reconstructions were forwarded and the distinction between impairment and disability was further, and specifically, separated (Shakespeare, 2006).

> Oliver (1996), a key architect of the social model, argued that impairment related to a missing or defective limb or a mechanism of the body that was compromised. However, for Oliver disability related to a disadvantage or restriction in a person's life which was caused by a social institution or a process that directly excluded people with impairments from mainstream social activities.

What are the key distinctions that Oliver makes in his definition of disability from those that are outlined in the medical model?

READER REFLECTION

The 'umbrella' organisation, the British Council of Disabled People, later expanded this defining statement to include other impairments such as those which were sensory and intellectual. Six years later a new group – the Disabled Peoples' International – further developed the UPIAS's definition by adding that disability was created by the imposition of barriers to inclusion that were erected by society against people with impairments. In the decades that followed, further initiatives such as the Disabled Arts Movement and the affirmative rights and international models of disability were born. These in turn brought a substantial and permanent reconceptualisation of the nature of disability into the hearts and minds of some elements of British society.

LEGISLATIVE FRAMEWORKS

Government policies during the last decades of the 20th century had been constructed upon conceptions of disability and impairment formulated by the World Health Organization (WHO). During the late 1970s the WHO commissioned Philip Wood, Elizabeth Bradley and Mike Bury to extend an existing classification of disease to include the consequences of long-term illness (Barnes et al., 2002). The resultant *International Classification of Impairment, Disability and Handicap* (ICIDH) (Wood, 1980) introduced a triad of definitions into British society.

READER REFLECTION

Note the definitions detailed below. Compare and contrast these definitions with other students and discuss how differing models of disability lead to such variance in definitions of disability and impairment.

Firstly then, the ICIDH define impairment as a deviation from a biomedical norm and a handicap as 'a disadvantage for a given individual resulting from impairment or disability of a role that is normal (depending on age, sex and social and cultural factors) for the individual' (Wood, 1980: 291). Furthermore, they define disability as a restriction of a lack of ability to perform an activity in a 'normal manner' because of impairment (Shakespeare, 2006).

In contrast, the Disabled Peoples' International would define impairment as the functional limitation within the individual caused by physical, mental or sensory impairment. Disability though would equate to the loss or limitation of opportunities to take part in the normal life of the community on an equal level with others due to physical and social barriers (Goodley, 2011).

Whilst the ICIDH's triad of definitions found favour with many social scientists and was observed to be useful in the accurate description of some dimensions of disabled people's experiences (Shakespeare, 2006), it was however subject to sustained criticism from disabled people's organisations. The criticism levelled at the classification system contended that the ICIDH had correlated impairment with disability and handicap. Thus, through this schema disability was caused by medical impairment and not (as the UPIAS observed) by societal barriers.

A further criticism was that the schema employed the guiding principle of 'normality' to classify a person with impairment against. Oliver and Barnes (1998) question how one judges the normality of psychological and physiological processes. They contend that normality as articulated within the ICIDH reflects a eurocentric view of society which is firmly predicated upon the values of healthy, male, middle-class professionals.

READER REFLECTION

In 1997, the WHO began to revise the ICIDH in light of the criticisms that had been levelled against it by disabled people's organisations. Within the ICIDH-2 (as it became known, or to give it its correct title, *International Classification of Functioning, Disability and Health*), 'disability' was replaced by 'disablement', and 'handicap' was reconceptualised as 'participation'. Disablement, within the new schema, operated on two levels: one incorporating environmental extrinsic factors, and the other incorporating intrinsic personal factors, such as fitness, health, gender, age or psychological well-being. However, impairment within the new schema remained unchanged.

For many people the WHO's new schema represented a step forward. However, for disabled people's organisations the 'ICIDH-2' remained problematic because it advantaged individual medical pathology over celebrating what people with impairments could actually do (Johnstone, 2001).

TAKING IT FURTHER

Read through the ICIDH-2 checklist (www.who.int/classifications/icf/icfchecklist.pdf? ua=1). What is your view of the usefulness, or otherwise, of a checklist such as this?

Now read Symeonidou's (2014) article in *Disability & Society*, 29(8): 1260–74. This paper details the dangers of the introduction of a classification system of disability based upon the 'ICIDH2' in Greece. Does this research support or undermine your view of a 'categorisation checklist'?

GOVERNMENT PERSPECTIVES

Interestingly, and despite the radical reconception of disability by the UPIAS and the WHO's more socially orientated employment, governments in Westminster, unlike governments in other European countries, chose not to move forward in their own conceptualisation of disability. Indeed, within legislative initiatives from the 1990s to the present day they have rigidly employed the original classification system (see Chapter 8 for a further comparative analysis). This has meant that the distinctions between impairment, handicap and disability have persistently remained as the benchmark not only for how society conceptualises but, moreover, for how it also measures disability (Johnstone, 2001).

THE 1990s AND THE DISABILITY DISCRIMINATION ACT(S)

In 1995 the Conservative government finally introduced legislation that made it illegal to discriminate against people with impairments in terms of employment and service provision (Borsay, 2005). The Act (Disability Discrimination Act, 1995) marked the end of a period of activism by disabled people's organisations (Pearson and Watson, 2007). After 14 previously unsuccessful attempts to push through legislation, those organisations finally hoped that 'a comprehensive anti-discrimination civil rights bill for disabled people' would be enacted (Evans, 1996: 1). Many anticipated that this legislation would provide a reconceptualisation of disability, one that would be based upon the social model developed by the Disabled People's Movement. However, the Act only adopted the construct of disability forwarded within the ICIDH. Whilst the Act provided a further elaboration of disability, the operational definition employed by it was based solely upon the discredited medicalised model (Evans, 1996).

> Disability, within this Act, was defined as follows:
>
> a person has a disability if he has a physical or mental impairment which has a substantial long-term adverse effect on his ability to carry out normal day-to-day activities. (DDA, 1995: 1)

The DDA then, rather than heralding a new era in society's conceptualisation of disability, actually reinforced the causal link between impairment and disability. Indeed, this legislation further promoted the medicalisation of disability. This was because it defined disability by the employment of medicalised measurements.

INFLUENCE OF THE NEW LABOUR GOVERNMENT

In 1997, the Blair government was elected upon a commitment to review the DDA. It was hoped by many that government would take the opportunity to amend disability legislation to emphasise a 'more social construct ... where disability is [seen to be] a product of ... external environmental factors (Keil et al., 2006: 169). However, its first piece of legislation, the Special Educational Needs and Disability Act (DfES, 2001), did nothing more than alter Part IV of the DDA in order to bring the educational provision into line with other discrimination legislation. As such, this legislation's definition of disability was based upon the medical model rather than the social model.

In 2005, legislation was again enacted. However, as with previous legislation the government chose not to expand its conceptualisation of disability. This Disability Discrimination Act only amended Part III of the DDA and thereby placed a general duty on public institutions to promote disability equality. More than a decade after the enactment of the DDA it was clear that government's conceptualisation and articulation of disability was, despite the activism and development of the social model by disabled people's organisations, stubbornly unchanged.

THE 2010 EQUALITY ACT

In 2010 an act was introduced into statute that replaced the DDA, this being the Equality Act. This Act offered legal protection not just to those who had an impairment or disability but also to those who possessed 'protected characteristics' (Brown, 2014: 129).

The Equality Act (2010) outlaws:

- direct discrimination
- associative discrimination
- indirect discrimination
- harassment
- third-party harassment
- victimisation.

(See Chapter 7 for further analysis.)

The Equality Act states that a person has a disability if:

a) the person has a physical or mental impairment; and
b) the impairment has a substantial and long-term adverse effect on the person's ability to carry out normal day-to-day activities.

According to Brown (2014) this Act is problematic, because instead of increasing an individual's protection, in law, it may actually dilute the rights of disabled people by grouping so-called 'at risk' individuals into one piece of legislation. Furthermore, Brown (2014) believes that the Act is still based upon the medical model of disability, as it focuses upon an individual's impairment and ability to carry out 'normal' day-to-day activities.

Trace the definition of disability that has existed since the 1990s in government legislation. Has the categorisation of disabled people actually changed?

READER REFLECTION

CONCEPTIONS AND BARRIERS TO INCLUSION

Moving away from our examination of the history of disability, we now turn to examine how society's conceptions of disability have been influenced by the 'picture' of disability created by the media. The media have a very powerful influence on people's lives and an important function in determining an individual's sense of reality (Orbe, 2013). The literature base references how stereotypical assumptions are inherent in our culture, and how the images reproduced within such media as books, films, television, newspapers, the internet and advertising have come to dominate people's conceptions of disability.

READER REFLECTION

An overview by Huws and Jones (2010) of research that has examined the portrayal of disability in the media, suggests it is an important source for the development of people's attitudes towards people with disability. They report that some studies have been critical of news reports about mental impairments because they are either too positive or they employ storylines that reinforce negative and inaccurate portrayal of people with disabilities.

Think about how disability culture is represented in one television series that you have watched. Which model of disability would prove the most valuable lens to understand how the show might impact its viewers' understanding of disabled people?

THE PICTURE PORTRAYED IN BOOKS AND NEWSPAPERS

The influence of the media upon conceptions of disability has a pernicious history. The media have for a long time stigmatised people with impairments by focusing upon the medical model's outlook that disability is a 'personal misfortune' (Shakespeare, 1994: 284). Over the last two centuries classic plays, novels and newspapers have presented people with impairments as pathetic, passive victims or ugly and depraved, such as in Charles Dickens's *A Christmas Carol* and *Nicholas Nickleby.* In the first text, two characters with impairments, Tiny Tim and a man with a visual impairment, are portrayed as pitiable and in need of society's help (Swain and French, 2000).

READER REFLECTION

Read the critique of Dickens's portrayal of disability below. Do you agree with the author that the portrayal of Tiny Tim should be seen as offensive?

I hate Tiny Tim

Tiny Tim is on the ropes in Charles Dickens's Christmas Carol. Sickly and dependent, Tiny Tim is getting shakier and shakier on that homemade little crutch. But he is saved from death by old Ebenezer Scrooge, who sees the light in the nick of time.

Now, before you go apoplectic at my assault on wee Tim, think about how he helps shape some of society's most cherished attitudes – charity, pity (for poor little Tiny Tim), for example. Tiny Tim, plucky, sweet and inspirational, tugs at the public heart ...

> I hate it. I hate it because this Tiny Tim sentimentality stereotypes people with disabilities and contributes to our oppression. When you think about a person with a disability as someone to feel sorry for, as someone to be taken care of and looked after, it is difficult to think about hiring them as a teacher, an architect or an accountant. (Stothers, 2008)

Now read this extract from *Nicholas Nickleby*. What might this extract tell us of societal conceptions of disability at this time?

> Pale and haggard faces, lank and bony figures, children with the countenances of old men, deformities with irons upon their limbs, boys of stunted growth, and others whose long meagre legs would hardly bear their stooping bodies, all crowded on the view together; there were the bleared eye, the hare-lip, the crooked foot, and every ugliness or distortion that told of unnatural aversion conceived by parents for their offsprings.

(See Marchbanks (2006) for an in-depth analysis of the intellectual impairments in the work of Charles Dickens.)

In addition, some famous storybooks have used their villains to demonstrate how disability has twisted and rendered as evil a person with impairment. For example, in recent research (Park and Hodkinson, 2017) into classic fairy tales, it was found that disability was often linked to characters who were an embodiment of evil, were tragic in nature, or indeed were the butt of jokes. Moreover, many of these stories included 'happily ever after endings' where the disabled characters either disappeared or were cured of their disabilities. The research concluded that the employment of children's classic fairy tales to support the national curriculum, as advocated by the government, was highly problematic. This was because of the manner in which disability was negatively formulated in these classic stories.

In general, then, books from the Victorian era forward have ensured that disability was employed to purvey emotive messages of courage, forgiveness and generosity (Shakespeare, 1994). Through such messages, the literature of the 19th and 20th century guaranteed that people with impairments were conceptualised as 'different' or as the 'other', an outsider trapped by their disability.

Newspaper reports within the British press have attracted similar criticisms as those outlined above. The construction of disability within newspapers is based upon the language used, the employment of image and the manner in which disabled people are 'framed' in 'stories' (Findlay-Williams, 2013). Within this medium, disabilist language is common, both in the tabloid and the so-called quality papers. Reports about people with impairments are usually featured for their sensation value, and stories of individuals who 'bravely manage' to achieve despite their impairment are commonplace. Stereotypical constructs, however, only serve to reinforce the belief that disabled people have 'something wrong with them', thereby devaluing people with impairments' contribution to society and helping to exclude them from participation in mainstream social and economic life (Oliver and Barnes, 1998).

TAKING IT FURTHER

Read 'Reporting it Right' (https://providers.dhhs.vic.gov.au/sites/dhhsproviders/files/2017-11/Reporting-it-right-media-guidelines-interactive.pdf).

Do you think this is a useful document in relation to how disabled people should be represented in the media?

THE PICTURE PORTRAYED IN FILMS AND TELEVISION

Portrayals of disability in film and television have been the subject of research. Apart from specific specialist programming (of which there is very little), people with impairments have been under-represented in British television and film productions (Contact, 1991), and when a disabled character does appear, for example in crime thrillers, they are often pictured as either the 'wicked' criminal or as the powerless and pathetic victim of a crime (Oliver and Barnes, 1998). In reality, television makes disabled people invisible and some observe this to be a form of social oppression (Barnes and Mercer, 2010).

If we examine films, we can observe that many villains are subject to an impairment, for example in the *Batman* films – here the Joker, the Penguin and Two-Face come to mind (Oliver and Barnes, 1998). And, in the 1946 film *It's a Wonderful Life* a principal character, Mr Potter, is portrayed as evil, twisted and frustrated – and this status is linked to that character's 'confinement' to a wheelchair (Swain and French, 2000).

An early content analysis of films and television showed that the most consistently employed picture of disability within this medium is that of the maladjusted disabled person

(Longmore, 1987). Furthermore, and despite recent positive constructions of disability in British soaps, it seems clear that the 'history of physical disability images in the movies has mostly been a history of distortion in the name of maintaining an ableist society' (Norden, 1994: 314). It appears, then, that ideologies of 'normalcy' are 'embedded within the narrative and visual/audio aspects of the film, the intent of the director/writers and cinematographers, the agendas and the commissioning/distribution and employment practices of the film industry, and in conceptualisations of wider film audiences and the way they are addressed, demonstrating that politics is always present in cinema' (Wilde, 2018: 5).

TAKING IT FURTHER

In the 90-year history of the Oscars, few disabled actors have been recognised with awards. Do you feel that the lack of representation of disabled actors, or indeed, the over-representation of non-disabled actors being cast as characters with disabilities, is problematic to society's conceptualisation of disability?

To help you develop your knowledge and understanding of this issue, it might be helpful to read 'The Oscars Love Movies About Disability, Not Disabled Actors' by Sophia Stewart (https://filmschoolrejects.com/oscars-love-movies-disability-not-disabled-actors/).

THE PICTURE PORTRAYED IN ADVERTISING

At the most rudimentary level, we may observe that people with impairments suffer from a lack of exposure within advertising campaigns that appear in Britain (COI, 2001). It is also apparent that the negative conceptualisation of disability evidenced in films, television programmes, stories and newspapers is further enforced with the campaigns employed by the advertising industry (Oliver and Barnes, 1998). Early charity advertising was formulated upon images of people with physical differences. The purpose of these campaigns was to 'evoke fear and sympathy in the viewer' (Barnes and Mercer, 2003: 93) and to establish a 'dependent, impairment active charity dynamic' (Hervey, 1992: 35–36). Indeed, charities generally have presented a distorted image of disability to recruit volunteers and publicise their cause, but most importantly so that they can raise money.

The picture of disability created by such advertising has been a major cause of concern for the disabled people's movement. This is because charity advertising has continued to emphasise the perceived inadequacy of people with impairments. Positively, though, in recent years some charities have shifted their campaigns to concentrate upon ability and not disability (Barnes and Mercer, 2010). However, these developments, whilst recognised as a step in the right direction, have also faced criticism because they do nothing to empower people with impairments. In more recent times therefore, whilst it is apparent that more disabled people are being seen in advertising, portrayals of disability in such campaigns are often superficial, tokenistic and misleading (Houston, 2017).

TAKING IT FURTHER

Take a look at the advertisement 'Canadian Tire's Hoop Dreams' (https://advertising anddisability.com/2017/03/09/canadian-tires-hoop-dreams/#more-1398).

Do you think, like the author of this web page, that this advert is significant because it is directed at the young and is designed to educate people in relation to tolerance, inclusion and community?

THE PICTURE PORTRAYED ON THE INTERNET AND SCHOOLS' INTRANETS

During the late 1990s third-wave technologies, those of computers, the Internet, multimedia and hypertexts, began to dominate pedagogical materials in schools and colleges (Hodkinson, 2012a). Although many people observed these digital technologies as positive, others believed that they should be treated with caution. In a study of digital technologies employed by schools, Hodkinson (2012a) found that the portrayal of disability was extremely limited and one that was bounded by medical deficit.

READER REFLECTION

A finding from my own research details that in the wealth of school-orientated images that were analysed such as playgrounds, classrooms, swimming lessons and school sports days, no picture of disability was observable (Hodkinson, 2012a).

Read the statement above. Consider what the effect of the 'invisibility of disability' in digital technologies employed in schools might have upon disabled children?

Although digital technologies have many positive aspects, there has been a growing issue in the employment of this medium over the last decade, namely cyberbullying (Slonje et al., 2013). Disabled children are some of the most frequent targets of such bullying. For example, it is suggested that around 65% of pupils with Asperger's have been subject to bullying (Subramanian, 2014). Social media platforms are not free of such harassment but operate by employing the cultural, economic and values replete in the wider society (Karppi, 2013).

Flaming is having an online fight that includes an exchange of insults and, at times, inappropriate language.

Trolling is starting a fight between two people on line.

> **Cyberstalking** is persistently sending intimidating or harassing messages through online platforms.
>
> (Source: Subramanian, 2014)

It would appear that trolling, flaming and cyberstalking are going to be growing issues in relation to disability bullying and hate crime in the future.

THE PICTURE PORTRAYED IN SCHOOL READING SCHEME BOOKS

The use of reading schemes in the UK has long been central to how children are taught to read in schools. The employment of schemes may be traced back to American texts of the 1930s and English texts of the 1940s such as the famous 'Janet and John' key words books. The importance of these books should not be underestimated as evidence denotes that 70% of British adults have learnt to read using such schemes. In 2017 research was conducted to analyse the picture of disability contained in reading schemes (Hodkinson, 2017). The research found that disability was almost invisible, and the images and text that were available represented disability in a highly stereotypical manner which was based on the ideology of the medical model.

TAKING IT FURTHER

Read Hodkinson's (2017) paper, 'Constructing impairment and disability in school reading schemes', *Education 3–13,* 45(3): 572–85. After reading this, consider how important it is that young children in early years settings and schools should encounter a realistic picture of disability.

CONCEPTIONS OF DISABILITY IN SOCIETY: A SUMMARY

Within our society it would appear, then, that the media, in all their forms, exert a powerful stimulus for the maintenance of disabling stereotypes. It may be seen that they form the bedrock upon which attitudes towards, assumptions about and expectations of disabled people are based. Barnes's (1992: 39) research concluded that it was these disabling stereotypes that were fundamental to the 'discrimination and exploitation … [that] … contribute significantly to the systematic exclusion from mainstream community life' that people with impairments experience.

It is salient to note, however, that some research studies may not have fully explored how the wealth of disabalist messages received from the media are inculcated by society. A perhaps more cautious stance to adopt, then, is that the media have a pivotal role in the dissemination of images and opinions, but in their relation to the formulation of society's conceptions of disability their role remains unclear (Hodkinson, 2012a).

This chapter has thus far outlined a number of stimuli, both historical and current, that it has been argued have the potential to influence society's conception of disability. It now turns towards a critical examination of how disability and inclusive education are operationalised within schools. What is problematic however to this analysis is that it draws upon a small research base and one mainly related to specific impairments. Furthermore, some of the research is dated, as well as being subject to methodological weaknesses. Despite this within the last thirty years there has been a growing interest in researching the attitudes that are displayed towards individuals with disabilities in modern-day classrooms (Wilson and Scior, 2014).

CONCEPTIONS WITHIN SCHOOL COMMUNITIES

Deal (2003) contends that educational communities are regulated by attitudinal systems constructed upon the 'normally' developing child. In addition, pupils' conceptions of disability and impairments are regulated by their interactions with older siblings and parents. Research suggests that conceptions of disability formulated through interactions within the home environment are mediated within school communities by powerful processes of socialisation (Hodkinson, 2012b).

> The catalyst to this mediation appears to be 'playful interactions', such as singing songs, telling jokes and participating in the games that occur through pupils' daily participation in school life (Shakespeare, 1994: 294).

Through this mediation process children and young people agree 'commonly held sets of norms for the physical body which they employ when interacting with people they consider to be different from themselves' (Shakespeare, 1994: 294). The difficulty for successful inclusive education for people with impairments is that they 'are often at the mercy of the other's construction of what it means to have a disability' (Lenney and Sercombe, 2002: 6).

A POSITIVE VIEW

Research over the past few decades has produced contradictory conclusions in relation to non-disabled pupils' conceptualisation of disability. Some studies (e.g. Harasymiw et al.,

1976; Hodkinson, 2007; Jacques et al., 1998; Siperstein and Gottlieb, 1997; Townsen et al., 1993) indicate that pupils, especially females, can and do display positive attitudes towards people with impairments, and that in general children hold a more positive view than those of their adult counterparts.

In one research study a number of children articulated positive views about the inclusion of disabled children who were wheelchair users. Two children's views are outlined below.

Yes, they should come into our class, because they are only humans with a wheelchair, and a wheelchair is like a bike, so it's a person with a bike.

Yes, because children come to school to learn and a wheelchair does not stop them learning. (Hodkinson, 2007: 71)

Whilst these findings are interesting, they are subject to limitation and it is important to recognise this when interpreting them. For instance, though Jacques et al. (1998) found that positive attitudes existed, these were based upon the implementation of co-operative learning programmes which are not normally available in the UK. Furthermore, Hodkinson's (2007) research, whilst revealing positive attitudes towards the inclusion of children with impairments, also discovered that these were based upon narrow conceptualisations of disability that were located within medical deficit. Moreover, both Hodkinson (2007) and Laat et al. (2013) revealed that children have more positive attitudes towards some disabilities than others. An important caveat, then, to the maintenance of these research findings, is that Harasymiw et al. (1976), Huckstadt and Shutts (2014), Hodkinson (2007), and to a lesser extent Townsen et al. (1993) determined that generally positive attitudes exist only for those children whose impairments most closely conform to the 'norms set by society' (Deal, 2003: 899).

Despite these limitations, it is pertinent to note that Jacques et al. (1998: 30) contend that the inclusion of pupils with sensory, physical or intellectual impairments can lead to significant gains in societal acceptance of disability. Furthermore, and despite some rather pessimistic findings, Hodkinson (2007) concluded that the majority of non-disabled children participants in his study had one of the major ingredients for successful inclusive education – namely that they appeared to be strongly committed to the ideal of equality in educational opportunity. This is a finding supported by Beckett (2014) who details that children can and do reference disability in terms of 'human rights,' 'fairness' and 'equality of opportunity'.

A NEGATIVE VIEW

These positive attitudinal findings however remain undermined by research which suggests that negative conceptualisations of disability dominate classroom environments (Beckett, 2014; Huckstadt and Shutts, 2014; Nowicki and Sandieson, 2002). Research also suggests that children with impairments are at risk of increased levels of bullying and teasing (see, for example, Gray, 2002; Martlew and Hodson, 1991; Mencap, 2007; Thomas, 1996), lower sociometric positioning in class (Jacques et al., 1998; Siperstein and Gottlieb, 1997; Zic and Igri, 2001), that young non-disabled children may be less interested in interacting with them (Huckstadt and Shutts, 2014) and that these individuals experience social distancing (Guralnick, 2002; Hodkinson, 2007; Weiserbs and Gottlieb, 2000; Zic and Igri, 2001).

> Hodkinson's (2007) study found that non-disabled children, even those who had had no interaction with a person with impairment, held negative attitudes towards disability, observing children with impairments to be less intelligent and more ugly, boring, cowardly and poorer than their non-disabled peers.

Furthermore, a survey by Mencap (2007) found that 82% of children with an intellectual impairment had been bullied, of which 58% had been physically assaulted. Additionally, the survey revealed that 79% of the participants were frightened to go out because of the threat of bullying. A more recent Mencap survey, in 2016, detailed that 6% of non-disabled people said they would feel uncomfortable using the same swimming pool as someone with a more severe learning disability.

TAKING IT FURTHER

Watch the video 'Here I am' (www.youtube.com/watch?v=D6i97xnZCfU) which takes a quote from *Atlantic* magazine in 1968, where an academic proposes that someone with Down's syndrome is not a person, and that there should be no guilt in 'putting them away' in a sanatorium or indeed to euthanise them. The quote is used by DJ Casey Rochell to turn 'shocking words' into something positive and upbeat (Mencap, 2016).

How might this video help change the minds of people that think disabilities are a burden on society?

Now read the following case study. How does it make you feel? Can inclusive education, or inclusion in society, ever become a reality without tackling other non-disabled people's views and attitudes about disabilities?

CASE STUDY 3.1
AMY'S STORY

When I was nine-years-old the girls in my class began to call me names and push me about. This used to happen every day but especially before we had PE lessons. I have Prader–Willi syndrome which means that I have constant hunger pains and I cannot stop eating. Last year the bullying became really bad and a group of girls pulled off my shirt in the PE lesson and shouted to everybody, 'Here comes the fat girl, look at her wobble.' I could not stop crying and I was so embarrassed as everybody just stared at me and laughed. I don't do PE now, I am just too scared.

AMY'S ADVICE TO PEOPLE WHO BULLY

Just think about what you do and the words you use. You can have a massive impact on somebody's life. If you had a broken leg, you would not be bullied for not being able to run fast would you? I cannot help being overweight. Please don't laugh at me; why don't you try to be my friend instead?

Having read this case study, what would your advice be to the children that bullied Amy?

What is worrying, for both pupils with impairments and educators alike, are the findings from studies such as Weinberg's (1978) which illustrate that negative conceptualisations of disability develop early, with children as young as four-years-old preferring non-disabled individuals to those who they perceive to be 'disabled'. These findings should be tempered by those of Jackson (1983) who suggests that, whilst people may express negative views, they do not always turn these into actions. Furthermore, although the discovery of negative attitudes is disturbing it is perhaps relevant to note Davis and Watson's (2001: 673) statement 'that disabled children encounter discriminating notions of "normality" and difference both in "special" and mainstream schools'.

Read and consider the responses of the non-disabled primary school children below to questions about disabled people. How might educators break the chain of poor understanding and bullying that exists in our schools today?

READER REFLECTION

Interviewer:	Do you think disabled people sometimes have children and families of their own?
Boy 1:	No, no, no, no, no!
Girl 1:	No!

Interviewer:	Why is that?
Boy 1:	Because they're disabled, they won't ever look after them because ...
Boy 2:	[Interrupts – ed.] They can't look after themselves! (Year Two, School D; original emphasis)
Boy 1:	Most of them can't [get a girlfriend/boyfriend].
Boy 2:	And people probably think that they're ugly. (Year Six)

(Source: Beckett, 2014)

A summary of the evidence outlined above, then, does not it seems provide an argument that undermines the premise that all children and young people can be successfully educated within mainstream school settings. However, the review does make clear that inclusive education is linked to how society conceptualises disability, and the number of barriers it places in the path of inclusion for people with impairments into mainstream educational settings.

CONCLUSION

In this chapter, you have gained knowledge and understanding of:

- how disability has been perceived by society;
- how definitions of disability developed in government legislation;
- the image of disability created by the media and children's storybooks, as well as internet technology; and,
- how societal attitudes towards disability can influence educational policy.

In the chapter we employed Finkelstein's construct to outline the development of the concept of disability. We discovered that, to some extent, the concept of disability did not exist before the advent of the Industrial Revolution. Indeed, it was contended that social engineering and the educational system formulated as a result of the Industrial Revolution created 'misfits' who were excluded by society. Later on we observed how the media influence society's concepts of disability and how the attitudes children develop at home can be transformed by the powerful socialising influence of the school environment. Finally, we examined research which outlined the experiences of children with impairments who had been 'included' into mainstream schools.

In the following chapters we will analyse how schooling for pupils with SEND has developed, and we critically examine whether government initiatives have enabled children and young people to become fully included within their local schools.

The 'Taking it further' activities in the chapter, along with the student activities, reflective questions and further reading detailed below, have been designed to make you think carefully about your own conceptions of disability and those that have dominated society over the past few hundred years.

STUDENT ACTIVITIES

At the start of this chapter, you were asked to make a note of your understanding of disability and consider how you have arrived at such an understanding. Having read this chapter has your understanding changed?

Using the resources available in most university education libraries, examine the picture of disability employed in ten school textbooks. How do your findings compare with those presented by Hodkinson (2007)?

REFLECTIVE QUESTION

You might like to read Beigi, A. and Hodkinson, A. (2018) A comparative analysis of the cultural representation of disability in school textbooks in Iran and England, *Education 3–13*: 27–36, and consider the similarities and differences of the picture of disability created in school textbooks in England and Iran.

FURTHER READING

Barnes, C. and Mercer, G. (2010) *Exploring Disability*. Cambridge: Polity. This is a very readable book that provides the background to the issues and concepts discussed in this chapter.

English Heritage (2014) 'Mental illness in the 16th and 17th centuries'. Available at: www. historicengland.org.uk/research/inclusive-heritage/disability-history/1485-1660/mental-illness-in-the-16th-and-17th-centuries/. This is a very useful website that provides a basic introduction to the history of specific impairments.

Park, J. and Hodkinson, A. (2017) 'Telling Tales': an investigation into the representation of disability in classic children's fairy tales, *Educational Futures*, 8(2): 48–68. Available at: https://educationstudies.org.uk/wp-content/uploads/2017/06/BESA-Journal-EF-8-2-hodkinson.pdf

SCOPE (2014) *Current Attitudes towards Disabled People*. This report provides very interesting data about how non-disabled people see those who have a disability. The facts that it reveals are at times disturbing. Available at: https://www.scope.org.uk/Scope/media/Images/Publication%20Directory/Current-attitudes-towards-disabled-people.pdf?ext=.pdf

SECTION II

HISTORICAL PERSPECTIVES OF SEND AND INCLUSION

4

THE DEVELOPMENT OF SEND: FROM BENEVOLENT HUMANITARIANISM TO THE HALFWAY HOUSE OF INTEGRATION

The major questions this chapter addresses are:

- How did special educational provision expand during late 1800s through to the early 1980s?
- How is categorisation employed to the provision of SEND?
- What is integrative education and how was special educational provision altered by the Warnock Report and subsequent 1981 Education Act?

INTRODUCTION

This chapter provides an outline of the development of special educational provision, from its embryonic beginnings in the late 18th century through to the birth of integrative practice in the late 1970s and early 1980s. During this period the legislation and service provision for children and young people with SEND were subject to radical change. The chapter considers how modern-day special educational provision is a result of its own history – a history that was shaped by the dominant societal values, beliefs and ideologies of the time. In addition, it examines how government legislation and reports, combined with the prevailing societal attitudes, led to changes in the policies and services which governed the provision of education for children and young people with SEND.

In Chapter 3 we observed that in Britain before the advent of an industrialised and mechanised society SEND as a concept did not exist, nor for that matter was there a need for it to exist. Children and young people with SEND were normally 'looked after' by their families or by the Church, and for those from the lowest echelons of society education was not needed to facilitate inclusion in Britain, as it was a largely agrarian-based society. However, by the late 1700s and early 1800s Britain was subject to change as the Industrial Revolution ravaged society. Although rapid industrialisation meant that Britain became the 'powerhouse of the world', a side-effect of this development was the creation of societal 'misfits' whose additional needs became barriers to inclusion within this new industrial age.

TAKING IT FURTHER

Consider why it might be important to understand the history of SEND and how this history might influence current practice in early years settings, schools and colleges.

This period created an underclass of citizens who were cared for with 'benevolent humanitarianism' (see Allan, 2003: 176). The 19th century bore witness to a phenomenal growth in charitable provision as the wealthier members of society felt a civic responsibility to provide aid for people they observed to be less fortunate than themselves (Lees and Ralph, 2004).

This form of humanitarianism, combined with a good dose of Methodism and Evangelicalism (Pritchard, 1963), led to the establishment of workshops and asylums for people who had sensory impairments that were not being catered for by 'ordinary' schools (Frederickson and Cline, 2002). By the mid-1800s, special institutions had been created for virtually 'every human ill, individual or social, moral or physical' (Lees and Ralph, 2004: 149). The provision for children and young people with SEND had, in a relatively short space of time, become firmly rooted in the ideology of the medical model.

THE FIRST SPECIAL 'SCHOOLS': A SINGULARLY VOLUNTARY ENTERPRISE

As with education in general, education for children and young people with SEND began through the enterprise of individuals and charities (DES, 1978). The first 'school' for children with visual impairments was opened, in Edinburgh, in 1760 by one Thomas Braidwood (Kitzel, 2017). He was followed in 1791 by Henry Dannett, who opened a school for the indigent blind in Liverpool. Then in 1841 the first church-controlled special school, 'the Catholic Blind Asylum', was established also in Liverpool. In 1851, there followed a school for children with physical impairments, 'the Cripples Home for Girls', which was established in Marylebone, London.

The following quote refers to the first few years of the operation of the Indigent School for the Blind in Liverpool. It paints a rosy picture of the educational provision provided by the school.

> At the opening of the present school ... the number of pupils was increased to seventy: in 1809 to one hundred: and the number at present in the school is one hundred and twenty. They are all of them usefully employed, and they exhibit a picture of cheerfulness and comfort which can scarcely be paralleled by an equal number of individuals of any description whatever collected under one roof. (Williams, 2005)

These early schools, however, were nothing like those we have today. Far from it. They were protective places available to a few where children, mainly from wealthy families, had little or no contact with the outside world (DES, 1978). As societal attitudes during the 19th century moved away from caring for children to sheltering them from society (Safford and Safford, 1996), this embryonic segregated education system was subject to further development as 'for personal and ideological reasons' segregated provision, based upon the medical model, prevailed and came to dominate the future system of education for children and young people with SEND (Copeland, 2001: abstract).

The philosophy of special educational provision at this time was driven by a doctrine which strongly emphasised self-help (Lees and Ralph, 2004). A contemporary belief was that work with children and young people with SEND could yield positive economic results (Johnstone, 2001).

This account from the 1860s clearly indicates the nature of education provided within special schools:

[In] ... many of the schemes for the improvements of idiots, a most important object was to enable those capable of reaping, the highest advantage, [was] to become adept in some useful branch of industry, and to make their work remunerative, exchanging their solitary and idle habits for social industrious and productive occupation. (*Edinburgh Review*, 1865: 56)

The curricula of many of these special schools were founded upon vocational education, including 'subjects' such as weaving, spinning, basket-making and music. Put simply, children were taught to earn a living (Higginbotham, 2017).

The table below outlines how special education developed in Britain. It provides an overview of the important legislation and events which helped shaped the development of special education from 1760 with the introduction of special schools through to the policy of integrating pupils into mainstream classrooms in the early 1980s.

KEY EVENTS IN THE DEVELOPMENT OF SPECIAL EDUCATIONAL NEEDS

1700s–1890s: BENEVOLENT HUMANITARIANISM

1760	First school for children with visual impairments opens
1851	First church school for children with physical impairments opens
1870	Forster Education Act – introduces compulsory state schooling
1872	Elementary Education Scotland Act – introduces compulsory state schooling in Scotland
1874	London School Board establishes a class for children with hearing impairments which is attached to a state school
1890	Education of Blind and Deaf Mute Act – compels school boards to provide education for children with sensory impairments in Scotland

1893   James Kerr is appointed as a medical officer to the Bradford School Board

1893   Elementary Education (Blind and Deaf children) Act – provides education in England and Wales for children with sensory impairments

1899   Egerton Commission reports upon the provision for children with sensory impairments

1899   Education (Defective and Epileptic Children) Act – requires school boards to provide education for children who have disabilities other than sensory impairments

1902–1944: THE ZENITH OF CATEGORISATION

1902   Education Act – creates local education authorities

1913   Cyril Burt appointed as London's first educational psychologist

1921   Education Act – constitutes five categories for the assessment of children with special educational needs and disabilities

1923   Hadow Report – accepts intelligence testing as a legitimate method of diagnosing mental deficiency

1944   Butler Education Act – requires all local education to meet the needs of 'handicapped' children

1945   The Handicapped Pupils and School Health Service Regulations – establish eleven categories for the assessment of disabilities

1960s–1980s: CHALLENGING THE ORTHODOXY OF SEGREGATION

1970   Education (Handicapped Children) Act – all children become subject of local education authorities

1978   Warnock Report – introduces the term special educational needs

1981   Education Act – introduces the Statement of Special Educational Needs and an integrative educational approach to the placement of children with special educational needs

(NOTE: For further and more detailed information on the Forster Act and the development of compulsory schooling, see Bartlett and Burton, 2012; 2016.)

THE 1870 'FORSTER ACT' – EDUCATION FOR ALL?

With the introduction of the 1870 Elementary Education Act (Education Scotland Act 1872), compulsory state schooling for all was developed 'to produce skilled workers who could compete in an era of growing industrial productivity' (Wood, 2004: 91). Through this legislation school boards were created to provide education where an insufficient capacity existed within the local charitable and voluntary provision (DES, 1978). Whilst the Act did not specifically include provision for children with SEND, it did nonetheless create a basic right for all children to be educated within local schools. However, it was only after its implementation, when large numbers of children with SEND who had previously been 'educated' at home entered mainstream education, that their 'difficulties' became subject to national recognition. It became obvious that many of these children were experiencing difficulties in making progress within ordinary schools, as elementary classes then contained large numbers of pupils who were taught by teachers with no specific special educational training. Both educationalists and society at large came to the same conclusion that pupils with SEND were hindering normal teaching activities. Moreover, they firmly believed that those children were limiting the educational progress of the other 'normal' pupils. The prevailing societal attitude, therefore, became one that was based upon a premise that pupils with SEND were unfit to be included in normal mainstream educational provision (Coune, 2003).

STATE-CONTROLLED SPECIAL EDUCATION: THE FIRST TENTATIVE STEPS

Shortly after the implementation of the Forster Act (1870), charity organisations began campaigning for the rights of children with visual and hearing impairments to be fully educated, and for the school boards to ensure that educational provision was fit to include all pupils. In the mid-1870s a few school boards, of their own volition, did indeed begin to make tentative moves towards catering for such children (DES, 1978). In 1874, for example, the London School Board established a class for children with hearing impairments at one of its state elementary schools. By 1888, 14 such centres had come into existence catering for some 373 children. In 1893, James Kerr was appointed as a medical officer to the Bradford School Board. His specific role was to assess pupils' mental processes and identify those who were not suitable for education in ordinary schools (Farrell, 2004). However, as progressive as these initiatives might have been they remained limited because special education incurred a higher cost than ordinary provision. Therefore, in practice very few boards were willing or able to provide specialised education. Indeed, in many areas children and young people with SEND were either isolated in ordinary schools or received no schooling whatsoever. This isolation in turn often led to these pupils being segregated from their peers and denied access to the normal opportunities and activities afforded by local schools and the wider community (Coune, 2003).

THE 1890S: THE FORMALISATION OF THE CATEGORIES OF SPECIAL EDUCATIONAL NEEDS AND DISABILITIES

On the 20th January 1886 a Royal Commission was established to investigate and report upon 'the condition of the blind in our United Kingdom' and to similarly report 'upon the condition and education of the deaf and dumb'. The commission was tasked with the examination of the problem of uneducable children and to establish how widespread this problem actually was

(Gibson and Blanford, 2005). The Egerton Commission, as it became known, reported back in 1889. It recommended that all school boards should provide an education for children with visual impairments from the age of five, and that children with hearing impairments should be taught by specialist teachers who should be paid more than mainstream teachers. The commission also recommended that each school board should appoint a medical officer to distinguish between children who were 'feeble-minded, imbeciles or idiots'.

'Feeble' derives from the Latin word flebilis, meaning doleful, sad and melancholy. It was used as early as 1611 in the Bible: 'Now we exhort you, brethren, warn them that are unruly, comfort the feebleminded, support the weak, be patient toward all' (Thessalonians, 5: 14 – see www.kingjamesbible.com).

During the early days of the 20th century a child would be determined as having a feeble mind if they scored 25 or below on an intelligence test. Other terminology employed at this time also related to an assessment of children's intelligence. Children were considered to be normal if they scored 100 or above in an intelligence test, or were labelled as:

- morons, if they scored 50 to 75;
- imbeciles, if they scored 25 to 50;
- idiots, if they scored below 25.

For further and more detailed information on the language employed to categorise children and people with SEND, see the paper by Marsh and Clarke (2002), 'Patriarchy in the UK: The language of disability', which is available online at the Disability Archive UK (www.leeds.ac.uk/disability-studies/archiveuk/).

The commission felt that 'imbeciles' should not remain in asylums but should, wherever possible, enter formal schooling. For pupils designated as 'feeble-minded', they argued that education should be provided in auxiliary schools which were to be separate from the mainstream (DES, 1978).

The report from the Egerton Commission was followed in 1890 by legislation in Scotland (Education of Blind and Deaf Mute Children Act) and three years later England and Wales followed suit with the 1893 Elementary Education (Blind and Deaf Children) Act. These acts required school boards to provide education for pupils with sensory impairments. In the years after their implementation pressure from teachers and medical officers over the plight of children with physical impairments led the government to establish the Sharpe Committee. Their major recommendation was that special schools should be established to make mandatory and effective provision for pupils who had disabilities other than sensory impairments (Gibson and Blandford, 2005). The subsequent Education Act of 1899 incorporated many of this committee's recommendations and so formalised the categorisation and segregation of children and young people with SEND within a two-tier education system.

The Act stated that:

> A school authority ... may ... make such arrangements ... for ascertaining what children in their district, not being imbecile, and not being merely dull or backward, are defective, that is to say, what children by reason of mental or physical defect are incapable of receiving proper benefit from ... instruction in the ordinary ... schools. (Roberts, 2007)

In summary, then, the development of mass schooling within the late 19th century ushered in the rapid expansion of a segregated special school system where 'children [with] particular difficulties were put together with other children who had similar needs' (Frederickson and Cline, 2009: 69). The provision of segregated schooling was reinforced because a system of payment by results designated that there was no benefit, for ordinary schools, in adopting inclusive practices. Indeed, the emergence of the special school system was firmly built upon the foundation that children and young people with SEND were different and could be 'categorised according to their difficulties' (Thomas et al., 2005: 3).

TAKING IT FURTHER

Reflect upon how 'payment by result' might have effected teachers' willingness to teach all children during the 19th and 20th century. Given that today's education system is dominated by grades and assessment, would you consider that children and young people with a SEND education might still be negatively affected by educational provision which is so dictated by results?

1902–1944: THE ZENITH OF CATEGORISATION

The Education Act of 1902 abolished the existing school boards created by the Forster Act of 1870 and replaced them with local education authorities. Educational provision was formally separated into two phases – elementary and secondary education. Whilst major developments were observable within mainstream education, the provision of education for children and young people with SEND remained largely unchanged until 1944. The development of special educational provision that was observed during this period was strongly influenced by Victorian notions of child-deficit.

The dominant societal ideology of the early 20th century, therefore, was that a pupil with SEND was simply different from the normal child and so it was no more than simple common sense to educate them outside of the normal school system (Frederickson and Cline, 2009). As a result, this period witnessed the evolution of a large variety of special school provisions. For example, there were open air schools for 'weak' children, day and boarding schools for children with physical impairments, and schools in hospitals and convalescent homes (DES, 1978).

The early part of the 20th century also witnessed the beginnings of educational provision for children deemed to have behavioural difficulties. For instance, the 1921 Education Act formally constituted five categories for use in the assessment of children who were judged to have mental 'handicaps' which would inhibit them from attending mainstream schools. Other children, adjudged to be uneducable, were to be removed from ordinary schools and accommodated in specialist wards and hospitals (Gibson and Blandford, 2005). To enable the assessment of children's mental processes required by this, local education authorities began to rely more heavily on the advice of doctors, medical officers and the developing field of psychological assessment.

CASE STUDY 4.1
BOB'S STORY

Read the case study below. What does Bob's story tell us about the state of special education during the period of the categorisation of children?

Hello, my name is Bob, and I attended a special school in a sunny seaside town in the North of England during the mid-1950s. I have a hearing impairment and my dad, who was hearing impaired too, taught me to sign when I was four. I loved to sign because I found it very difficult to speak and often people could not understand me. However, when I was six I was sent to this special school where I was told that I could not sign and that I must always speak when spoken too. The school simply thought that signing was wrong and that we should communicate like normal people. One day I was caught signing when I was in the playground. The teacher was very angry with me and told me that I had let myself down and that I had to try much harder to talk to people. He sent me to the head teacher who made me wear huge boxing gloves for a week. This meant that I could not sign at all and I felt very sad and very lonely. I wanted to talk to my dad about this as I knew he would understand but I had no way of getting in touch with him.

(Continued)

He lived 70 miles away and there was no phone and my writing was not that good then so I could not send him a letter. When he was allowed to visit two weeks later I told him what had happened and he confronted the head teacher but the school did not listen to my dad. They said to him if I signed again that I would be expelled and I would get no education at all. I spent six years in that school and I hated it.

CYRIL BURT AND THE RISE OF PSYCHOMETRICS AND EUGENICS

In 1913, at the age of thirty, a young lecturer from the University of Liverpool was appointed, on a part-time basis, to be London's first educational psychologist. Cyril Burt's remit was to be concerned with the 'backward, delinquent and maladjusted' children who had been referred for assessment by their teachers, school doctors, magistrates, care workers and parents (DES, 1978). This appointment was highly significant for the development of special educational provision because it added momentum to the 'burgeoning science' of psychometrics and eugenics (Thomas et al., 2005: 3).

Psychometrics is the measurement of knowledge, abilities and aptitudes through tests such as the intelligence test (IQ).

Burt advocated the employment of the developing technology of intelligence testing, which he amongst others strongly believed could provide statistical evidence to identify a child's intellectual deficit which would hinder their educational progress (Corbett and Norwich, 2005).

Burt believed strongly that:

> no grindstone can make a good blade out of bad metal; and no amount of coaching will ever transform the inborn dullard into a normal child. The pupil who is merely backward forms a different problem. He is a knife without edge – good steel that has never been sharpened. He hacks away at his daily loaf; but will never cut true or smooth until he has been sent off to the repair shop to be whetted and sharpened. (Burt, 1937: 9)

 **READER REFLECTION** Carefully read the quote from Cyril Burt in 1937 about children with SEND. Make a note of the problematic language employed. What are your thoughts upon the language that Burt employs? Do you believe it is the case that some children simply cannot be educated?

TAKING IT FURTHER

For more information relating to the background of the employment of IQ testing and eugenics you might like to read Chapter 4 of Sally Tomlinson's book, *A Sociology of Special and Inclusive Education* (Routledge, 2017).

Throughout the period of the drafting of the 1921 Education Act, Burt and others such as Schonell exerted their influence on policies effecting the educational provision for children and young people with SEND. Burt detailed that his psychometric testing revealed that some 15% of children 'suffered' an 'intellectual deficit' which would render them unsuitable for mainstream education. In addition, he contended that this group, consisting of three separate categories of children (those of 'sub-normal intelligence, mentally dull and inferior intelligence'), would only benefit from specialised curriculum and schooling. Burt maintained that:

> The ideal arrangement [for these children], therefore, would be a series of classes where promotion was slower or the increasing difficulty was less. Since backwardness affects scholastic and abstract work more than practical or concrete the curriculum would include a large proportion of concrete and manual work. (Burt, 1917: 38–39)

CASE STUDY 4.2
ANDREW'S STORY

Andrew is a ten-year-old boy who is struggling with all aspects of the formal curriculum, notably, maths, English and science. His teachers want to alter his curriculum so that it is based mainly upon art, PE and games. What do you think about the teachers' proposals? Should all children be entitled to a broad and balanced curriculum?

Burt's growing reputation within the field of psychology in general, and psychometrics in particular, was a catalyst for the expansion of a separate segregated education system based upon the categorisation of deficit (Thomas and Loxley, 2001).

In 1923, the Hadow Report accepted the principle that intelligence tests were a useful tool for the diagnosis of mental deficiency. The report did however contain a warning that no pupil should ever be treated as 'mentally deficient' based solely on the information gained from an intelligence test (infed.org, 2007). Despite this warning, Burt's contention that children with SEND 'suffered' from reduced cognition coupled with the notion of psychometrics and eugenics provided the legitimisation needed for the segregated special school system to be further expanded.

1944 AND THE 'BUTLER' EDUCATION ACT: THE ORTHODOXY OF SEGREGATION

In 1944, as the Second World War reached its climax, significant reforms were proposed to the education system in Britain. The 1944 Education Act established a general duty upon local education authorities to provide education within primary, secondary and further education based upon each pupil's age, aptitude and abilities. Sections 33 and 34 of the Act replaced Part V of the 1921 Education Act and required that all local education authorities should meet the needs of handicapped children within their area. The Education (Scotland Act) of 1945 made similar provision in Scottish schools.

The 1944 Act detailed that local authorities must:

> secure that provision is made for pupils who suffer from any disability of mind or body, by providing either in special schools, or otherwise, special educational treatment, that is to say education by special methods to persons suffering from that disability. (Roberts, 2007)

A further duty placed upon local authorities was to ascertain which children would require this special educational 'treatment'. In pursuit of this, local authorities were empowered to compel parents to submit their children to medical officers and psychologists for the purposes of an examination of their mental capabilities (DES, 1978).

The 1944 Act coupled with the Handicapped Pupils and School Health Service Regulations (1945) established eleven categories of handicap that children would be separated into.

These medical and quasi-medical categories (in part created by Burt) were:

- blind
- partially sighted
- deaf
- partially deaf
- delicate
- diabetic

- educationally sub-normal
- epileptic
- maladjusted
- physically handicapped
- children with speech defects.

The system of categorisation, based upon the ideology of the medical model, ensured that the causation of a child's learning difficulties was firmly located within the individual and not in the system of education they experienced. From this time forward then, after the requisite examination, any child who was deemed to be educable was afforded the right of access to state schooling. However, children who were judged to be 'severely sub-normal' were to be reported under the provision of the Mental Deficiency Act of 1913 as uneducable and sent to National Health Service training centres. The 1944 Act developed for all pupils, and not just those with SEND, a hierarchy of educational provision. Moreover, this hierarchical approach was observed to be an equitable method of service delivery because all children were seemingly enabled to reach a level of education that matched their level of aptitude and ability. Furthermore, the system of assessment used to categorise and segregate children was deemed to be stable, reliable and valid because it was based upon the 'science' of psychometric testing (Wearmouth, 2001).

During the decades that followed the 1944 Act children with SEND became excluded from ordinary schools because of their perceived differences. Those with illnesses were deemed delicate and so were sent to open-air schools; those with hearing impairments went to schools for the deaf; children with visual impairments attended schools for the blind, and so on. Children were labelled, categorised and dispatched to special school placements with many never having the opportunity to discover if they could make progress in ordinary schools. Furthermore, this period witnessed the birth of a new language of special education which substantiated the 'science' of segregation, and pupils thus stopped being children and were pigeon-holed as 'educationally sub-normal, maladjusted or disturbed'. Moreover, and seemingly worse, was the fact that society formulated other distasteful terminology that reinforced the nature of some children's differences. Within the segregated special school system children developed a clear idea of how they were viewed by their peers in ordinary schools and saw themselves as 'spastics, loonies and cripples'. The system of segregated provision and for those who were uneducable (the National Health Service training centres) led to children being stigmatised and denied access to the full range of educational opportunities afforded by ordinary schools (Frederickson and Cline, 2009). The delivery of education through a system of segregated special provision became the orthodox policy for the next three decades, one that was to become 'embedded in the individual and institutional consciousness' for generations to come (Thomas et al., 2005: 4).

(For further and more detailed information on the Butler Act and the development of the tripartite system of education, see Bartlett and Burton, 2012; 2016.)

READER REFLECTION

The overview of the history of the development of SEND up to the present day clearly identifies that special education was formulated upon the employment of categories that relied upon the premise that SEND was something an individual suffered from.

1. List what you consider to be the main points and issues related to special education thinking during this period.
2. Why is this type of thinking problematic for the formulation of educational provision for children with SEND?
3. What are the positives and negatives of employing labels for SEND?

THE 1960s–1980s: CHALLENGING THE ORTHODOXY OF SEGREGATION

The orthodoxy of segregation created by the 1944 Act was not subject to serious challenge until the late 1960s. Indeed, it was not until the Education (Handicapped Children) Act of 1970 (DoE, 1970) that all children finally became legally entitled to a 'full and broad' education, when the responsibility for children deemed to be severely 'educationally sub-normal' was transferred from health to local education authorities (Wearmouth, 2017). Throughout the late 1960s and into the 1970s parents, disability rights groups and educators began to subject the policy of segregated special school provision to increasing criticism. The argument that came to the surface was that continuing segregated education could not be justified either from a research or rights perspective (Frederickson and Cline, 2015). Demands were increasingly made, not only from the community at large but also from those adults who had experienced segregated provision that argued the idea of special schools was unjust. In line with the comprehensive movement of the 1960s and 1970s, society in general actively sought to break down the stigmatising barriers created by the 1944 Education Act (Thomas and Loxley, 2001). It was clear that people's understanding of SEND was shifting from the medical model's ideology of individual causation to one of societal responsibility.

This period of concerted societal criticism coincided with new research which cast serious doubt on the reliability and validity of the psychometric testing which had become the bedrock of the system of special school provision. The concern expressed by many researchers, educators and parents was that intelligence testing was based upon a model of child-deficit which was increasingly being seen as arbitrary and rigid. The prevailing argument was that psychometric testing was flawed because it failed to take into account the holistic nature of a child's education and how school environments could ameliorate or even add to a child's educational difficulties (Evans, 1995). It was clear, then, that a more social approach was needed for the provision of an education for those children and young people with SEND, one where schools would become more responsive to their needs. Furthermore, many people at this time believed that segregated education did not benefit pupils with SEND but instead negated the responsibilities of teachers in ordinary schools and colleges to devise and implement curricula for pupils who appeared unable to progress with their learning via normal instruction (Jenkinson, 1997).

As the 1960s progressed, psychometric testing and the employment of categories of disability were ultimately held to be a key factor that was limiting children's educational and life opportunities (Thomas and Loxley, 2001).

The end of the 1960s, and the beginning of the 1970s, also witnessed pioneering work by psychologists such as Wedell and Mittler. Within hospital settings they helped determine that 'the child-deficit model [of additional needs] was reaching the end of its usefulness' (Clough and Corbett, 2000: 12). The developing ideology of the time was that the 'integration of children [into ordinary schools] would facilitate access and participation in society, both as adults and children' (Frederickson and Cline, 2009: 74). Society's emerging acceptance of this ideology heralded the birth of a new integrated system of educational provision, but as history would show, this change in societal attitude did not signal the death throes of the ideology nor the practice of segregation.

THE WARNOCK REPORT

By the early 1970s educational professionals and parents had begun to step up pressure on the government to investigate the standards of national provision for children with additional needs. In 1973 Margaret Thatcher, the then Minister for Education, established a committee under the chair of Mary Warnock to:

> ... review educational provision in England, Scotland and Wales for children and young people handicapped by disabilities of body and mind. (Evans, 1995: 146)

The committee completed its work in 1978, and its final report made some 225 recommendations on the policy and organisation that governed the education of children with additional needs (Sturt, 2007).

The Report's major conclusions were that:

- categories of handicap should be replaced by a continuum of special needs and that a concept of SEN should be introduced (Gibson and Blandford, 2005);
- children's educational needs should be judged on the basis of multi-professional assessments and formally recorded (Evans, 1995); and,
- new terminology should be employed to describe pupils' SEN and that these needs would be located within speech and language disorders, visual and hearing difficulties, emotional and behavioural disorders and learning difficulties, which could be specific, mild or severe (Soan, 2005).

The recommendations contained in the Warnock Report criticised the orthodoxy of segregation and argued that the employment of handicap to categorise children was both damaging and irrelevant (Sturt, 2007). Warnock argued that the existing categories suggested nothing in the form of educational assistance and hence the provision that a child with SEND would require. Furthermore, the report recommended that rather than categorising children by deficit they should have their SEND identified and where possible those needs should be met within ordinary mainstream schools. The findings of the report's 'research' also indicated that as many as 20% of children could experience a learning difficulty at some time during their school careers, and that for some 2% of these children their difficulties would be so 'distinct that they would require an official statement of need' (Clough and Corbett, 2000: 4). The report concluded by stating that a child's SEND should be met through a continuum of integrated provision that should be mainly delivered in ordinary schools.

TAKING IT FURTHER

How far has SEND developed in the forty years since the Warnock Report of 1978? What do people think was the significance of this report? Was Warnock correct in her determinations about the future of SEND provision? To help you to consider these key questions you might like to read R. Webster (ed.) (2019) *How far have we come since the Warnock Enquiry – and where do we go next? Including children and young people with SEND in learning and life*, Oxon: Routledge.

THE 1981 EDUCATION ACT: THE LEGITIMISATION OF INTEGRATED EDUCATIONAL PROVISION

The Education Act of 1981 translated many of the recommendations in the Warnock Report into legislation. The term SEN was specifically defined and afforded legal status, and with this the employment of the categories of handicap (Gibson and Blandford, 2005) that had been in use since 1945 was ended. Furthermore, the Act clearly articulated how children with SEND should be assessed and how a Statement of Educational Needs should be formulated.

A Statement was a document which had legal status and was provided to parents, teachers and other professionals working with a child after a statutory assessment of that child's learning difficulties. It detailed a child's SEND and the educational provision that would be needed to address the barriers a child was experiencing. A Statement was only prepared for those children with the most severe and/or complex needs.

The statement of SEN was, in 2014, replaced by Education, Health and Care plans.

More importantly, though, the Act affirmed the principles of integrative practice by stating that children with SEND should, wherever possible, be educated alongside their peers within mainstream educational settings. However, it also built upon the recommendations of the Warnock Report and the 1976 Education Act and so reinforced the principle that children should only be integrated into ordinary schools if their needs could be reasonably met; that this should be efficient in terms of resources; and that it should not be to the detriment of other children (Wearmouth, 2001). Despite these caveats, the 1981 Act can now be viewed as a highly significant piece of legislation – because it was to influence the attitudes held by a whole generation of teachers in mainstream schools. From this time on, it was to become abundantly clear that pupils with SEND would be every teacher's responsibility (Coune, 2003).

It has been said that the Warnock Report and the subsequent 1981 Education Act changed the conceptualisation of educational provision for pupils with SEND by moving it away from an ideology based upon child-deficit and categories of handicap.

Think carefully about the knowledge and understanding you developed through reading Chapter 2 and then answer the following question. How was the ideology of special educational provision changed by the 1981 Act? Compare and contrast how SEND is located within the Children and Families Act 2014. What model(s) do these acts locate disability within?

READER REFLECTION

INTEGRATIVE PRACTICE: WHY DID IT ULTIMATELY FAIL?

Problematic for the aspirations of the 1981 Act was that as the 1980s progressed, the development of integrative educational provision became increasingly subject to a narrow conceptualisation.

Warnock (1999: 31), relating back to the 1970s, explains that:

> looking back on those days of the committee, when everyone felt that a new world was opening for disadvantaged children, the most strikingly absurd fact is that the committee was forbidden to count social deprivation as in any way contributing to educational needs. The very idea of such separation now seems preposterous.

Baroness Mary Warnock believes that her report was betrayed by schools who put financial gain before children. Watch the video, 'The cynical betrayal of my special needs children' (http://www.telegraph.co.uk/education/educationnews/8009504/Baroness-Mary-Warnock-The-cynical-betrayal-of-my-special-needs-children.html).

What other reasons does Baroness Warnock cite as responsible for the failure of special educational provision recommend by her Committee of Inquiry in 1978?

READER REFLECTION

TAKING IT FURTHER

To aid your consideration of the Warnock Report you might also like to read 'Warnock U-turn on special schools' (https://www.telegraph.co.uk/news/uknews/1491679/ Warnock-U-turn-on-special-schools.html), as well as R. Webster, (2018) 'Why the Warnock report still matters today' (https://www.tes.com/news/why-warnock-report-still-matters-today).

Whilst the 1981 Act should have provided a continuum of educational provision, the lack of a strong lead from central government over placement policies for children and young people with SEND (Dyson and Millward, 2000) instead created a system where enormous discretion over the development of integrative practice was placed in the hands of local education authorities (Jones, 2004). In addition, and despite Warnock and the 1981 Act championing the rights of parents, in practice they had no say over the educational placement of their children as the final decision always remained with the local education authority. Furthermore, the notion of the reasonableness of placement contained in the legislation, coupled with the lack of extra money to implement the Act, meant effective integration became subject to a postcode lottery (Farrell, 2004). This meant that whilst some local education authorities enthusiastically developed integrative educational practices, others chose to retain the existing system of segregated special school provision (Dyson and Millward, 2000). In practice, then, integration policies did not lead to a radical shift in educational provision: indeed, during the period 1983 to 1991 the proportion of children being educated in special schools only dropped by 12.5%, and in some local education authorities the number of children placed in segregated provision actually increased (Evans, 1995).

By the end of the 1980s integration had increasingly become subject to poor delivery and practice, and some would argue that this led to a system which failed to account for individual need. Ainscow (1995) contends that integration was reduced to 'making superficial changes [*and*] providing restricted provision for pupils … in schools where the communities had changed very little in attitudes and values' (Judge, 2003: 158). However, this contention may be seen by those who implemented an integrated system of provision to be unnecessarily pessimistic, as there were still many examples to be found of successful integrative practice within mainstream schools.

It does seems reasonable to suggest here that whilst integration heralded the establishment of a new level of individual and institutional consciousness, and that for some children and young people with SEND it enabled their access to mainstream education, this access was on the school's and not the child's or young person's terms. In respect of pupil rights to a full and broad education, history has shown that integration was to become something of a halfway house between the policies of segregation and those of inclusive education.

CASE STUDY 4.3

Read the following teacher's account which outlines how a child with Down's syndrome was eventually, and successfully, integrated into his local mainstream school.

NIGEL'S STORY

Nigel was eleven years old when he arrived at our school in September 1992. We had little warning of his arrival or his 'condition'. I must admit that I was a little worried about how I would cope with a boy who had Down's syndrome as I had had no training in how to teach these children.

Things got off to a poor start and Nigel had a bad first few days as the other children, especially the older boys, teased him terribly. I often found him hiding in the cloakroom as he was scared to go out onto the yard. I also found it very difficult to plan work for Nigel because he was so far behind the other children with his reading and writing. However, as the months went by things began to improve. I worked closely with his parents and the local Down's Association as well as spending many hours reading about his condition. However, in the playground things did not really get any better as many of the Year 6 boys still continued to tease Nigel and made rude remarks about him.

In the final week of the summer term we held our annual sports day with all the usual races and events. Nigel asked if he could take part in the 100 metres sprint as all the Year 6 boys had been talking about it. I must admit that both myself and Nigel's parents were concerned about this because he had a heart condition, and so we tried to persuade him not to take part. He, though, was adamant and so on a sunny morning in July he lined up with the other boys at the start line. The gun sounded and the Year 6 boys shot off at some pace. Nigel however could only manage a slow walk, and so by the time all the other boys had finished the race, he had barely started. At this point we expected the other boys to poke fun at him for being so slow. In fact, they all crowded round him shouting lots of encouragement and they all walked with him to the end of the track. As he finished a great cheer went up from the crowd and many of the Year 6 boys put their arms around Nigel. They had realised how much effort he had put into just taking part in the race. It was at that point I realised that he had finally been accepted, and that integrating him into our school had changed these children's perceptions of disability forever.

CONCLUSION

In this chapter, you have gained knowledge and understanding of:

- the expansion of special educational provision during late 1800s through to the early 1980s through an examination of the legislation that governs education;

(Continued)

- how categorisation is employed to the provision of SEND;
- integrative education and how special educational provision was altered by the Warnock Report and subsequent 1981 Education Act.

This chapter has introduced you to the major legislation, key reports and societal attitudes that influenced the development of special educational provision from the late 18th century to the end of the 1980s. This historical appraisal has revealed the seemingly dramatic shifts in the ideology governing the delivery of provision for children and young people with SEND. We have observed how 19th-century benevolent humanitarianism began, in the 1960s and 1970s, to give way to a belief that children did not need to be looked after and sheltered from society but rather that they should have their educational needs assessed, and moreover, that those should be met within ordinary mainstream schools. Whilst the 1981 Education Act is rightly observed as having been highly significant for the development of educational provision for children and young people with SEND, it did nonetheless create a legacy of ad hoc service delivery as well as failing to bring about the end of the Victorian principles which still maintained segregated educational practice.

However, despite the problems associated with the 1981 Act we may conclude that from the 1960s onwards very real progress was made in the provision of education for children and young people with SEND. By the end of the 1980s, it was clear to all that the education of pupils with SEND had developed more in line with the ideologies of social democracy and equity. But as the next chapter will show, the real historical significance of integration was that it paved the way for the new polices and practices of inclusive education to flourish.

The 'Taking it further' activities in the chapter, as well as the student activities, reflective question and further reading that are detailed below, ask to you to carefully consider how the terminology of SEND has been employed during the last century and in the first decade of the 21st century.

STUDENT ACTIVITIES

1. Discuss, with others, the following statement made by Oliver (1988: 20):

   From the introduction of categories such as 'idiots and imbeciles' in early legislation through the medical categories of 1944 to special educational needs in 1981, it could be argued that only the labels have changed; the underlying reality of an education system unable or unwilling to meet the needs of all pupils remains the same.

   Do you agree or disagree with these sentiments? Has the delivery of special educational provision actually changed?

2. With reference to the reading outlined below, examine what the lasting legacy is of the Warnock Report.

3. Consider how the terminology of SEND changed during the period covered by this chapter.

REFLECTIVE QUESTION

In your consideration of SEND you might ask yourself the question: have only the labels attached to disability changed and not the attitudes?

FURTHER READING

Glazzard, J. et al. (2015) *Teaching and Supporting Children with Special Educational Needs and Disabilities in Primary Schools* (2nd edn). London: Sage. This text provides a very practical guide to how special educational needs processes might be operated in schools.

Thomazet, S. (2009) From integration to inclusive education: does changing the terms improve practice?, *International Journal of Inclusive Education*, 13(6): 553-63. This article provides an expansive review of the evolution of inclusive education.

Wearmouth, J., Gosling, A., Beams, J. and Davydaitis, S. (2018) *Understanding Special Educational Needs and Disability in the Early Years: Principles and Perspectives*. London: Routledge. Chapter 1 of this text provides an excellent summary of the historical developments of SEND as it relates to early years provision.

5

THE EMERGENCE OF INCLUSIVE EDUCATION: FROM HUMBLE BEGINNINGS

The major questions this chapter addresses are:

- How did inclusive education develop during the 1990s?
- Should this inclusive education be perceived as a good development in the education of children and young people with SEND?
- What are the barriers that stalled the development of inclusive education?

INTRODUCTION

The aim of this chapter is to critically analyse the development of inclusive education from the 1990s onwards. It begins by defining inclusion from a number of differing and competing standpoints and relates how in the 21st century some people have begun to believe that inclusion is an illusionary concept. In addition, the chapter considers how the implementation of inclusive education during the late 1990s and early 21st century has been stalled by the barriers created by local authorities, schools, competing educational policy initiatives and by government.

At the commencement of this chapter, it would seem necessary to detail some contextual detail as to the policy of inclusion. Whilst it may be observed that the New Labour government of 1997 could claim ownership of inclusion, in reality it has a long history that lies outside the influence of current politicians.

The ideology of inclusion should not be viewed as a wholly new phenomenon; indeed, its origins go back to the late 1800s and those educational pioneers who believed in non-segregated schooling systems. However, in its current form, inclusion may be observed as the beginning of the end of a journey that began in the late 1950s when segregated institutions were subject to criticism by disabled people (Barnes and Mercer, 2010). Critics of 'special' education, with its 'systematic individualisation and medicalisation of the body and mind' (Barnes, 1997: 19) and employment of assessments of need as exercises of power (Oliver, 1996), began to argue that separating disabled children from their families, peers and local communities could only have negative effects (Morris, 2005). Morris (1991: 192) argues that it was this separation from 'common humanity' dictated by 'those who were not disabled' (1991: 71) that led to disabled people being seen as 'fundamentally different and alien' (Abberley, 1987: 14). During the late 1950s an opposing tradition was developed by disabled people (Barnes and Mercer, 2003), which was foregrounded by the premise that special schools lower expectations (Armstrong and Barton, 1999) and their continuance was nothing more than social oppression (Morris, 1991). In the 1960s policies of educational segregation became subject to increasing critique within the disability community (see Chapter 4). This questioning of policy heralded the birth of a new integrated educational system that was seemingly legitimised by the Warnock Report and the subsequent 1981 Education Act. For some these events began a journey towards inclusion; however, for others the last years of the 1980s witnessed integration being criticised as a policy that had failed to account for individual need (Ainscow, 1995). An argument forwarded by Oliver (1990a), Barton (1997) and others was that, from the perspectives of the social model, educational exclusion was generated by policy makers' and professionals' 'practices, attitudes and policies' (Morina Diez, 2010), which when combined led to the educational and social marginalisation of disabled people (Slee and Allan, 2005). The disability movement therefore proposed that 'the term inclusion ... as developed from the social model perspective should replace the term integration as developed by politicians' (Oliver, 1996: 15). A review of the literature base, whilst leaving no doubt that inclusion has gained status in schools, also suggests a tension in how it came to be defined and operationalised by government, educational practitioners and the disability movement (Armstrong et al., 2009; Hodkinson, 2012b).

THE EMERGENCE AND EVOLUTION OF INCLUSIVE EDUCATION

The evolution of inclusive education within the English educational system began with the election of New Labour in 1997 (Hodkinson, 2005). Upon taking office they acted swiftly, and through the imposition of the Green Paper (DfEE, 1997) and the subsequent Programme of Action (DfEE, 1998), set the tone for the central thrust of education reform throughout the last decade of the 20th century.

What became clear to observers was that the New Labour government had put inclusion firmly on the political agenda, as they stated:

we want to develop an education system in which special provision is seen as an integral part of overall provision aiming wherever possible to return children to the mainstream and to increase the skills and resources available to mainstream schools, and to ensure that the LEA support services are used to support mainstream placement. (DfEE, 1997: 44)

New Labour's inclusion policy though, whilst radical in nature to some writers and researchers, was criticised by others for promoting a narrow vision of inclusion. Clough and Corbett (2000: 9) suggest that this inclusive initiative did not go far enough because it only dealt with what might be termed locational inclusion. They believe that this early form of inclusion implied:

... schools will promote inclusion in society as adults. However, this is clearly a naïve view since many other factors are involved, such as appropriate curriculum, adequate transition planning and available support services.

The Labour government in its second term of office sought to address the apparent deficiencies of its SEND policy. In 2000, they introduced a revised curriculum that was designed to:

secure for all pupils … an entitlement to a number of areas of learning and to develop knowledge, understanding, skills and attitudes necessary for their self-fulfilment as active and responsible citizens. (DfES/QCA, 1999: 12)

Within the curriculum document itself, non-statutory guidance was offered on how inclusive practices could be fostered through the delivery of the core and foundation subjects. Thus, at face value it did appear that this government had fully committed itself to the ideology of inclusion.

GOVERNMENT INCLUSION IN THE 21ST CENTURY

The beginning of the new millennium witnessed the evolution of a variety of inclusive practices which were supported by a raft of government policies, initiatives and legislation. It appeared that these initiatives signaled New Labour's apparent acceptance of the ideology of inclusion by stating that 'the special educational needs of children will normally be met in mainstream schools or settings.' These initiatives impacted significantly upon educational provision in England and it would appear, at one level, that they clearly demonstrated New Labour's 'continuous drive to eradicate inequalities in our society' (Judge, 2003: 167). However, whilst New Labour's spin and political rhetoric intimated that inclusive education had become the bulwark of the English educational system, we will observe throughout this chapter that development of inclusive education was stalled by the problems of its definition, and of governments' acceptance of this form of education.

INCLUSION: THE DIFFICULTIES OF DEFINITION

A review of the last two decades of literature relating to SEND leaves no one in any doubt that inclusion in general and inclusive education in particular have become the new orthodoxy of educational thinking (Allan, 1999). Inclusion is the 'buzz-word' (Evans and Lunt, 2005: 41) that has gained high status and acquired international currency within the United Kingdom's educational and social policy initiatives. The term inclusion has become the common parlance which now permeates government policy within the area of SEND (see Chapters 6 and 7) (Rose and Howley, 2007). However, whilst this term might be widely employed, the question that dominates people's thinking is, what exactly does inclusion mean? Within the literature base, there are a plethora of definitions of inclusion and it is more than apparent that this is a concept that may be defined in a variety of ways.

 With another student, discuss how you would define inclusion.

 • Does inclusion relate just to the children with SEND?

 • Does, or indeed should, inclusion mean that all children and young people must always be incorporated into mainstream educational placements?

• Consider your educational journey in schools. Have you witnessed aspects of inclusive education? Share your thoughts with another student about what you have witnessed.

GOVERNMENT'S EARLY DEFINITIONS OF INCLUSION

From the late 1990s onwards, government legislation promoted an educational ideology which seemingly placed the inclusion of children and young people with SEND at the heart of the development of its educational practices and processes.

In 1997 the government defined inclusion as:

> ... [seeing] more pupils with SEN included in mainstream primary and secondary schools. By inclusion we mean not only that pupils with SEN should wherever possible receive their education in a mainstream school, but also that they should join fully with their peers in the curriculum and the life of the school. For example, we believe, that ... children with SEN should generally take part in mainstream lessons rather than being isolated in separate units. (DfEE, 1997)

During the last decade of the 20th century then, educational policy promoted inclusive education as the teaching of disabled and non-disabled children within the same neighbourhood schools. Further definitions suggested that all pupils, regardless of their 'weaknesses', should become part of the school community (Judge, 2003). Firstly, these definitions are difficult to accept because they appear to relate to what may be called locational inclusion. This is where pupils being educated together is more important than the attitudes or environment that each child is subjected to. As Barton (2003: 9) comments, 'inclusion is not about the assimilation of individuals into an essentially unchanged system of educational provision and practice.' A second flaw undermining these early government definitions is that they rely on categorisations and the language of medical deficit. Inevitably, definitions founded upon the medical model shackle an individual's inclusion to our entrenched societal views of disability. Moreover, the employment of the terminology of weakness and disability is observed by some to be both patronising and degrading. Definitions formulated in these terms do not promote inclusion but, conversely, encourage the return to integration and thereby tolerance, not inclusion, of children and young people with SEND.

To illustrate this point further let us consider the word 'weakness' as employed within some government documentation. In particular, imagine if you will, that Theresa May had been placed in a room with the late Professor Stephen Hawking and asked to discuss the relative merits of quantum physics or say quark theory – who would display a weakness then? Weakness, as utilised in this instance, is certainly different from how it is employed in government statements. This word, then, like 'disability', is subjective and bound within hierarchical societal notions of normality.

By employing the language of deficit, we do not instill pride, respect and value for all pupils, but rather refer to individuals who society feels are not able to be included because of impairment. Some people would argue that we must move away from this form of language and accept that recognition and a celebration of difference are the most important keystones of inclusion.

This principle is supported by Barton (2003: 10), who contends that:

Inclusive education is about the why, how, when, where and the consequences of educating all learners. It involves the politics of recognition and is concerned with the serious issue of who is included and who is excluded within education and society in general.

A third difficulty which early government definitions of inclusion encounter, is that they are framed within confusing and sometimes contradictory language. This has led some to contend that such government definitions cannot be embraced by everyone (Rose, 2003). For example, in 1997 the New Labour government, through the Green Paper (DfEE, 1997) and its 1998 Programme of Action (DfEE, 1998), trumpeted their commitment to the principles and practice of inclusion (Barton, 2003). Through policy initiatives such as these you might conclude that such inclusion is employed to ensure that the educational provision offers an opportunity for all pupils to achieve their full potential. However, even within these early definitions there exist contradictions, confusions and even an ambivalence which indicated that the New Labour government had not totally embraced an adequate definition of inclusion and that its commitment to this policy was qualified (Barton, 2003; Rose, 2003).

To be specific, within the 1997 Green Paper the government defined inclusion by using phrases such as 'wherever possible' and that it 'should generally take place in mainstream lessons'. This form of language places a qualification on the definition of inclusion. Furthermore, another contradictory statement employed is that 'children should be educated as far as possible with their peers' (DfEE , 1997: 4) and that the government would 'redefine the role of specialist schools to develop a specialist network of support' (DfEE, 1997: 4).

This form of qualification is again apparent in the government's Programme of Action (DfEE, 1998), where inclusion was promoted as 'when parents want it and where appropriate support can be provided'. Moreover, in the report from the Special Working Group, the commitment to special school education was reinforced, with comments such as 'the future role of special schools within the overarching framework of inclusion is strongly advocated' and 'The special school section enjoys the government's full support' (DfES, 2003: 2).

In June 1994 representatives of 92 governments and 25 international organisations formed the World Conference on Special Needs Education held in Salamanca, Spain. They agreed a dynamic new Statement on the education of all disabled children, which called for inclusion to be the norm. In addition, the Conference adopted a new Framework for Action, the guiding principle of which is that ordinary schools should accommodate all children, regardless of their physical, intellectual, social, emotional, linguistic or other conditions (see CSIE at www.csie.org.uk/inclusion/unesco-salamanca.shtml). The Salamanca Statement of Inclusion also detailed that academic achievement should be observed as being secondary to the development of the self through individual choice.

In recent times, the Salamanca Statement has been subject to criticism not least in its employment of contradictory and conflicted language use. For an overview of this critique, you may wish to read B. Byrne, (2013) Hidden contradictions and conditionality: conceptualisations of inclusive education in international human rights law, *Disability & Society*, 28(2): 232–44.

Let us pause, though, to reconsider again the definitions of inclusion offered above and analyse how their mediation and representation of inclusion stands at some distance from that of the Salamanca Statement. If we examine the first definition and consider the government's employment of words, another, more elusive and 'slippery' definition of inclusion materialises. The use of phrases such as 'seeing more pupils', 'wherever possible', 'that children should generally take part in', and a 'neighbourhood of schools' suggests that government intended to pursue a 'twin-track system' of SEND where the segregation of some pupils within the loci of special schools was acceptable (Barton, 2003). Pupils, therefore, were to be put there but not allowed here, present in an inclusive system but absent from a mainstream classroom.

It is apparent, then, that whilst the New Labour government documentation and legislation included a 'strong commitment to the principle of inclusion' (Croll and Moses, 2000: 47), it still observed inclusion defined in terms of a twin-track system which continued to promote the orthodoxy of segregation within special schools. Whilst the New Labour government supposedly based its definitions on the rights of all children and young people, this critical interrogation of its education policies and practices shows that it also acknowledged that its definition and operation of inclusion were subject to limits (Evans and Lunt, 2005).

INCLUSION: CAN IT BE A TWIN-TRACK SYSTEM?

On the campaign trail on the 27th of April 2010 David Cameron was confronted by Jonathan Bartley, a parent of a child with SEND. In retrospect, this incident has become a pivotal moment for analysing how Prime Minister Cameron believed effective education should be formulated. Read the conversation detailed below and watch the associated video, and then consider the view of special education put forward by Cameron and Bartley. What is your view on this issue? Should all special schools be closed and all children placed in mainstream education? Under New Labour was there actually a bias towards inclusive education? You might like to conduct your own research on this issue.

READER REFLECTION

Evidence to help you with your reflection

Mr Bartley, who has a son with SEND, asked Mr Cameron in the full glare of the television cameras why his manifesto lacked a strong statement about the benefits of inclusive education. Mr Cameron replied that his manifesto did support the inclusion of children with disabilities into mainstream schools. However, when people later read the Conservative manifesto in detail they found it contained a statement relating that vulnerable children should receive the highest quality of care, and that what Cameron called the ideologically-driven closure of special schools would end. It went on to say that the Conservatives would 'end the bias towards the inclusion of children with special needs in mainstream schools' (Conservative Manifesto 2010: 53). This statement about ending the bias towards inclusion is one that has become really important to parents, children, teachers and researchers in this area. Indeed Mr Cameron then said that special schooling and inclusive education was an emotive issue, and that under New Labour children were sometimes forced to go to mainstream schools even when they did not want to. He argued that special schools were an invaluable resource, and that even New Labour's first education minister, David Blunkett, who went to a special school, felt strongly about such schools.

> For further information on the 'Special school versus mainstream' debate see: www.theguardian.com/politics/2010/apr/27/david-cameron-schools-special-education)
>
> For special-needs children 'failed by mainstream schools': www.dailymail.co.uk/news/article-394206/Special-needs-children-failed-mainstream-schools.html, and
>
> Shaw, A. (2017) Inclusion: the role of special and mainstream schools, *British Journal of Special Education*, 44(3): 292–312.

For some educational professionals, however, the continuance of a separate system of segregated education creates a tension.

This tension created by the continuance of a separate system of education is clearly indicated in the following statement by the Centre for Studies in Inclusive Education (2005):

> The central message from the ... Department and Ministers is that special schools should continue and that their role should be enhanced through a variety of changes. We strongly disagree with this position and reject entirely the idea that there will always be a need for special schools for some pupils. There is nothing taking place in special schools that isn't also taking place in ordinary schools, somewhere. Special schools no longer have the monopoly on educating pupils who experience barriers to learning and participation, including those categorised as having complex and severe needs.

DEFINING INCLUSION: THE RIGHTS AGENDA AND THE IDEOLOGY OF FULL INCLUSION

For Glazzard (2014: 40) inclusion represents a proactive stance. It challenges educational settings to make adaptations and adjustments to cater for the needs of diverse learners. The purpose of inclusion is to provide all learners with equality of educational opportunity, and this right is guaranteed through equality legislation, which places a statutory duty on schools and other educational settings to make reasonable adjustments to break down barriers to participation and achievement.

Other educationalists though (Booth, 2000; Reynolds, 1989) would argue that inclusion is a concept that goes far beyond any single definition. For some people it should be a process inextricably linked to the 'goal of full inclusion' (Hornby, 2001: 4). Within that full inclusion it is generally accepted that all children should be educated together in terms of location, need, curriculum and attitudes, with no tolerance of or justification for the maintenance of a separate segregated system of education.

The ideology of full inclusion was formed and moulded by the world-wide pressure for civil rights during the 1960s and 1970s. This movement offered people with disabilities an avenue to voice their frustration and anger over what many perceived as the stigmatising and degrading educational experiences they had endured during their passage through the system of segregated special schools (Clough and Corbett, 2000). These frustrations translated into a real desire to deconstruct segregation and to then reconstruct an educational system which was based upon a philosophy of fraternity and an equality of opportunity (Thomas et al., 2005).

Ideas such as these took hold during the development of the comprehensive system of education during the 1970s. During this period a strong moral case for full inclusion was advanced and many people argued that it was simply the right thing to do. This growing desire for a fairer education system was lent further support during the 1980s and 1990s when research evidence, albeit limited, suggested that the differential outcomes for children with special educational needs in mainstream and special school placements were minimal (Clough and Corbett, 2000). Based upon this evidence it was also argued that the theoretical underpinning for the continuance of separate special educational provision was now redundant (Thomas and Loxley, 2001).

CASE STUDY 5.1
ENID'S STORY

I am now in my early nineties and so schooling seems a dim and distant memory to me. However, sometimes at night the horror of what I went through in my special school still haunts my dreams. I started going to this residential special school when I was five and did not leave until my sixteenth birthday. At the start I thought my school was brilliant; I loved the uniform, especially the straw hat and satchel I was given. However, this excitement did not last long. After a week I missed my family who lived over two hundred miles away. They could only afford to come and see me every two months or so and then we had only a couple of hours together before they had to leave. I felt so lonely and isolated and I missed all my brothers' and sisters' birthdays. I have felt throughout my life a stranger to my family and I still feel very sad about this. On the odd occasions I did manage to get home, the short time I had with my family was often spoilt by the local children. They would throw stones at me and call me a special kid or names that were worse than this. They did not know me and never bothered to find out why I was different. Why would they? Society at the time shut us away so that they would not have to think about people with disabilities.

What was worse, though, in the school was that you had the same teachers for over eleven years. I fell out with the English teacher when I was ten, and for the next six years he never let me forget it. Even in the evenings I could not get away from his constant ridicule. He hated me and I hated him. When I eventually left this school, I realised that I had not got any qualifications; they never really bothered with them at the school. This lack of qualifications affected the rest of my life as I always had low-paid and boring jobs. I hated my special school and I hate the idea that they are still in existence today. I think they should all be closed, and the sooner the better.

Despite such strong convictions and the moral stance taken by the full inclusionists, their conceptualisation of inclusion as a human rights issue has been the subject of criticism. For some, full inclusion is nothing more than a fervent campaign (Bailey, 1998), based upon an 'expressive zeal' (Low, 1997: 76) which fails to consider the practical realities of disability. It is thus contended that these practical realities make it difficult, if not impossible, to translate the theory of full inclusion into effective practice in mainstream schools. Croll and Moses' (2000) research supports this view: their work, with 38 education officers and head teachers across eleven local authorities, suggested that full inclusion was an unrealistic expectation, especially for those children and young people with complex and severe needs or for those who experienced emotional and behavioural difficulties. Farrell (2000: 10) suggests that full inclusion, based entirely upon the principles of human rights, is actually 'logically and conceptually naïve' because it fails to take into account mainstream children's right to receive a good education. It is arguments such as these that have led some to suggest that the ideology of full inclusion should be dropped in favour of responsible or cautious inclusion practices (Hornby, 2001).

In recent times, however, research has begun to show the benefits that inclusion can have for children, young people, schools and society. For example, Cairns and McClatchey (2013) have detailed that non-disabled children from inclusive schools did have more positive attitudes towards and a better understanding of disability because of their interactions with disabled children. This research finding is supported by numerous researches in Europe (de Boer et al., 2012; Laat et al., 2013). However, despite such positive steps forward Haug (2016: 1) states that 'No country has yet succeeded in constructing a school system that lives up to the ideals and intentions of inclusion, as defined by different international organisations.'

SHOULD THERE BE A CHOICE?

As we have seen, the government's failure to promote full inclusion is viewed by some to be a positive step forward in the development of an effective inclusive educational system. This is because by not promoting full inclusion the government appears to be advocating that inclusion should be by choice and not compulsion (Smith, in Tod, 2002). Notably, Mary Warnock subscribes to the premise of 'inclusion by choice'. Indeed, for some this notion of choice is vitally important, especially as the research suggests that some children and young people do not want to be forced into mainstream placements (Norwich and Kelly, 2004). Warnock believes that the special school sector, rather than being a place of last resort, should be regarded as offering a 'more productive and creative interpretation of the ideal of inclusive education for all' (Warnock, 2005: 1).

> Warnock contends that the single most effective way to improve educational provision for children who are 'fragile' and have 'learning difficulties' is small maintained schools. As she states:

> their right to learn we must defend, not their right to learn in the same environment as everyone else. For them we must emphasize their difference (i.e.) their needs as learners, not their similarities with all the rest. (Terzi, 2010)

BARRIERS TO INCLUSIVE EDUCATION

ACCOUNTABILITY AND STANDARDS

In common with many other educational initiatives and policy development, inclusion has become defined and controlled by the government's agents of accountability, performativity and standards. Indeed, in their relentless drive to improve standards, new systems of accountability, policed by autocratic inspection regimes, have been created. It has been argued that it is this 'accountability noose' (Grainger and Todd, 2000) of 'driving up standards' which has pushed educational provision towards an 'increasing emphasis on narrow conceptualisations of performance' (Booth, 2000: 12).

> **Standards agenda** – 'an approach to educational reforms which seeks to "drive up" standards of attainment, including workforce skill levels and ultimately national competitiveness in a globalized economy' (Ainscow et al., 2006: 296).
>
> **Performativity** – 'the emphasis on the use of outcome-related performance indicators. These are frequently expressed as quantitative measures of performance which drive the modern education system through the use of narrow performance indicators, which are then used to evaluate school effectiveness. School performance is . . . made public through the use of league tables and the publishing of inspection ratings' (Glazzard, 2014: 40).

Indeed, the inclusion agenda has not escaped the gaze of the operators of the regimes of accountability. As early as 2000 the Office for Standards in Education (Ofsted) had defined inclusion in relation to a statement of principles which promoted all learners, and as such its scope was broad (Ofsted, 2000). Furthermore, they (2000: 13) observed that an inclusive school was one in which 'the teaching and learning achievements, attitudes and well-being of every person matter'. Moreover, Ofsted contended that 'effective schools were educationally inclusive schools' (2000: 7). To ensure that schools delivered effective inclusive education Ofsted produced a checklist which they now employed when inspecting schools. Whilst we may observe that this checklist of principles is an improvement on government definitions which employed the language of deficit, we should still question whether inclusion can, or indeed should ever be, determined in relation to either the standards agenda or the metrics of accountability (Hodkinson, 2011).

Carefully read the case study below. Consider what the purposes of education are. Is education just about achieving high scores in examinations, and if this is the case what happens to those children who cannot do this?

CASE STUDY 5.2
PERFORMATIVITY AND ACCOUNTABILITY:
A DEPUTY TEACHER'S STORY

The standards agenda became a reality, a challenge and, for my school, a major concern.

I had been a deputy head for ten years and I used to work in a lovely small school based in a town in the Midlands. For years we were known as a school that included all children and we won awards for our teaching of children with SEND. Indeed, at one stage, we had 27 children who had a Statement. Our school then really reflected the rich diversity of life that exists out there in society. However, this ideal job changed dramatically when a new head teacher descended on our school at the same time as the Ofsted inspection regime began. Our new head was all about targets: how many children achieved well in their Standard Assessment Tasks. She had no time for the children who would not achieve this. When we had our first Ofsted inspection the report did not talk about the excellent work we did with children with SEND; rather it criticised us for not achieving national averages for Literacy, Numeracy and Science. The children that were once seen as a real asset to our school became observed, by some, to be a burden and a drain on our resources.

Later performance management came into being and my career became dependent upon examination success, and indeed my pay did also. I took early retirement a few years ago as I had become disillusioned with my job. I found myself asking, what is education for? Surely every child is entitled to an education that best suits their needs? What do we do with those kids who are different, those who will never have exam success – are we saying they have no worth?

TAKING IT FURTHER

Read the article 'Secret teacher: I am all for inclusion in principle, but it doesn't always work' (https://www.theguardian.com/teacher-network/2015/may/23/secret-teacher-support-inclusion-but-not-at-any-cost).

How does this article add to your growing understanding of the barriers to inclusive education?

Some have observed that the issue of school accountability is the biggest challenge to the development of inclusive education. It has been argued that English schools and colleges have become a laboratory for educational reform, and it is this coupled with accountability and performativity that has led to the progress of inclusion being 'painfully slow' (Ainscow et al., 2006: 296). For some the standards agenda has led to a backlash from teachers against the inclusion of pupils with SEND (Ainscow et al., 2006: 296).

CASE STUDY 5.3
TEACHER ATTITUDES TOWARDS INCLUSION

Read the following case study and ask yourself the following question: can inclusion ever become a reality when some teachers hold such attitudes towards children with SEND?

A school's effectiveness is mainly judged against children's attainment in Standard Assessment Tests (SATs) and examinations. For example, a primary school's success is judged by how many pupils achieve a level 4 in their SATs in numeracy and literacy. For some head teachers, but certainly not all, this level of accountability can cause a tension between on the one hand achieving academic success and, on the other, supporting pupils who may never achieve academic success as defined by the government. Such tension is illustrated by this head teacher, who is clearly struggling to develop effective inclusive education in her school.

> Now don't get me wrong: I fully support the principle of inclusive education, just not in my school and not when I am about to undergo an Ofsted inspection. I have a limited amount of resources and a limited amount of teachers. These children with SEND take up a lot of my teachers' time that would be better spent working with children who could, with a push, achieve a level 4 in their SATs.

> Whatever I or my teachers do these children will never get to a level 2 let alone a level 4. So there is no way that I am going to put my best, most experienced teachers with them; it would be an inefficient use of my resources. It is the number of pupils I get to a correct level that I am judged on and mine and the teachers' jobs depend on this, not how happy the children are or how many we include. If I'm being honest, as long as I can keep these children quiet and occupied they won't affect the education of the other children. I know that's not a politically correct thing to say but that is just the way it is. As far as I am concerned I cannot meet the government standards and be a paid-up member of the inclusive education club; it just does not work.

TAKING IT FURTHER

You might like to read the following paper that considers pre-service teacher attitudes towards inclusion in Bangladesh. Consider what attitudes these beginning teachers hold and how these might compare with your own views on the practicality of including all children and young people in mainstream schools.

Ashan, T. and Sharma, U. (2018) Hidden contradictions and conditionality: conceptualisations of inclusive education in international human rights law, *British Journal of Special Education*, 45(1): 81–97.

As Hanko (2003: 126) relates 'the national curriculum with its contentious league tables testing [and] … an excessively competitive academic results centred teaching climate [has] led to academic failure and disaffection for some'. He continues, 'inflexible forms of assessment of pupils' progress and schools' academic results have become threats rather than an indication of the need for support.' In relation to inclusion, the government's obsession with the metrics of accountability may be seen to have ensured that those schools and colleges 'whose reputation and financial viability have become dependent on surface success' (Hanko, 2003: 126) have become 'wary of accepting children whose low attainment and discipline may effect others' learning by depressing examination and SAT scores' (Fredrickson and Cline, 2002: 67).

For some commentators, inclusion linked to standards is simply unworkable. As Allan (2003: 178) states, inclusion 'is not about figures, politics or … dogma; it is about beliefs, faith, caring and the creation of community … It is about human rights and human beings.' Ainscow has argued that the development of peer friendships and relationships between schools, as well as developing all children, are of paramount importance rather than the employment of inclusion within the confines of the national curriculum. Dyson and Slee (2001) have also cautioned against correlating inclusion with educational performance. They believe that the pressure of enforcement, from bodies such as Ofsted, presents a very real danger that inclusion policy will be 'steam-rolled by the stronger standards agenda' (Dyson and Slee, 2001: 17).

Arguments such as these are proof positive that for many writers and researchers, inclusion is not, nor can it ever be, a summative measurable entity as Ofsted would like to have us believe. Perhaps, then, inclusion is a concept that does not have a single definition. Indeed, it could be argued that 'a definition is less important' but what actually is crucial is that schools achieve a 'meaningful understanding of the core values of inclusion' (Coles and Hancock, 2002: 9).

THE BARRIERS CREATED BY LOCAL AUTHORITIES

Over the past decade or so there have been significant developments in the role of the local authority within the system of English education (Ainscow et al., 2010). Whilst it has been argued above that government has a massive role in the standards agenda, we should not forget that the growing political commitment to raising standards has also led to a change in the way local authority education departments are now run (Ainscow et al., 2010). For some (Beveridge, 2004) the local authority is observed to be the guarantor of standards and of the rights of pupils and parents. However, increasingly some schools and colleges are reporting that their planning is being deliberately skewed by local authority advisors in their attempts to deliver on the government's standards agenda (Ainscow et al., 2006). There can be no doubt that local authority policy can exert a tremendous influence on the policy of inclusive schooling not just in terms of academic performance, but also in terms of its expectations of inclusive education and its views on the representation of parents, young people and children in the processes and practices of SEND (Beveridge, 2004). Indeed, most recently, whilst local authorities have continued with the pressure to increase standards, teachers remain uncertain as to what their role will be in terms of the new Code of Practice (DfE, 2014b) (see Pearson, et al., 2014).

In respect to the development of inclusion, local authorities perform a number of functions; not only do they create local policy, but also they decide, in the main, the level of funding for such education. These two functions are crucial to the successful implementation of inclusive education within local schools. However, in terms of special education, hindsight has revealed that local authorities have been accused of developing and maintaining a postcode lottery of SEND provision. Regrettably, it would seem inclusive education might be succumbing to the same difficulties that have already been witnessed in relation to the policy of integration.

For example, some local authorities' policies observe the building of new and more inclusive special schools; others develop inclusive provision by transferring monies from their special educational needs budgets to mainstream schools; and some no longer provide special schools for certain categories of need (Coles and Hancock, 2002). This variety of policy approaches means that families are once again being faced with unacceptable variations in the level of service provision. This means that for some children inclusion, like the policy of integration beforehand, will take the form of a school 'placement without adequate provision' for their individual needs (Corbett, 2001: 22). It would seem that whilst government rhetoric is advocating 'inclusion by choice' some families will be left with no option but the choice of inclusion.

A further barrier placed in the way of the provision of inclusive education is the 'complexity of funding arrangements' operating within local authorities (MacLeod, 2001: 191). Indeed, it might become the case that mainstream schools and colleges will not sign up to inclusion if they perceive there is insufficient funding for the support of individual children's needs.

It is interesting to note the Local Government Association 2018 response to the government consultation on SEND funding. They state: 'There has been a historic underfunding of high needs funding and a significant increase in the number of pupils with special educational needs or disabilities in schools. Whilst the additional funding announced earlier in the year was a step in the right direction, it was never enough to meet the needs of the increasing number of SEND pupils.' (See www.local.gov.uk/)

The issue of funding here is vital to the successful implementation of inclusionary practices and one that has undermined such policies in the past. However, it would be unfair to lay the blame for the creation of these barriers solely within the sphere of control operated by the local authority. Many authorities have been placed in an impossible position by the government, for whilst they have to continue funding special schools, they are also required to provide funding to support early intervention and inclusive educational strategies for all as well as cut funding for local services due to 'austerity measures'. The question to consider then is that if local authorities are not provided with adequate financial support, rather than being a catalyst to inclusion might they be left with no choice but to impose barriers that will inhibit the development of this educational initiative?

THE BARRIERS CREATED BY SCHOOLS AND COLLEGES

READER REFLECTION

Read the text below and consider what the prerequisites are for successful inclusive teaching.

The Council for the European Union believe that the successful inclusion of children and young people with SEND is based upon:

- increased use of personalised approaches;
- harnessing assessment to support the learning process;
- providing teachers with skills to manage and benefit from diversity;
- use of co-operative teaching and learning, and widening access and participation to education.

According to Rouse (2017: 19) successful inclusive education means also that teachers must 'accept the responsibility for creating schools in which all children can learn and feel they belong ... they are central in promoting participation and achievement'.

Inclusion for some children and young people is being stalled because the 'educational system is not fit to include' them because of the barriers of 'lack of knowledge, lack of will, lack of vision, lack of resources and (even) lack of morality' (Clough and Garner, 2003: 87). Successful inclusion, it may be argued, begins and ends with individuals, and everyone involved has to consider how their own practices can create or remove barriers to inclusion (Allan, 2003). Frederickson and Cline (2009) contend that for schools to become more inclusive they must critically examine how they might increase participation for the diversity of pupils that they serve within the local community. This examination, however, is difficult as it requires all teachers and support staff to challenge their own anti-discriminatory practices.

A school or college's approach to inclusion depends upon its teachers' attitudes and professional competencies. Training for the teaching of pupils with diverse needs has been an issue that has inhibited the successful implementation of SEND strategies in the past (Hodkinson, 2019). As far back as the Warnock Report (DES, 1978) the distinct lack of specialist training has been raised as a potential barrier to the successful implementation of SEND strategies. Twenty years later the Programme of Action (DfEE, 1998) again indicated the need for teachers to undertake specific training in relation to SEND, and the New Labour government indicated that successful practice was being inhibited by the same issue (DfES, 2004a). It seems reasonable to conclude then that despite continuing and widespread requests for the training of all teachers in the pedagogy of special educational needs, there remains a common feeling amongst educational professionals that the levels of training, to date, have been 'woefully inadequate' (Corbett, 2001: 22).

Key, then it seems, to the development of successful inclusive education, is the development of positives attitudes towards this form of education. Problematically, although teachers and trainee teachers seemingly have more positive attitudes towards inclusion than a decade ago (Humphrey and Symes, 2013), research continues to demonstrate that such positive attitudes are based upon effective training and 'successful' interactions with children with SEND. The issue of training is a significant one as research studies (see, for example, Hodkinson, 2005, 2006, 2009, 2019) have indicated that whilst a majority of teachers would support the concept of inclusive education, they can only do so with some reservations. Teachers, it would seem, are willing to support inclusion policies *if* they relate to children and young people with mild mobility or sensory difficulties (Corbett, 2001). There is however the suggestion that teachers do not have the same inclusive vision in relation to those children who exhibit extreme behavioural difficulties. Research in this area demonstrates that for these children and young people, teachers believe that exclusion is necessary purely on practical grounds (Corbett, 2001). If schools are to become more inclusive then it seems that support will be needed to develop a school ethos that not only enables all pupils to be supported but also provides for the needs of teachers as well (Hanko, 2003; Hodkinson, 2007, 2019).

CASE STUDY 5.4
'BEHAVIOURAL DIFFICULTIES'

The belief that teachers find it difficult to include children with behavioural problems is clearly outlined by these two quotes from teaching staff:

(Continued)

I think there's an issue with violent behaviour. I think that's something that's coming up especially with current society, and especially with recent things happening in schools' round the country. There is violence and young people use violence. I think there are health and safety issues here that have to be looked at by educational authorities rather than teaching staff. You cannot include children who are going to be violent in their behaviour. You cannot put other children and staff in danger can you?

A normal mainstream school is a very boisterous place, and it is just not the place for some children with emotional and behavioural difficulties, and sadly that is the nature of the beast. It's not the best thing to say I know, but I just think that a secondary school is not the place for them. The vulnerability of some of these children and the stress that it puts them under means that they would misbehave or possibly, you know, I am trying to think of a good word to say ... they would misbehave and they would just be, they could be, violent or whatever. It is just not the place for them.

TAKING IT FURTHER

Do you think that children or young people with significant behavioural issues should always be educated in mainstream schools and colleges? How do you think that the placements of these children and young people might affect the education of all pupils in early years settings, schools and colleges?

INCLUSION: A DEFINITION FOR THE 21ST CENTURY

Whilst full inclusionists', Ofsted's and government's definitions of inclusion prove interesting, it has been demonstrated that they are nonetheless subject to criticism. This has been the case because they attempt to define inclusion within the limits of institutional and societal control (Hodkinson, 2010). It has also been suggested that inclusion cannot be defined simply in terms of Ofsted's notions of academic achievement, nor can it be countenanced in relation to a process that forces inclusive education on every individual regardless of whether they want it or not. It would seem essential, therefore, that any definition of inclusion should be located firmly within the sphere of the individual and their right to choose. Furthermore, it would seem that any definitions should accept the sentiments of the Salamanca Statement where academic achievement is observed as being secondary to the development of the self through individual choice. From this perspective, then, it is perhaps more useful to define inclusion as a catalyst that requires schools, colleges and society to identify and overcome the barriers that inhibit a pupil's choices and their ability to achieve their full potential. Within such a definition, the controlling power of the state, its institutions and its vested interests, as well as the accountability of academic metrics, are diminished and replaced by an understanding of individual value and respect and a commitment to the development of the self.

CONCLUSION

In this chapter, you have gained knowledge and understanding of:

- the development of inclusive education during the 1990s;
- the benefits and drawbacks of inclusive education and the barriers that have stalled its development.

Within this chapter, we have learnt that educational policy is at a crossroads in respect of how it deals with inclusive education. We examined how the New Labour government placed inclusive education at the heart of its educational policy. What was revealed, during the chapter, was that the Coalition government of 2014 did not appear to have the same inclusive ideals. We also explored how since 1997 inclusive education has been stalled by various barriers created by schools, government and society. It was argued that if these barriers to inclusion are to be overcome it would seem clear that 'individual pupils … must be at the core of all we do' (Coles and Hancock, 2002: 1), and that the power of government influence in the implementation of inclusive education should be reduced. Despite the influence of such barriers we must however remember that many people would now argue that the teaching and learning of children and young people with SEND have improved substantially during the early part of the 21st century.

Yet the future evolution of inclusive education still holds many challenges for both teachers and pupils alike. It appears that we may not see more pupils with SEND being taught with their peers in local schools because of current government initiatives to 'end the bias towards inclusion'. This is a mistake and I believe that children, young people, parents and professionals must continue to argue for the development of inclusive education. However, this by itself will not ensure successful inclusion. Politicians must also guarantee that the professional development of teachers and adequate funding for schools are given a high priority within any future policy developments. Furthermore, if any government is to meet the needs of all children in local schools it must as a matter of urgency move away from the Victorian systems of accountability towards an education policy that allows local authorities, schools and families to work together in a partnership where mutual trust and respect, and not examination results, dominate.

Whatever happens during the next decade or so, you will through your reading of this chapter perhaps realise that Westminster needs to understand and take account of the mistakes of the past and employ that knowledge and understanding to inform its future planning. It must develop a clear vision for the education of children and young people with SEND, one that is supported by straightforward, co-ordinated and fully resourced policies. This chapter should have helped guide you to an understanding that if any government is to achieve an inclusive consciousness it must ensure that all pupils achieve their full potential and become a 'normal' part of society. This, it would seem, can only be realised by listening to children, young people and their families, and by ensuring that inclusion is by choice and not by compulsion.

In summary, then, this chapter set out to offer a critical overview of the emergence and evolution of inclusive education from the 1990s onwards whilst considering the barriers created by the government, local authorities, colleges and schools that have served to stall the development of SEND practice. Within the next section, we will locate how SEND, equality and inclusion are operated within the English legislative system. In addition, we will analyse how SEND and inclusion are formulated and delivered within other countries' educational systems.

STUDENT ACTIVITIES

Lani Florian is a professor of social and educational inclusion and her views on the term 'inclusion' are detailed below. Using the knowledge gained from this chapter and the previous ones you have read, decide whether inclusion has become too broad or indeed is a concept that has just replaced the term 'special', and in reality nothing in schools has actually changed over the course of the last twenty years.

There is uneasiness about the term 'inclusion'. On the one hand, it has been observed that narrow conceptualisations have resulted in simply replacing the word 'special' with 'inclusive', and nothing much has changed. On the other hand, there is a fear that the definition has become so broad that it is meaningless or, worse, that educationally important differences are being overlooked (Florian, 2008: 206).

REFLECTIVE QUESTION

By completing the activity and reading detailed above you would have needed to consider what the best way is of defining inclusion and inclusive education, and who should hold control of the inclusion of children and young people in mainstream schools. Should this be the local authority, the teachers, the parents or the children?

FURTHER READING

Robinson, D. (2017) Effective inclusive teacher education for special educational needs and disabilities: some more thoughts on the way forward, *Teaching and Teacher Education*, 61: 164–78. This text provides an overview of research into effective inclusion and teacher training.

Shaw, A. (2017) Inclusion: the role of special and mainstream schools, *British Journal of Special Education*, 44(3): 292–312. This research continues the 'special school versus inclusion debate' by suggesting that special schools continue to be important in the provision of SEND education.

SECTION III

OPERATIONALISING SEND AND INCLUSION

6

CURRENT LEGISLATION GOVERNING SEND AND INCLUSION

The major questions this chapter addresses are:

- How has legislation that governs SEND changed in recent times?
- How does SEND legislation operate in early years settings, schools and colleges in England?

INTRODUCTION

In Chapter 5 we considered the view that inclusive education and SEND practice was under threat because successive governments had introduced competing policy initiatives from the 1990s onwards. It was suggested that governments must put ideology to one side and develop a framework of SEND that is built upon straightforward and co-ordinated policies.

This chapter examines how SEND and equality legislation has changed in recent times. It provides an overview of legislation and policy and outlines the guiding principles that have informed these changes. Below is an overview of some of the important pieces of legislation that govern SEND and equality provision. It might be of some surprise to you that legislation from the 1970s still has a part to play in the development of SEND and inclusive educational provision in the 21st century.

- Chronically Sick and Disabled Person Act 1970. Available at: www.legislation.gov.uk/ukpga/1970/44/contents
- Children's Act 1989 (Section 17). Available at: www.legislation.gov.uk/ukpga/1989/41/section/17
- Children's Act 2004 (Children's Services) Regulations 2005. Available at: www.legislation.gov.uk/uksi/2005/1972/contents/made
- Mental Capacity Act 2005. Available at: www.legislation.gov.uk/ukpga/2005/9/contents
- The Equality Act 2010. Available at: www.legislation.gov.uk/ukpga/2010/15/contents
- Teaching Standards 2012. Available at: www.gov.uk/government/publications/teachers-standards
- The National Curriculum for England and Wales 2014. Available at: www.gov.uk/government/collections/national-curriculum
- Children and Families Act 2014. Available at: www.legislation.gov.uk/ukpga/2014/6/contents/enacted
- The SEN and Disability Regulations 2014. Available at: www.legislation.gov.uk/uksi/2014/1530/contents/made

---

THE CHRONICALLY SICK AND DISABLED PERSON ACT 1970

This Act was ground-breaking because it was the first in the world to provide rights and equal opportunities to people with disabilities (BBC, n.d.). This legislation introduced a code of practice to ensure that public buildings were accessible.

Consider the argument below which defines how important access to services is for all children. Consider also whether legislation is capable of ensuring equality of access. Mind-map what other issues should also be considered.

The Council for Disabled Children believe that all disabled children are children first and therefore they should have equal access to all the services available to children. Such services should include nurseries, playgroups, playgrounds, leisure services, children's centres and mainstream schools.

(Source: Council for Disabled Children, 2014)

READER REFLECTION

This legislation also required local authorities to support disabled people in accessing travel and educational activities outside of the home. Section 2 of the Act has been denoted to be the 'finest community care statute' that exists because of the manner in which it brought forward enforceable rights for disabled people in relation to community care services (see Bowen, n.d.: 1).

THE CHILDREN ACT 1989

This Act is one of the most significant to reach the statute book as for the first time it unified legislation relating to children and young people (Allen, 2005). It delivered the 'legal tools' to those who held parental responsibility for children and young people so that they could act in their best interest (Allen, 2005: 1). Section 3(5) provides that professionals as well as the local authority have a duty of care towards children and young people, and that they must 'do all that is reasonable in the circumstances for the purposes of safeguarding or promoting the welfare of the child' (NUT, 2013: 4).

This legislation has been amended through the Adoption and Children Act 2002 and the Children's Act 2004. This, and other legislation, has amended provision in terms of parental responsibility, special guardianship orders, care plans and local authority complaints procedures (Allen, 2005).

The Act provides that the following people have 'parental responsibility':

(i). The mother and father of a legitimate child (or the adoptive parents of a child who has been legally adopted).

(ii). The mother of an illegitimate child.

(iii). A guardian – the person appointed to act as the child's guardian – usually only when there is no-one else who has parental responsibility.

(iv). A person with whom the child is to live under what is called a residence order, and a local authority in whose favour a care order has been made, have parental responsibility.

(Source: Children's Act 1989. Available at: www.legislation.gov.uk/ukpga/1989/41/section/17)

According to the Council for Disabled Children (2014) the Children Act 1989 is the key legislation which provides services to support disabled children. It creates a duty on local authorities to provide services that safeguard and promote the welfare of children in need within their area. Sections 20 and 22 of the Children Act place a duty on authorities to ensure that children are consulted about their needs and the services provided to them (Joseph Rowntree Foundation, 1999).

This legislation though has been subject to criticism. For example, research conducted by the Joseph Rowntree Foundation (1999) suggested that the Act:

- was not ensuring children received adequate protection;
- was not ensuring that children's feelings and wishes were being taken into consideration about their placements in residential care;
- did not provide information about how many children were spending time away from home and what form of service provision was involved in their care.

The Children Act 1989 continued the tradition of ensuring that teachers had a duty of care towards their pupils – an idea that dates back to the 19th century. However, according to Hunt (2002) many teachers are unsure where the line between caring for a child as a teacher and the work of a social worker is to be drawn. Consider the following case studies: what should a teacher reasonably be expected to do in each circumstance?

CASE STUDY 6.1
Mrs AJAY'S STORY

Six-year old Paul attends his local school. His teacher, Mrs Ajay, notices that he is quite thin for his age. After talking with him, Mrs Ajay realises that Paul's parents do not always provide him with breakfast each morning. She decides to bring in a breakfast for Paul each morning to ensure he is eating well.

CASE STUDY 6.2
Mrs AUCHBRALLY'S STORY

Mrs Auchbrally notices that Jemma often comes to school in dirty clothing which in recent times has begun to smell. She decides that under her duty of care she should provide Jemma with a replacement uniform and that she should wash her dirty clothes at least twice a week.

CASE STUDY 6.3
Mrs KENON'S STORY

Mrs Kenon has successfully run a school canoeing trip for the past ten years for her secondary schoolchildren. However, this year she has decided to cancel the trip as she is unsure whether by organising such an adventurous outing that she would be maintaining her duty of care towards the children in her class.

THE CHILDREN ACT 2004 (CHILDREN'S SERVICES) REGULATIONS 2005

This Act came in to being as a response to the death of Victoria Climbié and other child abuse inquiries (Roche and Tucker, 2007) and was designed to strengthen the Children Act of 1989. This Act brought forward the biggest organisational change of children services that had been observed in recent times (Reid, 2005). The legislation aimed to ensure that schools were made available to be used by their local communities 365 days a year through the implementation of what was to be called the 'extended day' (Reid, 2005).

EXTENDED SCHOOLS

Extended schools provide a range of services and activities beyond the school day to help meet the needs of their pupils, their families and the wider community.

These services, normally entitled 'wraparound care', have importance for dealing with social inclusion issues, such as poor attendance, persistent late arrival at school, and a single point of access for parents and carers so that they may return to work or access appropriate training (see Roche and Tucker, 2007).

This Act provided the central pillar for New Labour's attempts to improve services for 'vulnerable children' and protect 'local communities' (Reid, 2005: 12). Parton (2011) notes that this legislation and the associated Every Child Matters agenda were the beginnings of a journey towards a radical reform of services and polices that related to children (see Roche and Tucker, 2007).

This legislation created the post of the Children's Commissioner and also created an electronic record for every child in England, Scotland and Wales. The purpose of these records was to ensure that when children moved across authorities their well-being would continue to be monitored. In addition, the legislation placed a duty on all service providers to work together to protect children and ensure that no child 'fell between the gaps' of provision. Moreover, it established Local Safeguarding Boards who became responsible for child protection in their area (*Guardian*, 2009). The objectives of such safeguarding boards were to co-ordinate service provision and ensure the effectiveness of that provision.

The Children's Commissioner promotes and protects children's rights and ensures that children are taken seriously. Further information is available at:

For England: www.childrenscommissioner.gov.uk/

For Wales: www.childcomwales.org.uk/

For Scotland: www.sccyp.org.uk/

For Northern Ireland: www.niccy.org/

To fulfil the requirements of this Act every authority had to appoint a Director of Children's Services (Lead Director in Wales) for children and young people to co-ordinate and oversee children's services. These Directors of Children's Services have three key roles:

- responsibility for promoting partnership working both corporately across the local authority and, in recognition of its leadership role, between the authority and its partners.
- to provide leadership to drive change.
- to ensure that the local authority implements the rights of children and young people.

The Children Act 2004 placed a duty on all schools, including independent schools, non-maintained schools and further education institutions, to exercise their functions with a view to safeguarding and promoting the welfare of their pupils by:

- creating and maintaining a safe learning environment for children and young people;
- identifying where there are child welfare concerns and taking action to address them, where appropriate, in partnership with other agencies;
- developing children's understanding, awareness and resilience.

(Source: Welsh Assembly Government, 2006: 54)

This legislation however brought forward challenges for those working in educational services because it called for a radical change in the culture of schools. From this time forward, schools were to become the centre of provision for the safeguarding and protection of children (Roche and Tucker, 2007). Many teachers found themselves having to undertake different forms of work from those they had traditionally been used to. For example, teachers were asked to become lead professionals who were responsible for ensuring that families could access services that were available on school premises (Roche and Tuker, 2007). Head teachers and senior management teams of schools were now to be observed as part of a complicated but totally integrated service for children and their families (Reid, 2005). Moreover, the role of local authority behavioural support staff and its education welfare officers was also significantly affected (Reid, 2005). One of the major criticisms of the Act though was that it was not backed by extra resourcing. Many authorities reported that they struggled to meet the cost of the increased level of services, especially that incurred by provision of residential accommodation for children (Batty, 2005). Furthermore, local authorities reported that they were having serious difficulties recruiting the necessary staff to ensure that the duties placed upon them by the Children Act were being met.

By employing internet and library resources examine whether the Children's Act 2004 was viewed as a successful piece of legislation. Were the initial difficulties overcome?

READER REFLECTION

A good place to start this examination would be with the internet resource: www.theguardian.com/society/2005/may/18/childrensservices

THE MENTAL CAPACITY ACT 2005

The Mental Capacity Act provides the legal framework to protect people who cannot make decisions for themselves due to a learning disability, mental health condition or any other reason. The Act came into force on the 1st of October 2007 and it is supported by its own code of practice. This legislation applies in England and Wales to anyone whose mental capacity is affected by 'an impairment of, or a disturbance in the functioning of, the mind or brain'. This act is based upon five key principles:

- **Presumption of capacity**. Every adult has the right to make their own decisions if they have the capacity to do so.
- **Maximising decision-making capacity**. People should receive support to help them make their own decisions.
- **Right to make unwise decisions**. People have the right to make decisions that others might think are unwise. A person who makes a decision that others think is unwise should not automatically be labelled as lacking the capacity to make a decision.

- **Best interests**. Any act or any decision made on behalf of someone who lacks capacity must be in their best interests.

- **Least restrictive option**. Any act or any decision made on behalf of someone who lacks capacity should be the least restrictive option possible. (See Mind, 2005.)

This legislation also set up the Office of the Public Guardian, which is responsible for protecting people who lack the capacity to make choices for themselves. They work with service providers, individuals and families to supervise how decisions are being made for those people who cannot make such judgments for themselves.

READER REFLECTION

Watch the 'Three Stories' (http://webarchive.nationalarchives.gov. uk/+/www.direct.gov.uk/en/disabledpeople/healthandsupport/ yourrightsinhealth/dg_10016888), a film about the Mental Capacity Act mentioned at the bottom of the web page. List the benefits of this legislation for the individuals who are shown in the film.

THE EQUALITY ACT 2010

The development of legislation to prevent discrimination on the grounds of disability began in the 1990s. In 1995 the Disability Discrimination Act (DDA) introduced the largest reform ever observed in terms of equality legislation (Hills, 2011). This Act introduced the legal concept of disability discrimination (Lockewood et al., 2012) and the premise that employers should make 'reasonable adjustments' for disabled employees.

MAKING REASONABLE ADJUSTMENTS

A term that causes consternation to some is that of 'reasonable adjustments'. This relates to educational institutions having to make some attempt to interpret the legislation when trying to meet the needs of children and young people with SEND. Obviously, the dilemma for teachers is what counts as 'reasonable' with regard to access to buildings and the curriculum.

Reasonable adjustments should be conceived as changes to the school layout, improved signage and information, relevant staff training and adaptation of the curriculum to ensure accessibility to education for children and young people with SEND. Reasonable adjustments therefore are about what is practicably achievable within educational institutions and individual situations based upon the resources available. Consequently, educational institutions are not required to make changes that are either impractical or beyond their means.

According to the Equality Act 2010 (see DfE, 2014c: 26) the school must make reasonable adjustments for disabled people:

- where something a school does places a disabled pupil at a disadvantage compared to other pupils;
- where schools expect to provide an auxiliary aid or service when it would be reasonable to do so, and if such an aid would alleviate any substantial disadvantage that the pupil faces in comparison to non-disabled pupils.

Review the term 'reasonable adjustments' and make a list of what you consider to be appropriate to adapt and modify within educational settings. In analysing this, try to make justifications for why you think certain adaptations are reasonable, whilst others are more problematic to achieve.

READER REFLECTION

TAKING IT FURTHER

To aid you in your consideration of this issue you might like to read:

Morley, D., Maher, A., Walsh, B., Dinning, T., Lloyd, D. and Pratt, A. (2017) Making reasonable adjustments, *British Journal of Special Educational Needs*, 44(2): 203–19.

or

Rieser, R. (2012) 'Reasonable Adjustments in Schools: A Checklist'. In *Implementing Inclusive Education* (2nd edn).

The guide starts at page 264 and is available online at: http://worldofinclusion.com/v3/wp-content/uploads/2014/01/Implementing-Inclusive-Education-promo-copy1.pdf

Over the next ten years or so the DDA was amended not least by the Special Educational Needs and Disability Act (SENDA) of 2001. SENDA (DfES, 2001) brought education within the remit of the DDA (1995). As such, it suggested that:

- An education a institution should not treat a disabled person 'less favourably' for a reason relating to their disability.
- An institution is required to make 'reasonable adjustments' if a disabled person would otherwise be placed at a 'substantial disadvantage'.

- Adjustments should be 'anticipatory'.
- The legislation applies to all admissions, enrolments and other 'student services' which include assessment and teaching materials.

In examining this legislation, however, many of its key intentions were vague and open to interpretation. For example, what can be determined as 'less favourable treatment', 'reasonable adjustments' and 'substantial disadvantage' had to be tested in the courts. In commenting upon the introduction of the new legislation, Bert Massie (chair of the Disability Rights Commission at the time) suggested that we all want to live in communities where we can participate fully and equally. Furthermore, we want all children to do well at school, to take part in all areas of school life and to reach their full potential.

READER REFLECTION

Imagine you are a teacher who teaches children with SEND in mainstream settings. The head teacher has provided you with the report from the Equality and Human Rights Commission (2017) which showed that children with SEND tend to do less well compared with their non-disabled peers both educationally and on into employment. The head teacher wants you to make some recommendations to the senior management team as part of introducing the new National Curriculum, with the specific aim of raising aspirations and attainment for children with SEND.

Make a list of the recommendations you consider vital in raising attainment for such children in your school. When you have completed your list, review the Equality and Human Rights Commission's advice in relation to making adjustments so that educational provision can be made effective for all children and young people (http://www.equality humanrights.com/sites/default/files/uploads/documents/reasonable_ adjustments_for_disabled_pupils_guidance_pdf.pdf).

In February 2005 the Labour government commissioned a review of equality law to 'consider the fundamental principles of discrimination legislation … and the opportunities for creating a clearer and more streamline, framework of equality legislation'. For Crowther (2007: 791), the decade from 1995 to 2005 witnessed a paradigm shift in legislation, moving from 'grudging acceptance' of the rights of disabled people to that of the positive duty of enforceable civil rights.

The process of modernising legislation came to an end when on the 24th of April 2009 a new single Equality Bill was presented to the House of Commons. This Act harmonised discrimination legislation into one statute and further enshrined the duties set out in the DDA (1995) (Porter et al., 2011). This legislation, then, details the legal duties that are placed on educational providers, employees and service providers to make reasonable adjustments so that disabled people can take part in education, use services and engage in work (Disability Rights UK). It is a large piece of legislation covering some 200 sections and 28 schedules. Section 6 covers the protected characteristics of disability and establishes who is, and is not, disabled for the purposes of this act (Wadham et al., 2012: 7).

This legislation makes it unlawful for an educational provider to discriminate against, harass or victimise a pupil, or potential pupil, in relation to the way it admits a child to school and provides them with an education. For the first time this legislation specifically covered the curriculum that pupils were introduced to. The Act also makes it unlawful to discriminate against pupils on the grounds of their:

- sex
- race
- disability
- religion or belief
- sexual orientation
- gender reassignment
- pregnancy or maternity.

In terms of the Equality Act there are four kinds of unlawful behaviour, namely direct and indirect discrimination, harassment and victimisation.

Direct discrimination – occurs when one person treats another less favourably because of one of the characteristics defined above.

Indirect discrimination – occurs when a provision, criterion or practice is applied generally but effects people with a protected characteristic to a greater degree.

Harassment – is the unwanted conduct to a relevant protected characteristic, which has the purpose of effect of violating a person's dignity or creating an intimidating, hostile, degrading, humiliating or offensive environment for that person.

Victimisation – occurs when a person is treated less favourably than they otherwise would have been because of something they have done.

(See DfE, 2014c: 10.)

Consider the following case studies and make a determination on whether the Equality Act was contravened and what, if any, of the four kinds of unlawful behaviour might apply.

READER REFLECTION

CASE STUDY 6.4
Mr JENKINS' STORY

During a school assembly Mr Jenkins, the head of year, belittles a child because of 'ticks and noises' that are resultant to the child having a condition called Tourette syndrome.

CASE STUDY 6.5
JAMES'S STORY

A school bans a pupil from taking part in Sports Day as they feel that, as James has Down's syndrome, he will not be able to run quickly enough. The head teacher is concerned that by James taking part in the event they will not be able to keep the sports day running to time.

CASE STUDY 6.6
Mrs BROWN'S STORY

Mrs Brown wants to send her four-year-old daughter, Anna, to the local state primary school. Anna, as a result of a disability, is not able to fully exercise control of her bowel movements. The school have told Mrs Brown that she cannot attend the school because the school's policy maintains that all children must be toilet trained. The school states that they are not refusing access to the school because Anna has a disability but are applying their toilet-training policy equally to all children.

CASE STUDY 6.7
ASHAM'S STORY

Asham is a bright and energetic boy who attends his local secondary school. He really enjoys his history lessons and has a wide circle of friends who play 'Fornite Battle Royale' on their gaming devices at lunchtimes. However, Asham has experienced frequent episodes of depression. He has been prescribed high doses of anti-depressant medication by his doctor. Ashram is not able to self-medicate, and his teachers are also not able to give him his medicine, as 'union rules' do not allow it. Given this difficult situation, the head teacher of Ashram's school has asked that he be taken out of school whilst he is on this medication.

In terms of the Equality Act, disability discrimination has a different status from that covered within the other protected characteristics (DfE, 2014c). To be specific, schools may treat disabled pupils more favourably than non-disabled pupils, and in some cases through the implementation of 'reasonable adjustments' are actually required to do so by law. The application of reasonable adjustments is provided to ensure that disabled pupils are 'put on a more level footing' with those pupils who do not have disabilities (DfE, 2014c: 11). The Act defines disability when:

> a person has a 'physical or mental impairment which has a substantial and long-term adverse effect on that person's ability to carry out normal day-to-day activities.' Some specified medical conditions, HIV, multiple sclerosis and cancer are all considered as disabilities, regardless of their effect. (DfE, 2014c: 25)

PUBLIC SECTOR EQUALITY DUTY (PSED)

The Equality Act also introduced a single Public Sector Equality Duty that applies to all maintained schools, colleges and Academies. This duty required public bodies, such as schools, to have due regard to:

- eliminating discrimination and other conduct that is prohibited by the Act;
- advancing equality of opportunity between people who share a protected characteristic and people who do not share it;
- fostering good relations across all characteristics – between people who share a protected characteristic and people who do not share it.

Advancing equality of opportunity means:

a) removing or minimising disadvantages suffered by people which are connected to a particular characteristic they have;

b) taking steps to meet the particular needs of people who have a particular need;

c) encouraging people who have a particular characteristic to participate fully in any activities.

(Source: DfE, 2014c: 33-34)

For early years settings, schools and colleges, then, having regard to the general duties of the PSED means that:

- decision makers must have 'due regard' when making a decision or taking an action, and must assess whether it may have particular implications for people with protected characteristics;
- equality implications should be considered before and at the time that they develop policy and take decisions, and they need to keep policies under review;
- educational providers functions need to be interrogated to ensure they are carrying out their equality duty seriously and rigorously;
- educational providers can't delegate responsibility for carrying out the duty to anyone else.

(Source: DfE, 2014c: 29–30)

These duties require all maintained early years settings, primary, secondary, special schools and colleges as well as Academies to take proactive steps to ensure that their disabled pupils, staff, governors, parents and caregivers, and other people using the school, are treated equally. The duty is not necessarily about changing the physical infrastructure of buildings or making adjustments for individuals. It is about embedding equality for disabled children and adults within the culture of the whole school's ethos.

It is important therefore to recognise that the PESD is not about trying to jump through the right hoops quickly. Rather, it is about developing a school approach to disability equality, and working towards achieving this over a sustained period of time. As we know, schools and colleges offer a diverse range of opportunities for interaction and engagement between different children, as well as employment opportunities for young people and the services they can provide to the wider community. Consequently, educational providers are potentially well placed to help challenge and overcome discrimination in society.

READER REFLECTION

In examining the PESD we can see this requires schools to carry out three general duties. Reflect upon these three points and consider what strategies educational providers could consider addressing to meet these requirements.

DISCRIMINATION TRIBUNALS

In relation to this Act, tribunals were set up to hear cases of the educational provision which contravened the general duty in relation to disability. These 'First-Tier' Tribunals hear cases brought by pupils or parents against a school. If a tribunal rules that there is a case to answer, it has the power to require a school or college to find a remedy, including putting in place the necessary measures to meet a child or young person's needs and help them catch up with other pupils (DfE, 2014c).

In summary, the Equality Act 2010 is a significant piece of legislation that 'simplifies, streamlines and strengthens the law' (Equality and Human Rights Commission, 2014). It offers individuals, including those with disabilities, greater protection from unfair discrimination, and sets new standards for public services to ensure that everyone is treated with dignity and respect. The legislation is supported by both a Code of Practice which outlines what exactly the legislation means and how it is to be applied, and the Equality and Human Rights Commission, which provide guidance and technical assistance.

These duties, then, represent a significant leap forward in legislative terms, with the emphasis moving away from minimum compliance towards an attempt to build a positive and sustained cultural change within early years settings, schools and colleges. The Equality Act strengthens children and young people with SEND rights in education and places a duty on educational providers to make reasonable adjustments. These duties require educational providers to eliminate discrimination and develop proactive approaches to make a real and positive change to the lives of disabled people.

> Information relating to the Equality and Human Rights Commission is available at: www.equalityhumanrights.com/

TEACHING STANDARDS 2012

Teaching Standards define the minimum level of practice expected of teachers (DfE, 2013c). They were developed to 'raise the bar for teaching and improve pupil performance and behaviour' in schools (Gove, 2011) and as such lay out the key areas in which a teacher must be able to assess their own professional practice.

The standards have minimal reference to SEND which teachers must take account of in terms of assessing their own level of professional practice. For example, they define children with SEN as:

> children who have a learning difficulty. This means that they either: have a significantly greater difficulty in learning than the majority of children of the same age; or have a disability which prevents or hinders them from making use of educational facilities of a kind generally provided for children of the same age in schools within the area of the local education authority. (DfE, 2013: 8)

They also designate that teachers should promote equal opportunities and make reasonable adjustments for those with disabilities in line with the Equality Act 2010. Whilst all of the standards are relevant for children and young people with SEND, the following standards would seem to have most relevance; that teachers:

5.2 – have a secure understanding of how a range of factors can inhibit pupils' ability to learn, and how best to overcome these;

5.3 – demonstrate an awareness of the physical, social and intellectual development of children, and know how to adapt teaching to support pupils' education at different stages of development;

5.4 – have a clear understanding of the needs of all pupils, including those with SEN; those of high ability; those with English as an additional language; [and] those with disabilities; and be able to use and evaluate distinctive teaching approaches to engage and support them.

READER REFLECTION Interestingly the standards do not mention inclusive education specifically. Imagine you have been asked to formulate two standards to support inclusive education what would you deem to be most important in terms of what teachers should be able to do?

These standards, though, are there for accreditation purposes and do not include the development of evaluative skills nor the values that underpin practice in working with children and young people with SEND. Allan (2003: 171) believes that earlier standards were just an 'official scrip' which was 'determinant and restrictive and which emphasised the discipline and control of children', not the support of children with complex disabilities. It would appear that these new standards do not alter, in any way, a teacher's ability to feel more confident and be more competent in their skill in identifying and addressing the personalised learning needs of all pupils.

THE NATIONAL CURRICULUM FOR ENGLAND AND WALES 2014

From 1989, curricula have changed significantly as successive governments have interfered directly in the teaching of pupils in state-funded schools (Carpenter et al., 2001b). The national curriculum forced a major rethink in schools into how education should be delivered (Carpenter et al., 2001b), not least for those children with SEND. On the whole, we may observe the National Curriculum as a positive development in that for the first time it provided an entitlement for all children to access the same curriculum. However, the introduction of national curricula since 1998 has led to tensions and some resistance from teachers of children with SEND. Many teachers feared that these curriculum initiatives would impede the learning of children with SEND because of the curriculum's reliance on subject-based teaching and its pernicious assessment regimes (see Carpenter et al., 2001a).

In 2014 a national curriculum was introduced to schools in England and Wales. This curriculum, according to the Department for Education, allowed teachers to adapt their teaching to meet the needs of pupils in their classrooms. The Department believed that this 'new freedom' would be particularly important in enabling teachers to meet the needs of pupils with SEND. To support SEND in this new curriculum the DfE awarded specialist contracts to the Autism Trust, Communications Trust, Dyslexia-SpLD Trust and the National Sensory Impairment partnership. The role of these trusts was to provide support and guidance to ensure that all children would acquire the 'essential knowledge and skills that they needed to succeed in life'. The government, through the Department for Education, also revised the national curriculum inclusion statement to reaffirm schools' duties to provide equality of learning in terms of their learning and teaching (see Chapter 1). The National Curriculum, then, determines the teaching interventions and support that schools must provide to enable all children to participate in every part of school life and to have full access to all teaching and learning activities. To enable full access to the curriculum, teachers are enabled to make reasonable adjustments to the teaching and learning activities they provide (DfE, 2014d).

Carpenter et al. (2001a: 6–7) detail that, regardless of whatever curriculum is in place in schools, a learner has the right to ask their teachers: 'What do I get out of this?' Amongst other things, they state that pupils should:

READER REFLECTION

- gain self-esteem
- increase independence
- develop knowledge
- make choices
- express preferences
- be active participants
- gain communicative skills.

With another student, add to this list the knowledge, skills and understanding that you feel children should gain from their time in school.

THE CHILDREN AND FAMILIES ACT 2014

In 2010 the leader of the then opposition party, David Cameron, detailed his conviction that schools should 'end the bias towards inclusive education' and that ideology should no longer control the provision of education for children with SEND. This conviction was adopted by the new Conservative/Liberal coalition that took power after the general election. The new government set to work to overhaul how SEND was to be managed in England. Initially, it launched a special educational needs and disability green paper, *Support and Aspiration: A new approach to special educational needs and disability*, with a view to initiate major legislative reform (Runswick-Cole, 2011). On the 13th of March 2014 the government received Royal Assent for its Children's and Families Bill.

Edward Timpson, the Children's Minister, commented that:

> Today's system for supporting children with SEN is based on a model introduced more than 30 years ago that is no longer fit for purpose. Enquiries and reviews of SEN provision ... have identified that the current system is complex, bewildering and adversarial. The evidence points to an assessment process which is inefficient, bureaucratic and costly, as well as insufficiently child-centred or user-friendly. Needs are sometimes identified late and interventions are not planned or implemented in a timely or effective way. Families tell us that they feel they have to battle at each stage of the system. (Perry, 2014a)

Key changes that were brought into effect by the Act were that it:

- replaced the Statements of SEN with a single assessment named as the Education, Health and Care Plan (EHCP);
- provided that children who have an EHCP have similar statutory protection to that afforded by the previous Statements;
- replaced the system of School Action and School Action Plus with one graduated approach;
- provided for parents and young people to manage their own personal budgets that relate to their support packages;
- placed a duty on health services and local authorities to jointly commission and plan services for children, young people and families;
- provided that local authorities must make known to parents and children what services are available within the local area in a document that will be known as 'the Local Offer';
- changed the manner in which adoption and foster services would be provided.

The government believed that this legislation would offer greater protection and support for children and that it would bring into being a new way of helping children and young people with SEND. The legislation was supported by a capital investment of £30 million to enable parents, young people and children to access from 1,800 trained Independent Supporters (Timpson, in Perry, 2014b). In addition, it introduced a Code which set out how the new assessment process for children and young people with SEND would be completed.

INDEPENDENT SUPPORTERS

These are individuals, trained by the voluntary, private and community sector, whose task is to provide guidance and support to parents of children with SEND during the processes of statutory assessment. The main function of these Independent Supporters is to help families build resilience and also reinforce the work of local authority parental partnership services (Council for Disabled Children, 2014).

THE SPECIAL EDUCATIONAL NEEDS AND DISABILITY REGULATIONS 2014

The revised Code has provided statutory guidance for how the duties, policies and procedures contained within Part 3 of the Children and Families Bill should be operationalised. It should be noted that children with disabilities who do not have a SEN are not covered either by the Children's and Families Act nor are they covered within the Code. Statutory provision for these children is detailed within the Children Act 1989, the Equality Act 2010 and the Health and Social Care Act 2012 (Nasen, n.d.).

The Code is a lengthy document running to 276 pages. Whilst it was broadly welcomed by Members of Parliament, the timescale for its implementation was regarded with unease by members of the Legislative Committee of the Houses of Parliament. This was because the Bill's passage through Parliament left only a few months before schools were expected to implement the Code, and so no time was left to provide workforce training (Perry, 2014a). To support the introduction of the code extra funding of £45.2 million was granted, and a further £70 million was made available to local authorities through the SEN Reform Grant (see Perry, 2014a).

The Code, then, sets out to provide advice to local authorities, maintained schools, early education settings (nurseries) and others with regard to undertaking their statutory duties to identify, assess and make provision for children's SEND. As such, it is informed by the guiding principles that:

- The views, wishes and feelings of the child or young person, and the child's parents must be taken into consideration. Under the new Act children, young people and parents must be provided with information, advice and support so that they can fully participate in the discussion and decisions in relation to their child's SEND.
- It is important that the child or young person, and the child's parents, participate as fully as possible in decisions, and that they are provided with the information and support necessary to do this. The Children and Families Act provides significant new rights for young people, especially when they reach the end of compulsory schooling at 16. Chapter 8 of the Code details how decision-making rights transfer from the parent to young children at 16.
- The child or young person's needs, and those of the child's parents, must be supported in order to facilitate the development of the child or young person and to help them achieve the best possible educational and other outcomes, and to prepare them effectively for adulthood. (DfE, 2014b: section 1.1)

Speaking about the new measures Edward Timpson, Children's Minister, said 'It's a radical overhaul that breaks down artificial barriers, and that champions children with SEN as never before from birth right through to adulthood' (Perry, 2014a).

READER REFLECTION

The Independent Provider of Special Education Advice service (IPSEA) commented in relation to this legislation:

'Don't panic! Much of the new law is still the same ... '

Whilst the Code was claimed to be a 'radical overhaul' of SEND policy, the question that remains is: 'Is this really the case?' Working with a peer, review the previous Code formulated under the New Labour government. Can you find any areas that still remain the same?

The Code maintains that mainstream schools must:

- use their best endeavours to make sure that a child or young person with SEND gets the support they need;
- ensure that a child or young person with SEND engages in the activities of the school alongside pupils who do not have SEND;
- designate a teacher to be responsible for co-ordinating SEND provision – the SEN co-ordinator (SENCo);
- inform parents when they are making special educational provision for a child or young person;
- prepare a SEND information report and arrangements for the admission of disabled children or young people; the steps being taken to prevent disabled children from being treated less favourably than others; the facilities provided to enable access to the school for disabled children; and their accessibility plan showing how they plan to improve access progressively over time;
- have a member of the governing body with specific responsibility for SEND;
- observe their duty under the Equality Act 2010 towards individual disabled children or young people, and make reasonable anticipatory adjustments to prevent discrimination and promote equality of opportunity.

ANTICIPATORY PROVISION FOR CHILDREN AND YOUNG PEOPLE WITH SEND

In practice, this means that educational providers should be making efforts to improve accessibility generally rather than waiting for a specific child with a particular need to arrive and to then address that need.

IDENTIFYING SEND IN EARLY YEARS SETTINGS, SCHOOLS AND COLLEGES

Early identification, assessment and provision for any child or young person who may have a SEND are crucial to that individual's educational and life outcomes. Consequently, the Code seeks to promote a common approach to identifying, assessing and providing for all children and young people's SEND. To reflect this, the Code advocates a continuum of provision. In many cases, this graduated approach will commence with educational institutions meeting learning needs through a differentiation of the curriculum. This would involve teachers tailoring their approaches to suit pupils' differing learning needs and styles. Such approaches enable teachers to become more skilled in mixed ability teaching which can benefit all children or young people and not just those with SEND.

THE GRADUATED APPROACH

The Code makes clear that education providers must have arrangements in place to support children and young people with SEND. As part of these arrangements clear guidelines for identifying and responding to pupils' SEND must be in place. The Code recognises that early identification of SEND coupled with effective provision will improve the people's long-term outcomes. In situations where children or young people do not respond to the differentiation of lessons mentioned above, and therefore do not make adequate progress, there will be a need for the educational institutions to do something additional or different. This SEND provision is described in the Code as a graduated approach.

> In terms of the Children and Families Act and the Code of Practice 2014 a pupil or young person has SEN where: their learning difficulty or disability calls for special educational provision, namely provision different from or additional to that normally available to pupils of the same age. (DfE, 2014b, section 6.15)

The first stage in identifying a child or young person with SEND rests with teachers who should, as part of their role, regularly assess all pupils' progress. The purpose of these assessments should be to identify those pupils who are not making the expected progress in terms of their age and individual circumstances. If after implementing 'high-quality and targeted' teaching, progress continues to remain problematic, a SENCo should assess whether or not a pupil has SEND in terms of its four broad categories. If after this assessment it is determined that the child might have a SEND, the educational provider must take action to remove barriers to learning and put effective SEN provision in place. This form of support should follow a staged process in which early decisions are 'revisited, refined and revised', so that the early years setting, school or college may correctly identify, address and evaluate the special educational needs provision that will best suit the individual pupil (see DfE, 2014b).

According to the Code, this 'school-based' support should follow a four-stage process:

Assess - Identify pupils who are making less progress.

Plan - Plan for teaching that increases progress and raises attainment.

Do - Actively seek to improve educational provision to meet a wide range of needs through well-differentiated provision.

Review - Schools will accurately review children's progress and the arrangements for increasing progress and attainment, and make changes to teaching and learning where necessary.

(See Nasen, 2014.)

READER REFLECTION

The Code advocates a continuum of provision, which is often referred to as a 'graduated approach' in which the early identification of SEND is essential to meeting the needs of the pupil concerned. Reflect upon this statement in relation to the strategies that teachers can put in place to ensure that early identification and intervention are achieved.

When the educational provider has been unable to help a pupil make adequate progress after implementing SEND provision, they will seek advice from the local authorities' support services or from health or social work professionals. This might, for example, involve speaking to a speech and language therapist about a specific language programme or an occupational therapist on how teachers might work differently with the pupil in class. It might also include gaining information about the pupil's home circumstances that might help explain changes in their behaviour and attitudes to learning. The school can then use this to work with others to resolve a pupil's difficulties. Central to this process should be active consultation with the pupil and their parents in order to ensure their needs are addressed, and that they play as full a part as possible in understanding any necessary modifications that may be considered. The Code also stresses the importance of working in partnership with parents in all aspects of a pupil's education, and of that pupil's participation in making decisions and exercising choices in relation to their own education.

EDUCATION HEALTH AND CARE PLANS

The test for considering whether a statutory assessment of SEND is necessary is whether the pupil concerned is making adequate progress. What 'adequate progress' is depends on the starting point and the expectations for a particular pupil. Essentially, however, what is considered to be adequate progress for a particular pupil is a matter for their teacher's judgment.

Most children or young people will have their SEND met by their early years setting, school or college, but this will not be possible all of the time. If a child's needs cannot be met by these institutions, the local authority may consider the need for a statutory assessment, and if appropriate, will then make a multi-disciplinary assessment of that child's needs. Following this, the authority may decide to formulate and implement an EHC plan which will specify those needs and the SEND provision that will be required to meet those needs.

THE CHILDREN AND FAMILIES ACT 2014: MOVING FORWARD BUT STANDING STILL?

In this section we will critically consider how this Act and its Code are operating in practice. Like most legislation, it is not unusual to find that changes in policy lead to controversy and criticism (Palikara et al., 2018) and a confusing picture as to the usefulness, or otherwise, of new policy and its associated practice. At this time, it is difficult to make a determination as to the effectiveness of this new legislative framework. However, worrying data are emerging which suggest that the new framework is not as effective as it was hoped it would be. It is important to remember that this new SEND assessment and provision was formulated so that practitioners and professionals would respond to the autonomous voice of children and young people (Harris, 2018).

A rather diverse picture has emerged as to how this policy is operating in practice. Detailed below are some of the 'headline facts'.

POSITIVES

(+) Early years settings are identifying children's SEND effectively, particularly those children who have complex needs.

(+) Staff in special schools are assessing and meeting the needs of children and young people with SEND with more accuracy than staff in mainstreams schools.

(+) Children in special schools tend to have access to the specialist support they needed.

(+) Children who have an EHC plan have improved outcomes over those with SEND who do not have a support plan. In addition, two-thirds of parents and young people are satisfied with the process of obtaining an EHC plan.

(+) The vast majority of parents felt that their views were now being included in the EHC plan.

(Continued)

(+) Official statistics demonstrate that the vast majority of EHC plans are being completed in designated time periods.

(+) Teachers feel more accountable and are taking on more responsibility for children with SEND.

NEGATIVES

(−) 74% of parents surveyed by the National Autistic Society found it difficult to access the support they needed and this had resulted in cases being taken to SEN tribunals.

(−) There are large variations in parents' and pupils' experiences in the EHC planning process across different local authorities.

(−) Overall, children and young people with SEND have not significantly benefitted from the introduction of the legislation.

(−) Many more children and young people with SEND are excluded from the educational system than is the case with their mainstream peers.

(−) Children and young people feel their views are not being consistently included in EHC plans.

(−) Parents are not confident that mainstream schools can adequately support pupils with SEND.

(−) Parents are not able to find enough information in relation to the 'local offer'.

(−) In two-thirds of local areas, inspected statutory assessment processes are not working well enough.

(−) Many practitioners do not have the requisite experience or training to enable them to assess children and young people who were struggling with their work.

(−) There is too little support for mental health in a time of significant increase in referrals.

(−) Multi-agency working is not effective in the support of the new legislation.

(−) Concerns are being expressed about the withdrawal of services and funding to support SEND provision.

(Sources: Boesley and Crane, 2018; CQC and Ofsted, 2017; Curran et al., 2017; Long, 2018; National Autistic Society, 2016; Palikara et al., 2018; Robinson et al., 2018)

Research examining the early implementation of this legislation suggests that many of the 'pathfinder families' experienced more joined-up thinking in relation to how education, health and care services responded to their children's needs, and that information sharing between these services had improved (Robinson et al., 2018). However, from the outset it became apparent that implementation of the new Code was being dominated by bureaucracy. Many SENCos felt that they had not received adequate support to implement the legislation, especially in how they should define SEND in terms of the Act (Curran et al., 2017). As Curran and colleagues report, the legislation led to many SENCos reviewing what was or was not SEND and that this in turn led to a reduction of children being registered as having SEND.

In the last few years, it has become apparent that special schools and early years settings are coping better with the demands of this legislative framework than mainstream schools. In such settings, data from inspection reports demonstrate that practitioners are assessing and meeting the support needs of children and young people effectively (CQC and Ofsted, 2017). In relation to the assessment of SEND, the evidence demonstrates that, in the main, EHC plans are a more powerful tool than the previous Statements in supporting the needs of children and young people (Boesley and Crane, 2018). Recently, 80% of parents surveyed agreed that their views, wishes and opinions had been taken into account in the formulation of the EHC plan (CQC and Ofsted, 2018; Holland and Pell, 2017). Further, evidence suggests that two-thirds of parents and young people are satisfied with the assessments relating to the EHC plan and felt that these plans would be successful (CQC and Ofsted, 2018). Problematically however, this positivity towards EHC plans and its processes is not consistent for all children and young people. For example, whilst the majority of SENCos observed that SEND reforms had had the greatest impact on parents in terms of engagement (Curran et al., 2017), the National Autistic Society reported that only 23% of parents engaging in assessment processes had been satisfied with the services they had received. Moreover, the National Deaf Children's Society reported that only 6% of parents had observed improvements in the support their children received (Curran et al., 2017). It would seem there are wide variations in the quality of assessment processes that are being operated by local authorities (CQC and Ofsted, 2018). It is also becoming clear that EHC plans are not always the holistic documents they were meant to be. Indeed, in many cases they are being dominated by an educational imperative rather than a wide-ranging assessment of a pupil's needs (Boesley and Crane, 2018).

In relation to multi-agency working, whilst early data suggested this was operating efficiently more recent data suggest otherwise. Indeed, one of the 'main themes' emerging from the implementation of this legislation is that multi-agency collaboration, especially as it concerns the formulation of an EHC plan, is causing concern (Palikara et al., 2018). For example, Boesley and Crane (2018) suggest that whilst SENCos felt that working with outside agencies was vitally important, it was the case that it was uncommon for other services to attend review meetings. In compiling a report for the House of Commons, Long (2018) found that in half the cases examined, access to therapy services was problematic, and mental health services were also poor in one-third of the cases examined. This lack of support was confirmed by the National Autistic Society, who detailed that parents of children with autism were fighting just as hard to find support for their children as they had under the previous legislative framework (see CQC and Ofsted, 2018). Further anxieties have been raised about the level of funding that has been allocated to implement multi-agency working. To be specific, SENCos have expressed concern that it is only when a child is in crisis that requests for support are taken seriously. The worry is that where children 'struggle in silence' nothing is actually being done and local authority support was 'disappearing in front of their eyes' (Boesley and Crane, 2018: 5).

In summary, it would appear that whilst this new legislative framework offers a 'direction of travel' (Holland and Pell, 2017: 308) that professionals, parents, young people and children support (Palikara et al., 2018), the implementation of SEND processes has not been as successful as had been hoped. The National Autistic Society summarised the pervading thoughts in relation to the new legislation:

[it] actually takes longer to bring about genuine cultural change in the way things are done at a local level than it does to change national law. (Long, 2018: 27)

To take a more expansive view, it would seem that in the forty years since the Warnock Report altered SEND practice, legislation still focuses on a child or young person's needs rather than their rights and entitlements. As Sayers (2018) comments this means that 'the problem' of SEND is still located within the child or young person. In this respect, Sayers' view is that SEND is still stuck in the realms of the medical model rather than progressing forward with more social-model-orientated solutions to societal problems. It appears to be the case, as with previous legislation, that there is a gap between the ideology and the implementation of the SEND framework in England (Palikara et al., 2018), and that children and young people's autonomous voices are not always being heard (CQC and Ofsted, 2018).

CONCLUSION

In this chapter, you have gained knowledge and understanding of:

- how legislation that governs SEND has changed in recent years;
- how SEND legislation is operating in early years settings, schools and colleges in England.

In this chapter you have learnt that during the last two decades there has been an increased impetus towards inclusive education for children and young people with SEND. Indeed, in the early part of the 21st century the shift had been dramatic. However, when parents want a special school for their son or daughter, they still have the right to state that preference. This seemingly indicates that autonomy and decision making rests with parents and with children themselves rather than local authorities. But in your reading of this chapter you will have realised that these new rights do not mean that every child or young person will actually go to the educational setting of their choice. Consequently, in times when early years settings, schools, colleges and local authorities are at the mercy of budgetary constraints, achieving the flexibility necessary to accommodate every pupil's needs with an educational placement of their choice is still highly problematic.

In summary, this chapter has detailed that the concept of inclusive education is beginning to become more of a reality for parents of (and for) children and young people with SEND. However, progress towards inclusion has not come about easily, and in reality there is still much work to be done if schools' cultures, ethos and philosophies are to become more like those envisaged within the Salamanca Statement. Although legislation has advanced in recent years, the ambiguity of inclusion still poses challenges for service providers.

As we move forward with the next phase of educational reform based upon the Children and Families Act 2014, the views of pupils with SEND should be considered as an integral component of the decision-making process regarding their educational choices. As we have observed though, this is not always the case. In more recent times, we have also seen a shift from inclusive education to the advocating of a more mixed economy of mainstream and special school provision. Who knows what the outcomes of such changes will be as we move through the 21st century? What is clear nonetheless is that inclusion involves a basic acceptance and empathy on the part of society that all pupils have the same entitlement to be valued and to access high-quality educational experiences, regardless of their individual needs. The initial findings in relation to the new Act do not suggest that inclusion for all will become a reality 'any time soon'. Indeed, in many respects it appears that inclusive education may actually be further away than ever.

Through the 'Taking it further' activities in the chapter, and the student activities, reflective questions and the readings detailed below, you will develop a deeper understanding of the workings of the legislation that govern how children and young people with SEND should be treated within our educational system. Developing a knowledge and understanding of such legislation and policies will be invaluable in your work with professionals, families, and children and young people with SEND.

STUDENT ACTIVITIES

Reflect upon what the concluding statement to this chapter means and how inclusion can be achieved over the forthcoming years.

The Equality Act 2010 requires educational providers to be proactive in promoting disability in schools. Discuss with a partner how such providers can meet this requirement in the future, both from a policy and a practice perspective.

FURTHER READING

Cook, A. (2014) 'Five Things Schools Need to Know About the SEN Reforms', *Guardian* (http://www.theguardian.com/teacher-network/teacher-blog/2014/feb/10/special-educational-needs-sen-reforms-five-things). This is a very readable piece that succinctly summarises for teachers the main changes in the 2014 legislation.

Palikara, O., Castro, S., Gaona, G. and Eirinaki, V. (2018) Professionals' views on the new policy for special educational needs in England: ideology versus implementation, *European Journal of Special Needs Education* (https://www.tandfonline.com/doi/full/10.1080/08856257.2018.1451310). This piece provides a detailed overview of policy implementation and how professionals have struggled with the challenges this has brought to their daily working lives.

SEN Policy Research Forum (2016) *An Early Review of the New SEN/Disability Policy and Legislation: Where Are We Now?* (http://blogs.exeter.ac.uk/sen-policyforum/past-policy-papers/) This policy paper reports on the first two years of operation of the 2014 Children and Family Act.

7

MULTI-AGENCY
WORKING

The major questions this chapter addresses are:

* What is the definition of multi-agency working?
* What are the key agencies and services, and how do they work together to support children with SEND?

This chapter will introduce you to the key definitions and the language surrounding multi-agency working. It also provides you with a background and context to the development of multi-agency working, as well as analysing legislation that governs this area of practice. Additionally, it examines some of the agencies and professionals that are involved in the day-to-day practice of supporting children and young people with SEND.

Section 25 of the Children and Families Act (2014) places a legal duty on local authorities to guarantee that education, training, health and social care provision is integrated around the child with SEND (DfE, 2014a). It states that the aim of this reform is to:

> ensure that services consistently place children and young people at the centre of decision making and support, enabling them to make the best possible start in life and challenging any dogma, delay or professional interests which might hold them back. (DfE, 2014a: 4)

Read the information below and consider how many 'professionals' might be involved with the child or young person with SEND and their family over the course of one year:

READER REFLECTION

> There are times that having all different people in my life is too much. I spend a lot of my time in hospitals. I wish there were less appointments and less doctors to see. (Cited in Stone and Foley, 2014: 49.)

MULTI-AGENCY WORKING: KEY DEFINITIONS

In developing an understanding of multi-agency working, confusion can arise because of the plethora of language that is employed to describe how various agencies and services work together to support children and young people with SEND (Hussain and Brownhill, 2014). It is important, therefore, that you develop an understanding of some of the more commonly employed language that dominates this area.

An example of the words used to describe multi-agency working:

* Integrated working
* Multi-agency/cross-agency/interagency/trans-agency

(Continued)

- Co-ordination
- Co-operation
- Collaboration
- Partnerships
- 'Joined-up thinking' and 'joined-up working'
- Cross-cutting
- Network
- Working together
- Interprofessional working.

(Sources: Kaehne, 2014; Payler and Georgeson, 2013; Stone and Foley, 2014)

The range of language detailed above and its inability to express with clarity its meaning demonstrate the complexity of this area. For example, what is the difference between 'cooperation' and 'collaboration' or indeed how in practice might 'partnerships' differ from 'networks' (Stone and Foley, 2014)?

WHAT ARE PARTNERSHIPS?

According to Farrell (2004) partnerships can be described as arrangements between two or more parties who have agreed to work co-operatively towards collective and/or compatible objectives in which there is shared authority and responsibility; a joint investment of resources; a joint liability or risk taking; and, ideally, mutual benefits. Taken together, the following factors identify the nature of partnerships:

- shared common objectives and goals
- shared risks and mutual benefits
- contributions from both partners
- collective authority, responsibility and accountability.

Underlying this definition is the notion that partnerships represent a better strategy to address specific projects or goals, in contrast to partners operating independent of each other. Indeed, this is certainly the case when working with a child or young person with SEND who may have a range of needs that have to be addressed. Consequently, a central feature of successful inclusion according to Rose and Howley (2007) is the commitment and desire for multi-agency and partnership working approaches.

CASE STUDY 7.1
ADELE'S STORY

Adele is a child who has restricted ranges of physical movement, and needs the services of a physiotherapist to support her physical activity and movement. Her physical development also needs to be supported within a school's Physical Education environment, so the PE teacher and physiotherapist need to work in partnership to support this child's physical development through the curriculum.

Reflect upon Adele's needs and then consider how partnerships between professionals might add value to the services that she is receiving. You should consider this from the perspectives of Adele, the teacher and the physiotherapist.

In trying to understand the language employed, in this area, Frost (2005, cited in Stone and Foley, 2014: 13) believes that more transparency might be achieved if we think about these ideas in relation to a 'continuum of partnership' that ranges from 'co-operation to integration'. Frost details four levels of such partnership, these being:

Uncoordinated – a freestanding service.

Level one: Co-operation – services work together towards consistent goals and complementary services, whilst maintaining their own independence.

Level two: Collaboration – services plan together to reach common outcomes and to overcome issues of overlapping, duplication and gaps in their service provision.

Level three: Co-ordination – services work jointly in a planned and methodical way towards shared and agreed aims.

Level four: Merger/Integration – here services would combine into one organisation in order to ensure effective and efficient service delivery.

(Source: Stone and Foley, 2014: 13)

According to Hussain and Brownhill (2014: 199) there are three major types of service provision available to children and young people with SEND. These are:

Universal services – These are services that all children and young people can access without a special referral, e.g. GPs, dentists, opticians, nurseries, schools, colleges and hospitals.

Targeted services – These services provide support for certain groups of children and young people and are often accessed, in the first instance, from within universal services. Such services might include children's centres, parental support and social services.

Specialist services – This form of service provision is usually required when universal services are unable to meet the individual needs of a child or young person. These services might include family support workers, behaviour support workers, speech and language therapists, physiotherapists, youth offending teams, dieticians, and child and adolescent mental health workers.

Carefully read each of the case studies below and consider which services would be the most appropriate to meet the needs of that child. You might also specify which individual professionals would be the most suitable to provide support.

CASE STUDY 7.2
AMIL'S STORY

Amil has recently transferred to St Mark's Secondary School. His teachers have noted that he is very quiet in class but that when he does speak they have difficulty in understanding what he has to say. Amil's head of year believes that he might have issues with his teeth but he is not sure what else might be affecting Amil's ability speak.

CASE STUDY 7.3
BEN AND HOLLY'S STORY

Ben and Holly's daughter is just coming up to her third birthday. She is a delightful, happy and very active child. Ben and Holly want to find out what is the best school for their daughter to attend.

CASE STUDY 7.4
PETER AND BETHANY'S STORY

Peter and Bethany are experiencing considerable issues in their family life. Bethany is having problems with heavy drinking and her husband Peter is undergoing long periods of depression. Both parents believe that the issues they are experiencing are exacerbated by their inability to cope with their five-year-old son, who displays extreme behavioural issues.

Within the context of SEND, Watson et al. (2002) suggest that multi-agency working necessitates the bringing-together of a range of professionals across the boundaries of education, health, social welfare, voluntary organisations, parents and advocates, all with the purpose of working towards holistic approaches to access and the entitlement of high quality services for young people. Thus, if as Bishop (2001) suggests, agencies and individual practitioners work together to support the educational development of children and young people with SEND through holistic approaches, this has the potential to significantly enhance their quality of life and social, physical, emotional and intellectual development. However, it has been the case that over the past four decades many disabled children and young people and their families have experienced barriers in trying to access opportunities and services. Research has strongly suggested that it is the complexities of service provision that have presented considerable obstacles for parents in developing and maintaining educational, home and social environments in which children and young people can thrive (Cavet, n.d.). The chapter now turns to consider how multi-agency working has developed over time and the challenge parents, children, young people and professionals experience in their attempts to provide co-ordinated packages of support.

Reflect upon the statement that 'Agencies and individuals working together will significantly enhance the quality of life for children and young people with SEND both in and outside of school.'

READER REFLECTION

Following your reflection consider the case study below and list what you see as the advantages and challenges of the various health and educational professionals working together to provide a holistic approach to supporting Adam's needs both in and outside of school.

CASE STUDY 7.5
ADAM'S STORY

Adam, who is eight years old, attends a special school, and has a profound physical and learning disability along with 'challenging' behaviour. In addition to his day-to-day schooling, he receives weekly physiotherapy, speech therapy and behaviour therapy, and attends a hospital clinic on a monthly basis.

MULTI-AGENCY WORKING: A BRIEF HISTORY AND OVERVIEW OF CURRENT PRACTICES

Multi-agency working is not a new phenomenon; indeed its roots may be traced back to the mid-1800s when health and social workers came together to try to reduce poverty in England

(Cheminais, 2009). More recently, multi-agency working has become a high priority for successive UK governments who have accepted that well-planned and co-ordinated strategic service provision positively enhances the lives of young children and young people and their families (Hussain and Brownhill, 2014). However, despite the rhetoric of the effectiveness of multi-agency partnerships, many serious case reviews have indicated that children and young people have been badly let down by professionals not working together (Hussain and Brownhill, 2014).

In the modern era, the need for multi-agency working developed out of the death of Maria Colwell. The subsequent inquiry, in 1977, found that a lack of communication between agencies and service providers was a major contributory cause in Maria's death. It was from this beginning that Child Protection Committees were established to co-ordinate the provision of child protection services (Hussain and Brownhill, 2014). From this date forward a raft of measures and initiatives have been produced and introduced to develop joined-up thinking and responses to the issue of social inclusion and child protection (Edwards et al., 2009). These included such things as the Children's Act 1989, Every Child Matters and the subsequent Children's Act of 2004, the Children's Fund, Sure Start, Local Network funding and extended schools initiatives (see Edwards et al., 2009). It seems that since the 1990s, multi-agency working has become a policy imperative for Labour, Conservative and Liberal Democratic politicians alike (Foley and Rixon, 2014).

CHILDREN ACT 1989

This Act and the 'Every Child Matters' agenda aimed to achieve a better balance, in integrated service delivery, between protecting children and young people and enabling parents to challenge state intervention. It also encouraged service providers to work in 'greater partnership'. The legislation additionally strengthened the rights of families, children and young people, and made it plain that health, education and social services should work together to support children and young people (Hussain and Brownhill, 2014).

READER REFLECTION

Farrell (2005) suggests the successful inclusion of children or young people with SEND occurs through ensuring there is a combination of:

- appropriate human resources;
- adequate resources for an adapted curriculum.

Imagine you are a head teacher who has to go to the school governing body to argue for more resources to support Robert, an eight-year-old child with cerebral palsy. Robert needs teaching assistant support in class and some additional resources to ensure the curriculum is modified to meet his needs. Consider how you would present your case to the governors and justify why and how you would argue for both human and curriculum resources for Robert.

CHILDREN'S ACT 2004

In 2004, the Children's Act (DfES, 2004b) identified the need for a wide range of professionals, organisations, schools and agencies to work together to enhance children's services. Indeed, the Act stated that these different agencies had a legal duty to cooperate with each other (Tarr, 2014). Through the encouragement of multi-agency partnerships, the government's Change for Children (see DfES, 2005b) agenda set out to provide a framework for more joined-up services in education, health, culture, social care and social justice for children and young people. The Children's Act encouraged proactive collaboration across a wide range of stakeholders, with the aim of promoting co-operation and shared working practices in order to improve the well-being of all children and young people.

CHILDREN AND FAMILIES ACT 2014

The Children and Families Act denotes that if children and young people with SEND are to achieve their ambitions then local education, health and social care services must work together to ensure that all children receive the correct support (Section 1.22). Indeed, the Act goes further in that Section 25 places a legal requirement on local authorities to ensure that integration between service providers takes place where this would promote well-being and improve the quality of service provision for children and young people with SEND.

Within the Code that supports this Act a chapter is devoted to how services should work together. This chapter details the:

- the scope of joint commissioning arrangements;
- how local partners should commission services to meet local needs and support better outcomes;
- how partnership working should inform and support joint commissioning arrangements;
- the role that children, young people, parents and representative groups such as parent carer forums have in informing commission arrangements;
- responsibility for decision making in joint commissioning arrangements;
- how partners should develop a joint understanding of the outcomes that their local population of children and young people with SEND and disabilities aspire to, and use it to produce a joint plan which they then deliver jointly and review jointly;
- how joint commissioning draws together accountability arrangements for key partners; and,
- the role of colleges as commissioners.

(Source: DfE, 2014b: Section 25)

The Act makes clear that joint commissioning arrangements must provide services for all children and young people aged 0–25, and that such arrangements should provide for those who have EHC plans as well as those who do not. This pooling of resources requires agencies not only to ensure everyone shares the same vision, but also to have the confidence to relinquish day-to-day control of decisions and resources whilst maintaining the high-levels of accountability and commitment necessary to the development of child-centred, responsive services for children and young people with SEND. In conclusion, therefore, the Act sets out the government's desire to reshape services for children and young people with SEND by offering more intensive support for those who need it.

The Children and Families Act provides examples of the types of services that might be involved in joint commissioning arrangements. Such services might include:

specialist support and therapies, such as clinical treatments and delivery of medications, speech and language therapy, assistive technology, personal care (or access to it), Child and Adolescent Mental Health Services (CAMHS) support, occupational therapy, rehabilitation training, physiotherapy, a range of nursing support, specialist equipment, wheelchairs and continence supplies and also emergency provision. They could include highly specialist services needed by only a small number of children, for instance children with severe learning disabilities or who require services which are commissioned centrally by NHS England (for example some augmentative and alternative communication systems, or health provision for children and young people in the secure estate or secure colleges). (DfE, 2014a: 40)

THE CARE ACT 2014

The Care Act of 2014 places a legal duty on local authorities to ensure that children's and adult services provide, co-operate and promote the integration of care and support and health services. The aim of such co-ordinated provision is that no young adult is left without the care and support they need to make the transition between childhood and adulthood.

THE CHALLENGES OF MULTI-AGENCY WORKING

Research by the Care Co-ordination Network UK (2004) has shown that, on average, families of children with SEND have contact with at least ten different professionals over the course of a year and can attend up to 20 appointments at hospitals and clinics. Therefore, it is vital that professionals and agencies work together through a multi-agency co-ordinated approach to support children and young people with SEND and their families (Atkinson et al., 2002). Indeed, this partnership working is hugely important as regards the provision of holistic services that provide the best chance of a child or young person with SEND succeeding and achieving physically, socially, emotionally and educationally. However, despite the evidence of the effectiveness of multi-agency working, Townsley and Robinson (2000) and Kirk and Glendinning (1999) suggest that the range, diversity and different levels of support that families of children and young people with SEND receive are in themselves problematic, and therefore multi-agency working is essential if streamlined services are to be offered.

The literature base also identifies a number of challenges that can serve to undermine the effectiveness of multi-agency partnerships (see Atkinson et al., 2002). These challenges normally centre around four broad areas, these being as follows:

- **Funding and resources**

  One of the major challenges involved with the development of multi-agency partnerships is the simple question, 'Who is going to pay for these initiatives?' This form of working, whilst being highly effective, is particularly demanding of staff time compared to that of single agency working.

- **Roles and responsibilities**

  Within any partnership arrangement a fundamental question is, 'Who should lead the multi-agency team?' Whose procedures and practices should dominate the approach taken with an individual child and their family?

- **Competing priorities**

  Each service provider in a multi-agency team may be held responsible by different government departments or indeed have different inspection regimes that they are accountable to. The question that can dominate multi-agency teams is, 'Who is accountable when something goes wrong?'

- **Communication**

  One of the major reasons for developing multi-agency partnerships was in response to the death of Maria Colwell. As stated above, the inquiry into Maria's death indicated that a lack of communication between professionals had been a contributory factor in this case. In 2002, a study by the National Foundation for Educational Research (Atkinson et al., 2002) found that communication was still an issue in all forms of multi-agency working. This lack of communication was evident not only 'on the ground' between professionals but also at a strategic and operational level.

TAKING IT FURTHER

Given the information that multi-agency working does not appear to be working effectively. Reflect upon how multi-agency approaches to supporting children or young people with SEND and their families can offer improved access to services. Do you see any limitations in multi-agency approaches other than those offered above?

THE KEY SUCCESS FACTORS INVOLVED IN MULTI-AGENCY WORKING

According to the research of the NFER (Atkinson et al., 2002) successful multi-agency working is based upon effective systems and practices that ensure good communication and adequate resources in terms of staffing and time, but more importantly that the professionals involved have the commitment and drive to ensure that this form of provision actually works in practice. It appears that successful multi-agency teams have a commitment and willingness, from all concerned, to engage in meaningful collaboration and co-operation. In addition, another key success factor is that all agencies understand their own roles and responsibilities as well as those of other agencies, and that multi-agency teams are led by people with vision and tenacity.

Lacey and Ouvry (2000) have examined the impact of multi-agency partnership working from both the professional and parental/child perspectives. In relation to the professional context, they identified the terms 'role release' and 'role expansion' to articulate what is required by individuals and agencies to address the government's changing children's agenda, and as part of the requirement to foster more joined-up approaches to the support of children with SEND. 'Role release' implies that professionals will be required to transfer their skills and share expertise (Graham and Wright, 1999) with other professionals, whilst in contrast 'role expansion' involves training professionals in the concepts and language of inter-disciplinary working. Thus what is crucial to effective multi-agency partnership working will be the ability of various professional disciplinary areas to be able to share ideas and resources, and to work much more co-operatively across professional boundaries.

In moving towards these partnerships Atkinson et al. (2002) identified some of the potential positive outcomes of multi-agency work with children and young people with SEND, and these include:

- access to a wider range of services;
- easier, more responsive and holistic approaches to services or expertise which work across professional boundaries, and which are more focused upon individual needs rather than getting caught up in any disputes or maintaining strict professional boundaries;
- improved educational attainment and a better engagement;
- improved support for parents; and,
- needs being addressed more appropriately and within a holistic, rather than single, disciplinary context.

In addressing these areas the Coalition government in 2014 set out to establish much more responsive services with timely support for children and young people with SEND and their families. Within education, then, we are increasingly likely to see the continuation of multi-agency team approaches towards ensuring that children and young people with SEND gain their full entitlement and accessibility to the curriculum. Consequently, it is worth reiterating that teachers must have a thorough understanding of the range of services that are on offer to support both children and teachers alike. The second part of the chapter turns to examine some of the key services and people that are involved in the multi-agency partnerships.

PARENTS

Carpenter et al. (2001a) state that parents and teachers have one common interest (i.e. the child), and that the government accepts this as an important principle in the partnerships between home and school. Indeed, in 1994, the government stated that:

> Professional help can seldom be wholly effective unless it builds upon parents' capacity to be involved, and unless parents consider [that] the professionals have taken account of what they say and treat their views and anxieties as intrinsically important. (DoE, 1994: Section 2:28, pp. 12–13)

Consider the statements made above in relation to parents and teachers. With a partner mind-map the areas in which a parent and teacher should work together to enable children and young people with SEND to be fully supported. You may also wish to consider what skills the teacher and the parent would need to bring to this form of collaboration.

READER REFLECTION

Parents play a crucial role in the education of their child, and research over two decades has indicated that their active involvement can result in better outcomes for their child (Lendrum, 2014). Indeed, the original 1994 Code of Practice stated that:

> Children's progress will be diminished if their parents are not seen as partners in the education process with unique knowledge and information to impart. (DoE, 1994: Section 2:28, pp. 12–13)

The original Code therefore was the first in a plethora of initiatives that were designed to include parents in the education of children with SEND. For example, the Special Educational Needs and Disability Act (2001) amended the 1996 Education Act by introducing the Parent Partnership Services whose work would be independent of local authorities. Such services provided parents with information, training, advice and support, as well as supporting networking and collaboration that informed parents what local SEND policy and practice were (NPP, 2013).

According to one local authority, Parent Partnerships Services should offer:

- access to a confidential telephone helpline;
- impartial information and advice around SEND issues;
- support in preparing for and attending meetings;
- help in filling in forms and writing letters/reports;
- initial support in resolving disagreements with the child's school and the local authority;
- contact details for other statutory and voluntary services;
- links to local parent support groups and forums;
- the chance to submit parents' views, which will help inform and influence local policy and practice training opportunities.

(Source: www.lancsngfl.ac.uk/projects/sen/index.php?category_id=186_)

In August, 2014, the Parliamentary Under-Secretary of State for Children and Families, Edward Timpson, wrote an open letter to parents. In this he detailed the government's commitment to high-quality partnerships with parents.

The Under-Secretary of State's letter stated:

> Like any parent, I want the best for my child. Every parent should expect people who provide support for their children to make sure that support is the best it can possibly be. And every child and young person has the right to expect a good education, and the support they need to become independent adults and succeed in life.
>
> The most important people in any child's or young person's life are their parents. You know your children best of all. What you as parents think, feel and say is important. You should be listened to and you need to be fully involved in decisions that affect your children. That's what the new system is all about.

Like previous codes of practices, the 2014 Code details the importance of parents and professionals working together to provide support to children and young people with SEND. As with the Special Educational Needs and Disabilities Act (SENDA) (2001), the Children and Families Act (DfE, 2014a) ensures that all local authorities provide children and young people with SEND and their parents with advice and information on the services and provision that are available in their local area. This information is provided within a document known as 'the Local Offer'. The government believes that effective participation of parents can lead to a closer fit between what families want and what local authority services can reasonably provide.

It would seem clear then that the role of parents in their children's education is crucial. Lendrum (2014) summarised some of the benefits of parents and professionals working in partnership:

- Engaged parents typically have higher aspirations for their children.
- Engaged parents facilitate and support extended learning opportunities.
- Parental involvement can increase a child's attendance at school.
- Parental involvement can lead to a child's improved behaviour and social skills.
- Parental involvement can lead to greater academic achievement.

It seems evident then that professionals working in partnership with parents can have a positive impact on the quality of life for a child or young person with SEND. However, in part, that level of impact is dependent upon 'the level and nature of engagement' of those involved in parental partnerships (Whittaker et al., 2014: 479). Whilst many parents of children and young people with SEND understand why they are involved with a range of professionals and the contribution that these integrated services can make, they nevertheless comment that they still experience fragmented provision and a lack of 'child-centredness' in such arrangements, and that they fail to observe clear examples of practitioners who can work efficiently and effectively together (Stone and Foley, 2014). As Townsley et al. (2004, cited in Stone and Foley, 2014: 51) state:

> The sheer number of professionals who may be involved in supporting a disabled child in the community can often lead to a lack of continuity and coordination and may leave families uncertain about who to contact regarding specific situation.

Todd's (2003) research (cited in Strogilos and Tragoulia, 2013) documented many parents' experience of dissatisfaction with service providers because they held different priorities and made different assumptions about the children's and families' needs. The Lamb Inquiry (2009) as well as the CQC and Oftsed Inspection (2017) stated that children with SEND were infrequently consulted about both their child's needs and aspirations, and what services the family believed would make a real difference to that child's education. The Lamb Inquiry also reported that for parents of children with SEND their confidence in working with schools was lower than that typically observed for parents whose children did not have

SEND (Lendrum, 2014). Strogilos and Tragoulia (2014) believe that there are serious gaps in the knowledge and understanding in relation to how parents and professionals should collaborate within applied educational settings.

Read the blogs below from parents of children with disabilities. Write a list of the factors that have influenced these parental partnerships positively or negatively.

The relationship that you develop with your child's teacher when your child has multiple learning difficulties is an extremely complex one that sometimes requires a lot of time and patience. You not only have to support your child, you also have to support the teacher too by listening to them and politely giving them suggestions as to how they might teach your child more effectively and respond to his or her needs. There are those teachers who simply do not understand my son's autism and others who do not want to understand. Look, I am not an expert; I have had good relationships with teachers and some really bad ones. I would recommend that developing a good working relationship is everything, and you need to try to seek the teacher's point of view and you need to work hard to get them to see you point of view too.

My daughter Beth has ADHD and a hearing impairment. She was not diagnosed with ADHD until she was 12. By the time she was 14 education had become a real battle. We had to fight to get her a statement of SEN. We had to fight to ensure that Beth got the specialised teaching that was set out in her statement. The school do not really talk to us anymore, and we often find that they have passed on information to the paediatrician without even having the courtesy to inform us that they have done so. School is just one big stress factor for Beth now, and I am sick of dealing with teachers who cannot be bothered to find out how me and our Beth actually feel about how we are being treated by the system.

Governments over the past three decades have attempted to address uncoordinated and fragmented services that children and young people with SEND and their families experience (Foley and Rixon, 2014). One such example is the Scottish government's website 'Getting it right for every child' (http://www.scotland.gov.uk/Topics/People/Young-People/gettingitright). The Scottish government believe that this should be the bedrock for multi-agency working.

CORE COMPONENTS

Getting it right for every child is founded on ten core components which can be applied in any setting and in any circumstance:

1. A focus on improving outcomes for children, young people and their families based on a shared understanding of well-being.
2. A common approach to the proportionate sharing of information where appropriate.
3. An integral role for children, young people and families in assessment, planning and intervention.
4. A co-ordinated and unified approach to identifying concerns, assessing needs and agreeing actions and outcomes, based on the *Well-being Indicators*.
5. Streamlined planning, assessment and decision-making processes that lead to the right help at the right time.
6. Consistent high standards of co-operation, joint working and communication where more than one agency needs to be involved, locally and across Scotland.
7. A *Named Person* for every child and young person, and a *Lead Professional* (where necessary) to co-ordinate and monitor multi-agency activity.
8. Maximising the skilled workforce within universal services to address needs and risks as early as possible.
9. A confident and competent workforce across all services for children, young people and their families.
10. The capacity to share demographic, assessment, and planning information – including electronically – within and across agency boundaries.

HOLISTIC APPROACHES TO INCLUDING CHILDREN AND YOUNG PEOPLE WITH SEND WITHIN EDUCATIONAL SETTINGS

One of the central components of successful inclusion is the ability of a wide range of professionals to work together to provide a co-ordinated support service to specific children and young people with SEND. In relation to effective inclusion, Vickerman (2007) argues that taking a holistic approach to children and young people with SEND is vital if teachers are to be aware of all the needs and issues they may face. In addition, it is highly important that teachers, SENCos and schools have access to the necessary resources, information and guidance to be in a position to take appropriate action to effectively include children and young people with SEND. As a result, Kirk and Glendinning (1999) would argue that the types of support teachers are likely to need when assisting pupils with SEND are those from specialists such as physiotherapists, occupational therapists, educational psychologists, nurses, and speech and language therapists, and sometimes specialist agencies such as will be required to support particular disabilities or mental health. In drawing together this multi-disciplinary team of professionals, the knowledge and understanding that can be gained by teachers in order to give a comprehensive understanding of a child or young person with SEND are critical. Furthermore, teachers listening and reflecting upon the advice and guidance given by each professional will help to ensure that they provide a co-ordinated and person-centred approach to the specific needs of children (Jahoda et al., 2006).

SERVICES THAT WORK WITH CHILDREN AND YOUNG PEOPLE

CAMHS refers to the Child and Adolescent Mental Health Services which are provided by the National Health Service (NHS). Their role is to assess and treat children and young people who experience emotional, behavioural or mental health difficulties. They also provide support which covers depression, anorexia and bulimia, self-harm and abuse, as well as a range of other issues. Each local authority will provide NHS CAMHS referral and assessment services through multi-agency teams comprising nurses, therapists, specialist psychologists and support and social workers, as well as a range of other practitioners and professionals (for further information see https://youngminds.org.uk/find-help/your-guide-to-support/whos-who/).

TAKING IT FURTHER

Read the 2016 Children's Commissioner Report, 'Lightning Review: Access to Child and Adolescent Mental Health Services' (www.childrenscommissioner.gov.uk/wp-content/uploads/2017/06/Childrens-Commissioners-Mental-Health-Lightning-Review.pdf).

What does this report suggest are the failings of the CAMHS? What do young people really want from CAMHS?

Another professional group who might work with children or young people is occupational therapists. In order for occupational therapists to qualify and practise they are required to have a thorough appreciation of aspects of anatomy, physiology, neurology and psychology in order to assist with the assessment and support of children or young people who often have functional difficulties. These therapists are primarily of use to teachers, children or young people, in that they have specific skills in observation and activity analysis and the implementation of carefully graded activities to develop, learn or relearn skills in order for children and young people to live independently. Furthermore, and in specific relevance to supporting children and young people with SEND, paediatric occupational therapists' appreciation of neurology, child development and cognitive psychology offers teachers an insight into the functioning of gross and fine motor skills and movement in order to help them plan effective educational programmes (Lacey and Ouvry, 2000).

In contrast, physiotherapists have a knowledge and appreciation of anatomy and physiology, and are experts in analysing movement. They are particularly focused on aspects of children's movement based on the structure and function of the body, and physical approaches to promoting health, treatment, preventing injury, and the rehabilitation and management of particular disability conditions. Consequently, in relation to supporting children and young people with SEND, physiotherapists can help teachers to improve the quality and range of movements that are central to successful learning and participation.

Speech and language therapists can offer essential information in helping children who have speech errors and communication and language development needs. They are of particular importance to teachers in helping them to ensure such children are able to communicate and interact in effective ways with their peers and tutors. In addition, teachers can reinforce any particular language programmes that are being worked on with a child with SEND. Educational psychologists, on the other hand, will focus on learning outcomes, student attributes and instructional processes which directly relate both to the classroom and the school. In addition, they can support pupils and teachers in ensuring that individual needs are clearly understood, by which they can plan for effective and supportive educational programmes.

As part of the statutory assessment of SEND under the Code (DfE, 2014b) an educational psychologist can also help gather information for teachers, parents and professional support agencies. Furthermore, they are able to assist in evaluating children and young people's thinking abilities and assessing individual strengths and difficulties. Together, the parents, teachers, SENCos and educational psychologist can formulate plans to help children and young people learn more effectively, which is critical to the co-ordinated and multi-disciplinary partnership approaches (Keers et al., 2004) of supporting children and young people with SEND.

Educational psychologists are professionals who work with children and young people in early years and educational settings. These professionals are 'experts' in learning difficulties, social and emotional problems and issues around disabilities, as well as more complex developmental disorders. They offer a specialised service to support teachers, parents and the wider community, as well as children and young people (see the British Psychology Society: http://careers.bps.org.uk/area/educational).

In 2013 there were 1,799 educational psychologists working across 115 local authorities. The vast majority of educational psychologists work in stand-alone educational psychology services, but a significant number do work as part of multi-agency teams (Troung and Ellam, 2013). In research conducted in 2013 (Troung and Ellam, 2013) 81% of the educational psychologists surveyed reported that they could not meet all the requests for their help, and some reported that they could not meet the basic statutory aspects of their role.

Watch the short video available at the website address given above. Make a list of the services offered by educational psychologists. Do you think, based upon the information given, that educational psychologists are simply expected to do too much?

READER REFLECTION

SPECIAL EDUCATIONAL NEEDS CO-ORDINATOR (SENCo)

The key link in the co-ordination of service provision for a child with SEND, their families and service providers within the school context is the special educational needs coordinator (SENCo). According to section 6.85 of the Code, a SENCo has to be a qualified teacher who normally holds a National Award in Special Educational Needs Coordination. A SENCo has a very important role to play in determining, with the head teacher and governors, the strategic development of SEND policy and provision in their school. The SENCo also has day-to-day responsibility for the operation of SEND policy and co-ordination of the educational provision made to support children with SEND. Another major part of the role of a SENCo is to provide other teachers and colleagues with professional guidance and to work to support families so that all children with SEND in their school receive appropriate support and high-quality teaching (DfE, 2014b: Sections 6.87–9).

According to the Code (DfE, 2014b) the key responsibilities of a SENCo are:

- overseeing the day-to-day operation of the school's SEND policy;
- co-ordinating provision for children with SEND;
- liaising with the relevant Designated Teacher where a looked-after pupil has SEND;
- advising on the graduated approach to providing SEND support;
- advising on the deployment of the school's delegated budget and other resources to meet pupils' needs effectively;
- liaising with parents of pupils with SEND;
- liaising with early years providers, other schools, educational psychologists, health and social care professionals, and independent or voluntary bodies;
- being a key point of contact with external agencies, especially the local authority and its support services;
- liaising with potential further providers of education to ensure that a pupil and their parents are informed about options and a smooth transition is planned;
- working with the head teacher and school governors to confirm that the school meets its responsibilities under the Equality Act (2010) with regard to reasonable adjustments and access arrangements;
- ensuring that the school keeps the records of all pupils with SEND up to date.

READER REFLECTION Using the table below, outline in your own words what you see as the different roles the professionals listed above play in supporting children and young people with SEND. You should then relate this specifically to how these professionals can support teachers, parents and children in order to ensure you have a full grasp of the varying roles professionals take in supporting children and young people with SEND.

Table 7.1 Supporting children with SEN

Professional	Your understanding of their role	How can these professionals support teachers, parents, and children and young people?
Occupational therapist		
Physiotherapist		
Speech and language therapist		
CAMHS		
Educational psychologist		
SENCo		

According to Sloper (2004), health authorities should ideally have arrangements for ensuring that local primary care trusts and general practitioners have the necessary information to support children and young people with SEND from both a health and wider educational context. Health authorities should, as part of their expectations and requirements, be able to identify arrangements for the early identification of children with particular difficulties whilst providing advice, support and assessments as to whether they think a child or young person has a SEND or not. Norwich (2007) believes that specific information from health authorities can be of help in identifying young children with physical, sensory or developmental difficulties or particular medical conditions, and as a result could provide schools with the necessary interventions and support to ensure effective access and inclusion within the educational system. Because of this, health authorities, as part of their partnership working with local authorities, should seek to:

- ensure all schools have a contact (usually the school health service) for seeking medical advice on children who may have a SEND;
- co-ordinate health services' advice for a statutory assessment and proactively participate in multi-agency meetings on assessments and formulating EHC plans;
- co-ordinate the provision to be made by the health services for a child or young person with SEND;
- make sure that there are appropriate mechanisms so that health advice is provided for annual review meetings and transition planning when appropriate.

Section 3.59 of the Code (DfE, 2014b) states that health services must be involved with children and young people with SEND. It states:

> Health services for children and young people with SEN or disabilities provide early identification, assessment and diagnosis, intervention and review for children and young people with long-term conditions and disabilities, for example chronic fatigue syndrome, anxiety disorders or life-threatening conditions such as inoperable heart disease. Services are delivered by health professionals including paediatricians, psychiatrists, nurses and allied health professionals such as occupational therapists, speech and language therapists, rehabilitation trainers, physiotherapists and psychologists. In addition, public health services for children ensure a whole population approach to health and wellbeing including preventative services such as immunisation for the whole population and targeted immunisation for the most vulnerable.

Section 3.61 states:

> The multi-disciplinary child health team, including paediatricians, therapists, clinical psychologists, dieticians and specialist nurses such as health visitors, school nurses and community children's nursing teams, provide intervention and review for children and young people with SEN and disabilities and should contribute to supporting key transition points, including to adulthood. They aim to provide optimum health care for the children, addressing the impact of their conditions, managing consequences for the families and preventing further complications.

READER REFLECTION

Using the table below, review your understanding of the roles of health, education and social services in terms of the services, advice and guidance they can offer to each other, and what the benefits for you as the teacher and the child with SEND are likely to be.

Table 7.2 Benefits of health, education and social services agencies

Authority	What is your understanding of the role of each agency?	What are the benefits of collaborative working for the teacher of children with SEND in PE?
Social services		
Health authorities		
Education authorities		

CONCLUSION

In this chapter, you have gained knowledge and understanding of:

- the definition of multi-agency working; and,
- the key agencies and services that work together to support pupils with SEND.

In this chapter, you have learnt that parents, teachers, SENCos, health and social services, schools, and youth services all play a pivotal role in supporting children and young people with SEND. In addition, you have developed an understanding that the government aims to ensure services are responsive to the needs of families and that they offer further support at earlier stages with packages which are tailored to individual needs. Furthermore, this chapter has evidenced that despite such government commitments over a number of decades, it remains the case that children and young people are still being failed because of the lack of effective multi-agency working. The chapter concluded by arguing that a commitment on the part of all those involved in supporting children and young people with SEND and their families to holistic and multi-disciplinary partnership approaches is essential if such children are to learn and progress in their schooling in the future.

The 'Taking it further' boxes in the chapter, as well as the student activities, and further reading detailed below, are included to develop further your knowledge and understanding of the workings of multi-agency services which aim to support children and young people with SEND and disabilities.

STUDENT ACTIVITIES

The 2004 Children's Act identified the need for a wide range of professionals, organisations, schools and agencies to work together to enhance children's services. Discuss what the advantages of educational services working in partnership to support children and young people with SEND can bring to the development of a quality education system.

This chapter has covered some of the major service providers and professionals who work within multi-agency teams. Working with your peers, produce an electronic resource that provides information for parents as to the role of the following professionals in relation to SEND:

- school nurses;
- family support workers;
- community mental health workers;
- CAMHS.

FURTHER READING

Crutchley, R. (ed.) (2018) *Special Needs in the Early Years: Partnership and Participation.* London: Sage. In Chapter 9 of this text Estelle Martin provides an outline of multi-agency services, as well as considering the policy and practice, and how the 'voice of the child' come together to provide person-centred approaches to SEND.

Foley, P. and Rixon, A. (eds) (2014) *Changing Children's Services: Working and Learning Together* (Working Together for Children Series). London: Policy. This text concentrates on the ongoing and fundamental changes that have been happening to children's services across the United Kingdom. It reviews and critically examines the realities of multi-agency working and questions the effectiveness of closer working relations between the professionals that support children with SEN.

Walker, G. (2018) *Working Together for Children* (2nd edn). London: Bloomsbury. This text provides a practical, detailed and expansive account of the systems and processes of multi-agency work that surround individual pupils and their families.

8

INTERNATIONAL PERSPECTIVES ON SEND AND INCLUSIVE EDUCATION

The major questions this chapter addresses are:

- What are the policies and international legislation that govern inclusive education on the 'world stage'?
- How are pupils with SEND educated in Poland, India and the United States of America?

This chapter provides a comparative analysis of the world of SEND and identifies the key themes that impact upon the quality of education that children and young people with SEND receive. In Part A of this chapter you will be introduced to a range of international policies related to SEND. In contrast, Part B examines the policies and practices of specific countries. It commences by examining a European country (Poland) before moving on to examine how SEND and inclusion is conceptualised in the USA and India. Consequently, it is envisaged that after reading this chapter you will have a grasp of international policy related to SEND, alongside an appreciation of how different countries interpret this in practice.

INTRODUCTION

If we accept the ideology of inclusive education, we have to believe that all people, no matter where they are located in the world, should have access to high-quality education. At the beginning of the 21st century inclusive education was high on the international agenda. Indeed, in 2010 the World Education Forum stated that achieving Education for All would happen by 2015 (Srivastava et al., 2013). The 'human ideology' of inclusive education then has 'appealed globally' and has often been described as a global movement with a global agenda (Johansonn, 2014). However, despite such 'humane' ideology, inclusion has experienced difficulties in converting its initial idea into a practical reality upon the world stage. For example, despite the UNESCO Convention against Discrimination in Education being formulated in 1960 it is still the case that millions of children, youths and adults experience exclusion from education. Inclusion, then, whilst being high on the agenda of many countries since the Salamanca Statement of 1994, still witnesses that 72 million children throughout the world are not in school. UNESCO estimates that more than half of this number are girls; seven out of ten of these children live in sub-Saharan Africa, or South or West Asia; and the most 'blatant educational exclusion' is experienced by disabled people. Indeed, UNESCO suggests that one-third of all out-of-school children are those who we might consider are disabled.

READER REFLECTION

Read this extract from UNESCO's education page:

Education is not simply about making schools available for those who are already able to access them. It is about being proactive in identifying the barriers and obstacles learners encounter in attempting to access opportunities for quality education, as well as in removing those barriers and obstacles that lead to exclusion. (www.unesco.org/new/en/education/themes/strengthening-education-systems/inclusive-education/)

Throughout the chapter, make a note of the barriers and obstacles that learners face in their struggles to access high-quality learning placements.

Reflect upon why you think some international countries 'get on the inclusion bandwagon'. As part of your consideration identify what the main reasons are for some countries taking this a step further and actioning inclusion, whilst others do not move beyond rhetoric and philosophical statements.

READER REFLECTION

PROBLEMATISING INCLUSION WITHIN INTERNATIONAL POLICY

One of the many issues with the internationalisation of inclusive education is the fact that this concept has remained largely unproblematised and therefore has operated at a superficial level (Byrne, 2013). For example, the United Nations (2006: 66) defines inclusion as ranging from 'full-time placement of all students with disabilities into one regular classroom or placement into the regular classroom with varying degree of inclusion, including a certain portion of special education' (Byrne, 2013: 3). This definition would seem to be at odds with those 'full inclusionists' located within the English context (see Chapter 5). Furthermore, within the Salamanca Statement 'integration and inclusion' are used interchangeably and other issues of terminological ambiguity are detailed. Notably, the Statement indicates that the 'special needs' of children with disabilities should be considered (Byrne, 2013). This form of ambiguity leads some to believe that inclusion as a concept within the international agenda is one which is heavily diluted, and that its original 'reformist intent' has been undermined (Byrne, 2013). For other researchers, such as Armstrong et al. (2011), the concept of inclusive education is simply a western construct that has difficulty translating into the many and varied international contexts.

Within inclusive education Smith and Thomas (2006) suggest that the international debate has, for too long, focused on whether children and young people with SEND should be educated in special or mainstream schools, rather than concentrating on the quality of education and support they receive.

Consider the statement below. With another student detail what other barriers might stop the development of inclusion bearing in mind that countries have widely different cultures, traditions, languages and histories:

READER REFLECTION

Inclusive education is not an 'indigenous concept to India' but rather has developed as a result of Western influences in special education. Indeed, it may be observed that within the national language of Hindi no direct translation of this terminology exists. (Hodkinson and Devarakonda, 2011)

PART A: INTERNATIONAL ACTION TO DATE AND FUTURE POLICY DIRECTIONS

Legislation governing the international formulation of special education and inclusive education:

- 1948 – Article 26 of the Universal Declaration of Human Rights
- 1959 – United Nations Declaration on the Rights of the Child
- 1960 – UNESCO Convention against Discrimination in Education
- 1966 – Article 13(1) of the International Covenant on Economic, Social and Cultural Rights
- 1989 – UN Convention of the Rights of the Child
- 1993 – Standard Rules on the Equalization of Opportunities for Persons with Disabilities
- 1994 – Salamanca Statement and Framework for Action
- 2006 – UN Convention of the Rights of Persons with Disabilities

(See Byrne, 2013, for an insightful examination of the deficits in such international legislation.)

During the last thirty years, there has been an increasing pattern of UN conventions setting out the expectations of member states towards SEND. In 1993, for example, the UN Standard Rules on the Equalisation of Opportunities for Persons with Disabilities noted that the rights of disabled people had been the subject of significant attention within the UN over the previous three decades. It highlighted that the most important outcome of the International Year of Disabled People (1981) was the introduction of the World Programme of Action Concerning Disabled Persons. This programme emphasised the right of disabled people to the same opportunities as other citizens (Davis, 2000). A further significant development was that disability was to be considered a function of the relationship between disabled people and their environment. This programme highlighted the importance of countries' interaction with disabled people and the agencies that supported them (see Chapters 3 and 4).

As part of the shift towards social models of disability, a global meeting of experts to review the implementation of the World Programme of Action was held in Stockholm in 1987. It suggested that guiding philosophies should be developed to highlight the priorities for action in the years ahead, and that the basis of these should be a recognition of the rights of disabled people. Consequently, the meeting recommended that the UN General Assembly convene a special conference to draft a convention on the elimination of all forms of discrimination against persons with disabilities.

TAKING IT FURTHER

Although UN conventions and treaties are to be welcomed, in reality many people argue that whilst there has been a dramatic increase in disability being included in treaties, to truly mainstream disability rights the UN must move beyond just mere policy references (Skarstad and Stein, 2017). Consider this statement as you read through the rest of this chapter. Is it the case that disability rights are accepted at the level of international policy but not really actioned in practice?

THE UN CONVENTION ON THE RIGHTS OF THE CHILD (1989)

In 1989 a Convention on the Rights of the Child instigated the first legally binding international agreement to address human rights, including civil, cultural, economic, political and social rights for young people. The reason for implementing this convention was that world leaders decided that children needed a special convention because people under eighteen years of age are often in need of special care and protection that adults do not require.

The convention, set out in 54 articles, identified the basic human rights that children everywhere should have, which include:

- the right to survival;
- an opportunity to develop to the fullest;
- protection from harmful influences, abuse and exploitation;
- full participation in family, cultural and social life.

(Continued)

Alongside these were four core principles:

- non-discrimination;
- a devotion to the best interests of the child;
- the right to life, survival and development;
- respect for the views of the child.

READER REFLECTION

Consider the barriers to successful inclusive education. How might these undermine the four core principles of the United Nations Convention of the Rights of the Child?

The core principles identified above support the notion of equality of opportunity discussed in more detail in Chapter 1, and suggest what countries should do to tackle those barriers to the participation of children and young people (including those with SEND) within society. The articles noted below specifically relate to this development of international inclusive SEND policies and practices.

Article 2: All human rights applying to children without discrimination on any ground particularly.

Article 12: The right of the child to express an opinion and to have that opinion taken into account, in any matter or procedure affecting the child. This emphasises the notion of empowerment and the self-advocacy of children to have a voice in decisions which impact upon them.

Article 23: The right of disabled children to enjoy a full and decent life, in conditions which ensure dignity, promote self-reliance and facilitate the child's active participation in the community. It also advocates the right of the disabled child to special care, education, health care, training, rehabilitation, employment and recreation opportunities. Moreover, all of these are to be designed with the intention of fostering the child to achieve the fullest possible levels of social integration and individual development.

Article 28: This states the child's right to an education, and that it shall be provided on the basis of equal opportunity.

Article 29: This states that a child's education should be directed at developing that child's personality and talents, and mental and physical abilities, to their 'fullest potential'.

Historically, the UN Convention on the Rights of the Child (1989) was not the first to address children, as its instigation marked the thirtieth anniversary of an earlier declaration of the rights of the child in 1959 and the tenth anniversary of the International Year of the Child in 1979. But since its adoption in 1989, and after more than sixty years of advocacy on children's rights, what was significant about this convention was that it was ratified more quickly and by more governments (except those of Somalia and the USA) than any other human rights instrument. Indeed Nind et al. (2003) suggest that pivotal to the successful implementation of the convention was that it was at the time the only international human rights treaty that expressly gave non-governmental organisations (NGOs) a role in monitoring its implementation under Article 45a. The uniqueness of enabling NGOs in supporting the UN convention lay in the fact that for the first time this gave organisations (excluding government representatives) an opportunity to influence and shape the policies and practices of international child development, including those with SEND.

In summary, the 1989 convention was a paradigm shift in UN policy direction through which children with SEND were considered as being integral to any successful international strategy development for young people (Thomas and Loxley, 2007). Therefore as the disability movement sought to assert their human rights to be included within society (Slee, 1998), this convention continued developing a trend of including children with SEND as an integral component of children's development activities.

Article 12 of the UN Convention on the Rights of the Child gave the right to any child of expressing an opinion and to have that opinion taken into account in any matter or procedure affecting them. Furthermore, it gave NGOs a pivotal role in its implementation.

READER REFLECTION

Reflect upon the above statement and consider how the voice of children and young people with SEND can be heard, and how this can shape inclusive education policies and practices in the future.

UN STANDARD RULES (1993)

Following substantial debate by international member states of the UN, a total of 22 rules were established which provided a benchmark for policy making and action covering the entitlement and accessibility of disabled people in society. In relation to education, Rule 6 is significant, in that it states that countries should recognise the principle of equal educational opportunities for pupils with disabilities within integrated settings. This seemingly reinforces the encouragement of the social model of disability and the new orthodoxy of inclusive education.

Indeed, in order to implement inclusive education, the UN suggested member states should have clear policies which are understood at school as well as wider community levels. These should allow for a flexible curriculum alongside on-going teacher training and support (Rose, 2001). Moreover, the UN argued that where 'ordinary schools' cannot as yet adequately make inclusive provision, special school education could be considered. However, such provision should prepare the student for inclusive education. Thus, these UN rules constituted the first articulated drive towards inclusive schooling for children and young people with SEND.

Central to the international drive for inclusion was the responsibility of schools, teachers and policy makers to change their structures to accommodate the diversity of all children and young people with SEND (Vickerman, 2007). As such, individuals and agencies supporting children and young people with SEND have had to respond to what has become a significant policy and practice shift from segregated schooling through to an acknowledgement of the entitlement to mainstream education.

READER REFLECTION

A significant development of the UN Standard Rules on the Equalization of Opportunities for Persons with Disabilities (1993) was a recognition that disability was to be considered a function of the relationship between disabled people and their environment, which is commonly referred to as the 'social model of disability'.

In reviewing the statement above, reflect upon what issues you think early years settings, schools, colleges and teachers would have to adopt in implementing the social model of disability within international educational provision.

THE SALAMANCA STATEMENT (1994)

The Salamanca Statement (see Chapter 5) was a significant directive in that it called upon the international community to work towards inclusive schools by implementing practical and strategic changes across the world. In June 1994, representatives from 92 governments and 25 international organisations attended the World Conference on Special Needs Education in Salamanca, Spain, and agreed that inclusive education should be considered as the norm rather than the exception (O'Hanlon, 1995).

The conference also adopted a new framework for action which advocated that 'ordinary schools' should accommodate all children, regardless of their physical, intellectual, social, emotional, linguistic or other needs. The framework for action stipulated that disabled children should attend their neighbourhood school, which should make appropriate provision to accommodate their needs. The statement argued that 'regular schools' with this inclusive orientation were the most effective means of overcoming discriminatory attitudes, creating welcoming communities, building inclusive societies and achieving education for all (Mittler and Daunt, 1995).

The World Conference (Salamanca Statement, 1994) called upon all international governments to:

- give the highest policy and budgetary priority to improve education services so that all children can be included, regardless of their differences or difficulties;
- adopt as a matter of law or policy the principle of inclusive education and seek to enrol all children in 'ordinary schools' unless there are compelling reasons for doing otherwise;
- develop demonstration projects and encourage international exchanges with countries with more progressive inclusive policies and practices;
- ensure that organisations of disabled people, along with parents and community bodies, are involved in the planning and decision making of policies and practices for children with SEND;
- place greater effort into pre-school strategies to promote inclusive practices;
- ensure that both initial and in-service teacher training addresses the provision of inclusive education.

The Salamanca Statement (UNESCO, 1994) called upon international communities to endorse an inclusive approach and support the development of SEND as an integral aspect of all education programmes. Furthermore, the statement also reinforced the importance of multi-disciplinary and multi-agency approaches to the successful adoption of inclusive educational practices (see Chapter 7). Moreover, non-governmental organisations were asked to strengthen their collaboration with official national bodies and become more involved in all aspects of inclusive education. UNESCO was asked to:

- ensure that SEND formed part of every discussion dealing with 'Education for All';
- enhance teacher education related to SEND and inclusion, and gain support from teaching unions and related professional associations;
- stimulate the academic community to conduct more research into inclusive education and disseminate the findings across international boundaries;
- use its funds to create an expanded programme for inclusive schools and community support projects to enable them to launch inclusive education pilot projects in those countries with less advanced education systems.

The framework for action within the Salamanca Statement (UNESCO, 1994: 11) states that 'inclusion and participation are essential to human dignity and to the enjoyment and exercise of human rights. Within the field of education this is reflected in bringing about a genuine equalisation of opportunity.' Thus, SEND provision must embody proven methods of teaching and learning in which all children can benefit, but at the same time it must recognise that human differences are normal and that learning must be modified to meet the needs of the child, rather than the child fitting into existing processes. As such, the fundamental principle of the inclusive school is premised upon the notion that all should learn together, where possible, and that 'ordinary schools' must recognise and respond to the diverse needs of their students, whilst also having a continuum of support and services to match those needs.

READER REFLECTION

Reflect upon your views and perspectives in relation to the Salamanca Statement, which argues that '"regular schools" with an inclusive orientation are the most effective means of combating discriminatory attitudes; creating welcoming communities; building inclusive societies; and achieving education for all.'

As part of your reflection and justification or opposition to the statement above you should identify some key points based on the chapter so far to justify your comments.

THE UN CONVENTION ON THE RIGHTS OF PERSONS WITH DISABILITIES (2006)

In December 2006, the UN Convention on the Rights of Persons noted that only 45 of its 192 member states had specific legislation protecting the rights of disabled people. This first convention of the new millennium set out to encourage the enactment of laws and policies with the aim of including disabled people in everyday life, and at the same time providing equal access to educational services for everyone. Indeed, the treaty was created to have a concrete effect on the lives of disabled people by ensuring that laws were not only put into policy but also implemented in practice (Fisher and Goodley, 2007).

> By 2018 the convention had been signed by 177 parties and ratified by 161 states (www.un.org/disabilities/documents/maps/enablemap.jpg).

It has been estimated that the worldwide number of children under the age of eighteen with a disability varies between 120 and 150 million (UNESCO, 2004). Moreover, two-thirds of people worldwide with disabilities live in developing countries, and these countries in particular suffer from the resultant waste of potential which goes hand in hand with the exclusion of people solely due to their disability (Timmons, 2002). A key feature of the UN Convention emphasises the need for international co-operation, and that all phases of the new international development programmes should include a disability dimension. As such, developing countries will receive support from a range of international agencies to implement the 2006 UN Convention on the Rights of Persons with Disabilities, with the aim here being to raise the aspirations and achievements of those children and young people with SEND.

In summary, this convention centres upon the instigation of a significant 'paradigm shift' from medical models to a social model approach (see Chapter 2). Central to future international developments in SEND is the need for a commitment that no child or young person is discriminated against on the basis of their disability, and that all should have access to a high-quality educational experience. However, whether this is located within mainstream or segregated school settings is subject to much international debate as countries' differing cultures and financial situations determine the quality and nature of education provided for children and young people with SEND (Smith, 2006; Warnock, 2005).

TAKING IT FURTHER

For the latest information which relates to the United Nations and disability you may wish to view their website. This is available at www.un.org/development/desa/disabilities/

PART B: A REVIEW OF CONTRASTING INTERNATIONAL PERSPECTIVES

Part A of this chapter offered an international context to the various UN declarations and ideologies being promoted to support children and young people with SEND. However, as discussed earlier the countries involved have adopted different approaches and interpretations to these directives. The second half of this chapter seeks to provide an overview of various countries' approaches to the inclusion of children and young people with SEND.

CASE STUDY 8.1
SPECIAL EDUCATIONAL NEEDS AND INCLUSION IN POLAND

Poland is a European country whose territory was defined at the end of the Second World War. It is relatively homogeneous, and compared to many European nations has added a relatively low number of migrants to its education system (Pajak-Wazna, 2013). After a period of communist control it now has a parliament and a cabinet system of government.

(Continued)

In Poland formal education begins at the age of 6 in reception classes, and from age 7 to 12, children move into the primary phase of education (Grades I to VI). Similar to the United Kingdom, secondary education begins at age 12 and lasts until the age of 16 (Starczewska et al., 2014). Statistics, cited by Starczewska et al. (2014), suggest that some five million people in Poland have a disability and that a significant proportion of these are children.

From the 18th century disabled people's right to life has been protected by the state. In 2004 Poland ratified the Convention on the Rights of Persons with Disabilities (Ćwirynkało, et al., 2017). Therefore, education acts have created the possibility for children with disabilities to be educated within the public education system. In addition, in the last few years, there has been a societal push towards the development of inclusive education (Baran and Winzer, 2017; Ćwirynkało et. al., 2017) and this has witnessed more opportunities for children with SEND to be educated in mainstream schools. However, a barrier to inclusive education is the fact that whether a child is or is not admitted to mainstream schooling is based upon the decision of professionals located in the 'Guidance and Counselling Centre' (Sheligevich-Urban, 2011).

In Poland, another barrier to inclusive education centres on the training of teachers. For example, beginning teachers experience five training modules which relate, amongst other things, to educational theory and practice, in order to become qualified practitioners. Three of these modules, namely those which relate to pedagogy, are mandatory, but the module relating to SEND is optional (Czyż, 2018). It is interesting in this respect to note that research suggests it is more experienced teachers who have the more positive attitudes towards inclusive education than newly qualified teachers (Ćwirynkało et al., 2017; Czyż, 2018).

READER REFLECTION It would seem then that whether a child is or is not educated in the mainstream in Poland rests with the decisions made by professionals. Who else do you think should be involved in making the decision to educate a disabled child in a mainstream educational setting?

DEFINING INCLUSION IN POLAND

In a research project I was involved with, we found that the majority of the teachers defined integration as including children with disabilities into mainstream schools. Indeed, one of the teachers believed that inclusion was an alternative to integration, and that both those words meant the participation of children with special educational needs in mainstream schooling. Another participant denoted that integration was a 'willingness to bring children with disabilities and without disabilities closer together, willingness to co-operate and interact, mutual understanding'. For one teacher, integration was conceptualised around the need for specialised support; they commented that 'pupils with disabilities are in a mainstream class, supported by special educational needs teachers'. Thus for these teachers integration was inclusion – the concept was interchangeable (Starczewska et al., 2012).

In 1994 Poland signed the Salamanca Statement and this committed it to move from a system of segregated special schools to a policy of inclusive education. However, a review of the literature available for education in Poland still denotes that integration and inclusion are employed interchangeably by educational professionals (see Starczewska et al., 2012).

BARRIERS TO THE DEVELOPMENT OF INCLUSIVE EDUCATION IN POLAND

The highest number of pupils integrated into the mainstream are those with moderate learning disabilities, followed by those with physical disabilities and then those with social and emotional difficulties or children who have sensory impairments (Starczewska et al., 2014).

Research from Poland suggests that 'integrative' education is a being stalled by the fact that:

- teachers are having difficulty in including older children (Starczewska et al., 2012);
- schools cannot satisfy the individual needs of its pupils (Wapiennik, 2005);
- 'integration' is not leading to the closure of special schools (Gajda, 2008);
- the training of teachers in special educational needs is problematic (Czyż, 2018).

TAKING IT FURTHER

Read the information below. What are the major issues, in terms of teacher training, that are stalling the implementation of inclusive education?

Through this research, it was found that the qualifications required of teachers in Poland were specified in the Act on the Charter of Teachers (1982, amended in 2004). This Act states that teachers must at least have an undergraduate degree and a teaching certificate to be able to teach children. According to Wapiennik (2005), the quality of education for teachers at the university level was usually outdated and lacked pedagogical knowledge in the field of intellectual disabilities. More recent legislation, though, has specified new standards for training within the area of special needs. However, this still requires only a minimal knowledge of special education (Starczewska et al., 2014).

Starczewska et al.'s (2014) summary of Polish inclusive education is somewhat pessimistic in that it states:

> inclusion is a concept that has little meaning in the Polish educational system. Furthermore, the review highlights the difficulties that pupils with disabilities have in gaining access to mainstream integrative provision and the lack of appropriately trained school personnel to facilitate high-quality teaching and learning. It would seem that in relation to the inclusive segregation continuum, Poland's education system is far closer to the segregation end, particularly for children with profound disabilities living in its rural hinterlands.

READER REFLECTION From the knowledge and understanding you have gained from this chapter, do you believe that Starczewska et al.'s (2014) study is a reasonable summary of the state of inclusive education in Poland?

CASE STUDY 8.2
THE UNITED STATES OF AMERICA

The United States of America (USA) is a country made up of 50 states; it covers some 3.8 million square miles and is populated by around 318 million people. The United States is the fourth-largest country by land mass and third-largest by population (US Census Bureau, 2014). It is reported that 53.9 million school-aged children have a disability (Koller et al., 2018).

Education in the United States is provided by both the public and private sector. In the autumn term of 2014, some 49.8 million students attended public school in America and 5.0 million pupils attended private schools (NCES, 2014). Education is compulsory for children who have reached their fifth birthday, and state education ends at 16 or 18 depending upon individual states. It is organised into grades, ranging from kindergarten and first grade through to the twelfth grade, which is the final year of high school.

INCLUSIVE EDUCATION IN THE UNITED STATES

Whilst some developing international countries may be working towards ensuring all children and young people have a basic right to education, in the USA around 96% of children with disabilities are presently educated within mainstream schools, and almost half spend the majority of their school day in 'general inclusive' classrooms as opposed to being withdrawn for segregated lessons. However, despite this positive picture some researchers (see Kirby, 2016) suggest that two dominant viewpoints still exist in the American education system today: that disability is a deviance and should be eradicated, and that special education should be delivered within a segregated system. Despite inclusive education in the USA being 'far from perfect' (Sen, 2018: 20), research presents a picture which demonstrates a progressive increase in the number of children and young people with SEND being included in mainstream settings since 1976. Furthermore, Public Law 108–446: Individuals with Disabilities Education Improvement Act of 2004 continues to advocate the inclusion of children and young people with SEND within mainstream education settings. This law not only advocates accessibility to a high-quality education for children and young people with SEND; it also promotes accountability for results, enhanced parental involvement, the use of proven practices and resources, greater flexibility and reduced paperwork burdens for teachers, states and local school districts (Sen, 2018).

The Individuals with Disabilities Education Act (IDEA) is the main federal programme within the USA that authorises state and local aid for special education and related services for children with disabilities, including those students with learning disabilities. On the 3rd of December 2004 President Bush signed IDEA, which made significant changes, including new provisions regarding how schools could determine whether a child had a specific learning disability and how they could receive special education services (see http://idea.ed.gov/).

As a result, the USA can be considered as one of the more progressive international countries that has actively promoted the full inclusion of children and young people with SEND. Indeed, the country has had a long history of policy and practice developments in inclusive education, dating back to 1975 when President Gerald Ford advocated that every public school district in the country must provide all its students with disabilities (aged from 3 through to 21 years of age) with an individualised, free and appropriate public education that was to take place within the 'least-restrictive environment'. President Ford's desire to foster educational environments that were 'least restrictive' was initially introduced in 1975 through the 'Public Law 94–142: Education of All Handicapped Children Act', and this has since been regularly updated in 1983, 1990, 1997 and 2004.

The notion of 'least restrictive environments' is worth taking note of. According to Winnick (2005), the least restrictive environments for children and young people with SEND are within mainstream education and so this should be used whenever and wherever possible. However, Warnock (2005) has argued that for many children with SEND, segregated schooling may be the most appropriate environment for some to have the best access to education. This highlights the complexity of developing SEND provision within countries' national laws as well as with regard to UN directives which promote full inclusion within the mainstream.

READER REFLECTION

The IDEA has three main phases:

Stage 1: 'Get 'em in' – involving opening the doors of public schools to children with SEND.

Stage 2: 'Get 'em through' – involving teacher educators, related support services, staff and parents working to keep children and young people with SEND from dropping out.

Stage 3: 'Get 'em ready' – involving preparing children and young people with SEND for further education, employment and independent living.

Reflect upon the three points from IDEA above and consider the strategies that need to be in place to ensure each of the stages are fulfilled for children and young people with SEND.

According to Block and Obrusnikova (2007), the US model of inclusion is rooted in the philosophy of educating children and young people with SEND alongside their non-disabled peers, whilst at the same time supporting them fully from initial entry and access to school, through modifications to schools and curricula, and then on into preparation for employment. This model exemplifies the notion of fostering the 'least restrictive' environments (Winnick, 2005), suggesting that a child or young person with SEND should have the opportunity to be educated with their non-disabled peers to the greatest extent possible, whilst also having an entitlement to the same activities and programmes that any other non-disabled person would be able to access.

READER REFLECTION

American law does not clarify the nature of the least restrictive environment. However in a landmark case (*Daniel V. the State Board of Education* (1989), cited in Daniel, 1997) it was determined that pupils had a right to be included in both academic and extracurricular programmes of 'general education'.

As part of this significant ruling case it was acknowledged that in determining what constituted a 'least restrictive environment', four fundamental factors should be considered. Namely:

* the educational benefits of integrated settings versus segregated settings;
* the non-academic benefits of inclusion (primarily social interaction with non-disabled peers);
* the effect of a pupil with SEND on their teacher and peers;
* the costs of all supplementary services required for a child or young person with SEND to stay within an inclusive setting.

Read the four fundamental factors noted above and then devise your own definition of the term 'least restrictive environment'. Try to identify factors additional to those noted above that you would use to determine the most appropriate inclusive setting for children or young people with SEND.

CASE STUDY 8.3
INDIA

India is a country that cannot be easily quantified or described. It is a unique nation of historical traditions and modern developments where incredible poverty sits side by side with immense wealth. India is the world's largest democracy and it is estimated that it has 17% of the world's population (UNICEF, 2003). In India, there are 16 officially recognised languages as well as over 314 spoken dialects, and four major religions.

India has 200 million children who are eligible to attend schools, of which it is estimated some 20 million require SEND provision (Singh and Agarwal, 2015). The Indian school system, then, is the second-largest in the world. From 2002, children in India up to the age of fourteen have had a right to access eight years of free education. However, whilst it is a country that is working hard to ensure that all children attend school it is noticeable that the Indian government is faced with a very difficult task to fulfil their aim of free universal primary education for all. Indeed, despite the government's attempts to include all children, it is still the case that between 35 million and 80 million children do not attend school (Singal and Rouse, 2003). Furthermore, it is also reported that 53% of children drop out of school before they reach Grade VII. UNESCO believes that, despite intensive efforts and a very real commitment to provide universal education, the Indian government is failing on this educational promise.

THE STATE EDUCATION SYSTEM IN INDIA

The Indian education system provides a mainly uniform structure of provision across the 28 regional states (Singal, 2006a). Nursery and pre-primary education is not compulsory and there is also a great discrepancy in educational provision between rural and urban areas (Singal, 2006b). State education in Indian commences when a child is six years of age, and the first five years of education are within primary education (Grades I–V). Grade VI–VII begins at age eleven where pupils are educated in what are known as upper primary classes (Singal, 2006a). The main focus of the state educational system in India is upon the provision of basic reading, writing and numeracy skills (Singal, 2006a).

Since the 1990s the education system has changed substantially as many private and charitable bodies have moved in to deliver educational programmes on the state's behalf. Singal (2006a) estimates that nearly one-quarter of education is now provided by private or non-governmental organisations (NGOs).

READER REFLECTION

Read the following information which relates to the Indian education system and consider what barriers face the Indian government in its aim to provide universal free primary education to all of its children. Do you think, as Sharma does, that it is only through legislation that these barriers can be overcome?

The Hindu Business Line (2007) believe that education in India is mainly delivered in poorly lit classrooms where large classes are often taught by a person who may not have completed state education themselves. India, then, is a country which is so large, where resources are so scarce and in which societal attitudes are sometimes so damaging, that it is only through well-directed legislation that all children might be included in schools.

THE DEVELOPMENT OF INCLUSIVE EDUCATION IN INDIA

Within the Indian context the education of children and young people with SEND was mainly conceptualised within a segregated special schooling system. Up until the 1970s, many educational and medical professionals believed that pupils with SEND were simply not capable of being educated in mainstream settings. However, the last two decades or so have observed significant and major educational reforms in India which have been influenced by international developments (Raghavan, 2014). In 1994, India endorsed the objectives of the Salamanca Statement and began to promote a policy of inclusive education (Raghavan, 2014). In 1995, the Indian government passed the landmark Person with Disabilities (PWD) Act which ushered in a new era for children with disabilities in India (Das et al., 2013).

The Person with Disabilities Act was observed to be a landmark step in Indian education as it required all of its central and state governmental institutions to provide free and appropriate access to children with disabilities. As part of this legislation state schools were required to keep 3% of all its places for pupils with SEND. India, then, is one of the few countries that employ positive discrimination to ensure that all of its pupils have the right to be educated.

In 2000 it was recommended (NCERT, 2000) that the Indian education system would be improved if it were based upon an inclusive educational model. From this time forward the Indian government has launched a multitude of initiatives, such as the Integrated Education for Disabled Children and the District Primary Education Programme, to speed the development of inclusive education.

BARRIERS TO THE DEVELOPMENT OF INCLUSIVE EDUCATION IN INDIA

From the beginning, the development of inclusive education was stalled because politicians, teachers, pupils and parents had no clear understanding of what inclusion meant. Indeed, many educators referred to inclusion as a western construct and, as such, inclusive education has often been dismissed or misunderstood (Madan and Sharma, 2013). This issue has meant that inclusion and integration have been employed interchangeably within policy and legislative acts and by education professionals alike (Gupta et al., 2018). This terminological ambiguity has led to a lack of clarity and indeed even an elusiveness in professionals' understanding of the practice of inclusive education (Madan and Sharma, 2013).

A further barrier to inclusion is that the location of children and young people with SEND in schools is controlled by professionals such as psychologists and special educators. These professionals judge whether children have the capabilities, in terms of communication, mobility, dressing and toileting skills, that would enable them to be able to access mainstream schools. It is apparent that this power to exclude children and young people has been widely employed, as it has been reported that during the first decade of inclusive education there was a twofold increase in the number of children attending special and segregated schools (Singal, 2005).

A major barrier to the government's commitment to inclusion is the teachers who are required to operate inclusive education within the schools themselves. Sharma and Deppeler (2005: 4) believe that Indian universities 'fail to train teachers adequately' about educating children in inclusive settings. It is somewhat disturbing to note that the vast majority of Indian school personnel in post today do not have the requisite training to enable them to provide successful inclusive education (Hodkinson and Deverakonda, 2011). For example, it was reported in Delhi that nearly 70% of mainstream teachers had not received any SEND training or any experience of teaching pupils with SEND (Das et al., 2013). A further issue is that of professionals' attitudes towards children and young people with SEND. Practitioners in India, it would seem, view inclusive education not as a fundamental human right but as 'an act of kindness' (Singal, 2006a). Other researches note that many teachers do not believe that all children should be educated in the mainstream, and more worryingly that some teachers hold negative attitudes regarding pupils with SEND (Shama, 2002; Singal and Rouse, 2003; Singal, 2006b). What is apparent is that whilst significant numbers of children and young people with SEND are included in the mainstream system, many simply drop out because of a lack of sensitivity displayed towards their educational needs (Panda, 2005). This has led researchers to call for more interventions to develop positive teacher attitudes concerning the inclusion of children and young people with SEND, as they believe this is critical to the success of inclusive education in India (Gupta et al., 2018).

In summary, it would seem that despite the good intentions shown by the government towards the development of inclusive education, the latter part of the 20th century witnessed the Indian education system struggling to cope with the vast number of children and young people with SEND who wanted to access the system (Manni, 2000). It seems the case, in the 21st century, that cultural and religious stigma still have a major and negative effect on the human rights of people with disabilities in relation to the provision of educational services in India (Dickinson, 2018). Moreover, inclusive education is being stalled by poor teaching practices, limited curricula and a lack of infrastructure (Sawhney, 2015). This has led many to believe that, in general, teachers in India only accept inclusion in theory and not in practice (Tiwari et al., 2015).

READER REFLECTION   Imagine you are a government education minister who has been tasked with the responsibility for meeting UN international directives on promoting the inclusion of children and young people with SEND within mainstream settings in one of the countries detailed above. Make a list of the ways in which you would tackle this complex challenge and what policy and practice directives you would advocate. In addition, consider which key agencies you would need to engage with in order to ensure you have fully consulted and represented all stakeholders' views.

This review of differing and different education systems shows how the United States contrasts with Poland and India in its development of inclusive education for children and young people with SEND. The review of these countries' education systems also demonstrates the complexities and variations of how they are working towards establishing acceptable levels of schooling for all (Baker and Zigmond, 1995). Indeed, it demonstrates the unique role of the UN and the significant challenges it faces in working with its member states to encourage international commitments towards not only inclusion but also, for some countries, the commitment to a basic right to education. However, in noting these varying perspectives this chapter will now move towards an examination of internationally significant initiatives established in the late 1980s and early 1990s (Kavale, 2000; Snyder et al., 2001) which have been instrumental in encouraging access and the entitlement of children and young people with SEND to be educated within ordinary schools. A key factor will be the ability of international governments, policy makers, teachers and parents to work together to share and disseminate practices with the ultimate goal of raising aspirations and the entitlement to high-quality, appropriate education for all who are marginalised and under-represented within society.

READER REFLECTION

INTERNATIONAL DIRECTIONS IN INCLUSIVE POLICY AND PRACTICE

As noted earlier in this chapter, the first UN convention of the new millennium, the Convention on the Rights of Persons with Disabilities (UN, 2006), was adopted by the UN General Assembly on the 13th of December 2006 and has been signed by a total of 101 governments to date. Due to the diverse international views and stages of development that are encompassed by inclusive policies and practices, this was a challenging convention to agree. However, the negotiators succeeded in shifting the position on education from one of a choice between segregated or mainstream education to the right to attend inclusive primary and secondary schools.

The convention is based upon a 'paradigm shift' (Norwich, 2007; Pijl et al., 1997) from a medical model to a social model approach. This movement in philosophy has been fundamental in moving international SEND developments forward to a position of society changing and responding to the needs of children and young people with SEND, whilst at the same time recognising their fundamental right to an education that is inclusive. In addition, the convention also recognises the complexity of interpreting inclusive education (which is more than merely about location, and more importantly includes the context within which the schooling takes place).

The Chair of the ad hoc committee which negotiated the convention applauded the role that disabled people and their organisations had played in the development process, with over 800 agencies taking part in the negotiations. This acknowledges the significant shift towards self-representation and the empowerment of both disabled people and the organisations that represent them to determine their futures. Article 24 requires signatories to ensure that all disabled children and young people 'can access an inclusive, [high] quality, free primary and secondary education on an equal basis with others in the communities in which they live' (UN, 2006: Article 24, 2b). It continues by stating that 'reasonable accommodation of the individual's requirements' (Article 24, 2c) should be made along with the support that is provided, 'within the general education system, to facilitate their effective education' (Article 24, 2d). What is particularly significant within the convention is that Article 24 allows for the possibility of segregated education for children with sensory impairments, thereby 'ensuring that the education of persons, and in particular children, who are blind, deaf and deafblind, is delivered in the most appropriate languages and modes and means of communication for the individual, and in environments which maximise academic and social development' (Article 24, 3c).

Article 24 marks a significant step forward in the development of inclusive education for children and young people with SEND, with its main features recognising that:

- all disabled children and young people are entitled to an education in an 'inclusive system';
- disabled people should not be excluded from the general education system on the grounds of their disability;
- a focus upon removing barriers to the development (to their fullest potential) of disabled people's personality, talents and creativity, as well as their mental and physical abilities, is paramount;
- all disabled people should receive the support they need within general education systems;
- large classes make inclusive education more difficult and this should be challenged when implementing the convention;
- every state will need to engage with disabled people's organisations in implementing the articles and convention;
- disabled people's organisations need to develop their capacity to advocate for inclusive education;
- all disabled learners need to be consulted.

READER REFLECTION

Read the key points noted above from Article 24 of the UN Convention on the Rights of Persons with Disabilities (2006) and compare how these have developed since the late 1980s and early 1990s' directives. In doing so, try to summarise what you see as the central components of inclusive education for children and young people with SEND in the 21st century.

Efforts to include disabled people within international development activities have been gaining momentum. For example, in 1997 the UN, in collaboration with the National Research and Development Centre for Welfare and Health in Finland, published a document entitled 'Disability Dimension in Development Action: Manual on Inclusive Planning'. This set out to serve as a tool by which development theories could be translated into good practice. Various agencies have issued publications and strategic plans since that have addressed the inclusion of disabled people; and the adoption by international states of the UN Convention on the Rights of Persons with Disabilities (UN, 2006) should provide a further impetus for the study and practice of this critical worldwide development work.

There is growing recognition among organisations of the need to include children and young people with SEND in educational activities; however, there remains much room for the expansion of such programmes, as well as more documentation of good practices. Indeed, the World Bank found that during the fiscal years 2002–2006 only 5% of new international lending commitments had a disability component. Therefore, in March 2007 the World Bank issued a guidance note to assist its projects in better incorporating the needs of disabled people, integrating a disability perspective into ongoing sector and thematic work programmes, and adopting an integrated and inclusive approach to disability. These developments represented a significant paradigm shift as they identified disability as an issue to be considered in all programming, rather than as a stand-alone thematic issue. Within this framework there is still space for disability-specific actions and programming, based on the needs of the particular international contexts of individual countries.

The UN convention obligates states to be proactive in taking measures to ensure that disabled people participate in all facets of society, on an equal basis with others. However, all such efforts should be guided by the overall goal to integrate and include disabled people in every aspect of programme development, although finding the appropriate methods of doing so will not be possible without the participation of disabled people at every stage of this process. Thus, empowerment and the self-representation of disabled people, combined with an international commitment to acknowledge the rights of children and young people with SEND to a high-quality education, will be paramount if this new millennium is to see a major change in the policies and practices of inclusive education.

In 2014, UNESCO worked with governments and international partners to address exclusion from education in all its forms. As a result of this international co-operation UNESCO formulated 'Ten Questions on Inclusive Education'. This document, they believe, is useful in assessing the success, or otherwise, of a country's attempts to deliver 'Education for All'.

TEN QUESTIONS ON INCLUSIVE EDUCATION

1. Beyond the figures, what do we know about the excluded?

   UNESCO detail that exclusion has many faces such as poverty and marginalisation. What is it that countries are doing to ensure that children avoid the 'enormous risk' of missing out on an education?

2. Why, when schools are promoting access, do they not ensure that the access is to quality education?

   UNESCO suggest that it is not enough to simply include children but also that governments must implement strategies to keep children at school and examine what they are actually learning, and importantly in what conditions are they studying.

3. How does inclusive education promote successful learning?

   UNESCO believe that inclusion must be accompanied by policies to enhance educational quality and that such policies should work on a principle of 'access to success'. This they believe has implications not only for children but also for teachers, the curriculum and ways of interacting across the schools and their communities.

(Continued)

4. What are the principles of inclusion?

   How we define and operationalise inclusion is very important for UNESCO as this affects how the curriculum and pedagogy are organised and how school systems are managed.

5. The notion of inclusion is still often associated with children who have special needs. Why?

   Too often, UNESCO state, inclusion programmes are targeted at one marginalised or excluded group at the expense of another, and they believe this results in second-rate opportunities for all children.

6. How does education need to change to accommodate everyone?

   Inclusion involves a change in how teachers, children and parents view schools and education in general. Inclusive education according to UNESCO is an approach that must transform education systems in order for them to respond to the diversity of all learners.

7. How do curricula need to change to improve learning and encourage the inclusion of all pupils?

   UNESCO state that the curriculum has an instrumental role to play in fostering tolerance and promoting human rights. They believe it is a powerful tool for breaking down barriers, and transcending cultural, religious and other differences. An inclusive curriculum, they argue, must take the gender, cultural identity and language background of a child into consideration.

8. Teachers have a foremost influence on learning. Yet their status and working conditions in many countries make it difficult to promote inclusion. What can be done to improve their lot?

   Teachers are the linchpins in any educational system and as such are of critical importance to attempts to introduce inclusive education. As a result UNESCO believe that teachers' attitudes and practices towards learners from different backgrounds are crucial to the success of polices for Education for All.

9. Is inclusive quality education affordable?

   An argument sometimes levelled at inclusion policies is that it is an expensive form of educational system. UNESCO believe that educating all children for success is more cost effective than students continually failing in education systems and having to repeat schooling.

10. Does inclusive quality education lead to more inclusive societies?

   UNESCO state that exclusion starts very early in life. A holistic vision of education is imperative. Comprehensive early childhood care and education programmes improve children's well-being, prepare them for primary school and give them a better chance of succeeding once they are in school. All evidence shows that the most disadvantaged and vulnerable children benefit most from such programmes.

(Source: www.unesco.org/new/en/education/themes/strengthening-education-systems/inclusive-education/)

CONCLUSION

In this chapter, you have gained knowledge and understanding of the policies and international legislation that govern the delivery of inclusive education on the 'world stage' and how pupils with SEND are educated in Poland, India and the USA.

This chapter has detailed that governments, international agencies and organisations are all working with renewed vigour in this millennium towards the goal of equality for children and young people with SEND following the adoption of the UN Convention on the Rights of Persons with Disabilities at the end of December 2006. According to the UN there are approximately 650 million people with disabilities in the world (of which 120–150 million are estimated to be children), who represent 10% cent of the global population. An estimated 80% of these disabled people live in developing countries, with many in conditions of poverty and deprivation (Kristensen, 2002). In reading this chapter, it is important to understand that in both developed and developing countries, the evidence suggests that disabled people are disproportionately represented amongst the world's poorest countries.

In this chapter, you have learnt that although international inclusive education has progressed significantly in some countries, there is still much to be achieved in offering a fundamental right to a basic education for some children. This chapter has made plain that despite the rhetoric and the very real attempts to ensure that inclusive education and the United Nations Millennium Goals became a reality by 2015, it is the case that these goals were not realised. In concluding your reading of the chapter, it is important for you to understand that it is clear that international legislation and initiatives, to date, have not ended the struggle for universal education for all. However, it is also important to realise that this should not preclude professionals and parents from having high aspirations for all of the world's children. Furthermore, it should not impede governments and professionals working tirelessly to ensure that children throughout the world have their individual educational needs met.

The student activities and reading outlined below are included to deepen your knowledge of the international definitions and systems of inclusive education. In addition, they aim to challenge the notion that the system of inclusion in England is 'so good' that it deserves to be operationalised throughout the world.

STUDENT ACTIVITIES

Using the 'Ten Questions on Inclusive Education', critically examine inclusive education in England. Is the English educational system a good example of inclusive education for other countries in the world to copy?

The UN Convention of 2006 noted in this chapter advocates that disabled people are actively involved in the decision-making process about their services. Reflect upon what strategies you could implement to ensure this goal is achieved when developing inclusive educational policies and practices.

FURTHER READING

Blanford, S. (2017) *Achievement for All in International Classrooms: Improving Outcomes for Children and Young People with Special Educational Needs and Disability.* London: Bloomsbury. This book provides an overview of SEND policy, provision and practice in a number of international contexts.

Ghosh, N. (ed.) (2016) *Interrogating Disability in India: Theory and Practice.* London: Springer. Chapter 1 of this text provides a very readable overview of the history of disability in India.

9
CONCLUSIONS

In this chapter you will gain knowledge and understanding of:

- the key themes examined in the book
- the future direction of SEND and inclusion.

INTRODUCTION

This book has provided an overview of the key themes in SEND and inclusion. That overview has been based upon an examination of the history, current legislation and international perspectives of SEND and inclusion. What should have become clear to you through reading this book is that education systems both in the UK and across the world are experiencing real difficulties in finding ways to ensure that all of our children and young people are included in early years settings, schools and colleges (Wearmouth, 2017).

This chapter brings together the key issues examined within the book. We will review these issues in order to draw out the complexities of SEND and inclusion and then consider what the future directions of inclusive education might be. The purpose of this review is to enable you to construct your own understanding of the key issues, and reflect upon your attitude and feelings towards them. The key issues we will examine in this concluding chapter are the barriers to inclusive education and how we might move beyond these.

TAKING IT FURTHER

As we near the end of the book, reconsider your attitude and feelings to the concept of SEND. Has your view of the practical usefulness of this concept changed? If it has, consider what has been the main driver for this change.

Previous chapters have navigated you through a series of complex and diverse issues related to SEND and inclusion. We have referred to the work of Farrell (2000), who commented that SEND is dominated by professionals, families and administrators who try to work together to meet children's needs. We observed, though, that underpinning such working relationships are a range of educational policies and ideologies that provide a regulation to the provision of inclusive education in early years settings, schools and colleges. If we are to fully understand the context of SEND and inclusion, we must be able to recognise the complex interplay between these practical, professional, political and ideological worlds (Norwich, 2002).

The discussion within previous chapters acknowledged that SEND operates on a continuum in which there is no clear distinction between pupils who have a SEND and those who do not (Postlethwaite and Hackney, 1989). Conceptualising differences such as disability and the SEN of children and young people is therefore complex and often fraught with difficulties, as there so are many contrasting and opposing views as to what counts as a SEND. Such views are constantly changing as new ideologies, policies and practices emerge. However, what is important in the development of your understanding is that current thinking and the practice of SEND and inclusion are dominated by its history.

In reviewing the development of current legislative frameworks, the book provided you with a comprehensive overview of the early education Acts, from the late 19th century through to the transformational Warnock Report (DES, 1978) and on to the 1981 Education Act. We saw how the work of Warnock in 1978 stimulated the drive towards inclusive education. Forty years later, though, it was detailed how data continue to show that approximately one in five children are still identified as having a difficulty with learning that requires extra help to be given in class. Consequently, it would seem that the complex and diverse nature of SEND continues today as does the debate on how support for these pupils should operate and where the teaching of these children and young people should be located. Given this history, it would appear necessary that if we are to move forward with inclusion we need to reframe the debate on SEND, and the models of disability and inclusive education, both within the UK and for international settings.

REFRAMING DEFINITIONS OF SEND

There can be no doubt that SEND has, over the last four decades, become the orthodoxy of education worldwide. SEND is a high-status construct that has gained currency within educational and social policy initiatives as well as in early years settings, schools and colleges. For some SEND is an uncomplicated, straightforward term – one that is based simply upon providing the best support so that a child's educational needs might be met. However, in the harsh reality of practice and policy imperatives, it is apparent that SEND does not represent an uncomplicated or uncontested ideological construct. I wish at this point, therefore, to reframe this construct to demonstrate that perhaps it is a term that has outlived its usefulness.

Let us begin this reframing by refreshing our memories as to the legal definition of SEN that operates within the Children and Families Act 2014:

1) A child or young person has a SEN if he or she has a learning difficulty or disability which calls for special educational provision to be made for him or her.

2) ...

    a) A child of compulsory school age or a young person has a learning difficulty or disability if he or she: has a significantly greater difficulty in learning than the majority of others of the same age, or

    b) has a disability which prevents or hinders him or her from making use of facilities of a kind generally provided for others of the same age in mainstream schools or mainstream post-16 institutions.

3) A child under compulsory school age has a learning difficulty or disability if he or she is likely to be within subsection (2) when of compulsory school age (or would be likely, if no special educational provision were made).

SEND, defined in these terms, has changed little since the Warnock Report. What we must realise though is that policy terminology, such as SEND, operates within educational policies that do change over time. It is clear that such policies serve either to stall or accelerate inclusive education. For example, if we examine current government definitions of the purposes of education we find that 'Perhaps what is most important is that we must ensure that more people have [the] knowledge and skills they need to be a success in a demanding economy', and that 'education is the engine of our economy' (Nik Gibb, Schools Minister, 2015).

What becomes abundantly clear is that SEND and inclusion operate within a political arena where academic success (based upon good GCSE/'O' levels) and contributing economically to society dominate. However, if inclusion is to become a political and practical reality it must be based upon a human rights approach, which would necessitate a redefinition of how education frames success and its employment of 'special' in SEND. For some children and young people, framing success only in terms of good GCSEs or obtaining a good university place will mean that their 'educational career' is doomed to failure before it has begun. As Albert Einstein supposedly wrote, 'Everybody is a genius. But if you judge a fish by its ability to climb a tree, it will live its whole life believing that it is stupid.' SEND then is a construct that, rather than supporting all children to experience success, has actually, because of competing policy initiatives, ensured that some children have always been doomed to failure.

MODELS OF SEND

The practical operation of SEND is complicated not only by political ideology, based upon economic success, but also upon ideology encapsulated in the models of disability that we reviewed in Chapter 3 – the psycho-medical, biopsychosocial, social and rights-based models. We observed that in recent times rights-based models have come to the fore and that their core principle is that all children should attend mainstream educational provision based within their local community. This model of disability challenges the widely held belief regarding the legitimacy of segregated education based on the premise that it is impossible to include all children within mainstream education. This has been a point of much debate and consternation encapsulated within the 'special school versus mainstream' debate, as professionals, parents, children, disability rights groups and government continue to discuss what the most appropriate educational location is for a child or young person with SEND.

However, the question I pose here is this: can any of these models, or the plethora of others detailed in the literature base, ever really capture the complexities of the life and aspirations of a child or young person with SEND? In addition I would also ask, who are these models really designed to help? As with the definition of SEND, conceivably they are more for researchers and professionals than those who are struggling to obtain a good education. Perhaps, in the realisation of a truly inclusive education system it is time to devote less energy to purely theoretical models, and invest more in working together with children and young people to listen to and hear their views on the education they want to experience.

INTERNATIONAL DIMENSIONS

To further our discussion of the definitions of SEND and inclusion we have realised that this term also operates within distinctive international perspectives and settings (see Chapter 8). Such perspectives and settings as we observed are also driven by policy and ideology. Two aspects of international policy related to SEND that are worth returning to here are the 1994 Salamanca Statement (UNESCO, 1994) and the UN Convention on the Rights of Persons with a Disability (2006). We saw that many international communities and educational authorities adopted a philosophy of 'inclusion' to address their social and moral obligations to educate all children. Indeed, the UN convention of 2006 obligates international member states to undertake proactively the appropriate measures to ensure disabled people participate in all facets of society, on an equal basis with others. However, we have observed that the UN failed to meet its Millennium Goal and that there are still millions of children and young people with SEND out of education or segregated in special school settings. Despite policies signed at an international level that prioritise inclusion, politicians are still finding difficulty in determining the appropriate balance between mainstreaming and segregative strategies. Thus, whilst the goal should be to integrate and include disabled people into all aspects of schooling, finding the appropriate methods of doing so is proving to be highly problematic. What remains clear two decades after the Salamanca Statement is that the empowerment and self-representation of disabled people, combined with an international commitment to acknowledge the rights of children and young people with SEND to a high-quality education, will be paramount if educational settings are ever to see a major shift in the policies and practices of inclusive education.

The consultation and empowerment agenda is moving with vigour and purpose within the field of SEND. Review your interpretation of the empowerment/human rights agenda and how you can respond to this when working with children and young people labelled as SEND.

READER REFLECTION

FUTURE DIRECTIONS FOR INCLUSIVE EDUCATION

We observed that during the late 1990s and early part of the 21st century, New Labour took a 'powerful inclusion stance' (Coles and Hancock, 2002: 10), and by adopting a top-down approach to policy implementation they forced their own version of inclusion upon early years settings, schools and colleges. Therefore, whilst it might appear that New Labour was committed to the ideology of inclusive education as defined by a previous minister of education as 'ensuring that every child has the opportunity to achieve their full potential' (DfES, 2004a: 2), it also appeared that their particular view on inclusion was not without its critics. Indeed, New Labour's attempts to define inclusion along a continuum that placed inclusive education in the realms of 'equality for all' actually led to more children attending special schools than ever before. It was suggested in earlier chapters that whilst New Labour was well versed in 'inclusion-speak' its motivational drivers and its inclusion policy were like its definition of inclusion – highly suspect. However, by 2010 inclusion had become yet another buzzword that had, like SEN, gained status and acquired international currency within educational and social policy initiatives. What we observed though, in previous chapters, is that inclusion is a concept that might be defined in a variety of ways.

From 2010, we have witnessed a fundamental change in the ideology which underpins the provision for children and young people with SEND in England. It became clear that the government of the day did not observe inclusive education to be the sole objective of educational provision for children and young people with SEND. Indeed, as commented upon in Chapter 1 this government made clear through the tone of its rhetoric that the medical model of disability had been returned to the centre of educational policy and provision. Indeed, any hope that 'full inclusionists' might have had that all special schools would be closed were cast aside by Prime Minister Cameron's conviction to end the ideological bias towards inclusion. Whilst Cameron determined that policy and provision should, quite rightly, not be driven by ideology, the employability emplaced at the centre of legislation would itself appear to be an example of Conservative ideology driving the governing principles of educational provision. The stories of 'special school survivors' that you have read suggest strongly that government interference and ideologically driven policies were nonetheless unsuccessful in the past because they failed to take into consideration the views and wishes of those who are important – namely children and young people. Experience has shown that policies since the 1940s that include the notion of pupil voice have not delivered on this commitment. Perhaps it is time for politicians from every political party to begin thinking about who education is really for. Is it for children and their families or is it so that we may produce economic units of production? This question is significant for all children and young people but especially for those who have SEND.

READER REFLECTION   Review what you see as the key developments and changes in SEND policy and practice since 2010. Consider the strengths and weaknesses of these initiatives and the impact they have had upon children and young people with SEND.

REFRAMING INCLUSION

Inclusion, we might conclude, is a construct that is built upon the absolute presence of all children in mainstream classrooms – 'no ifs, no buts'. As a society, it is perhaps comforting to believe that our educational system has moved far beyond exclusion based upon historical categorisation and the medical model. However, as you have observed, this is not the case, and with the application of current government's policies, we actually seem further away from making inclusion happen than ever. This is because we are still operating a system based upon segregation and categories, and educational practice that appears to be simply coated with the rhetorical guise of inclusive practice (Hodkinson and Burch, 2017).

What we find, then, is that in attempting to define inclusion we produce a construct contextualised in the wider underworld of politicians, politics and ideology. The analysis of inclusive education located in this book leads to a belief (both in the UK and throughout the world) that, as a word, 'inclusion' is simple but 'inclusive education' in practice is complicated. It has become clear, therefore, that inclusive education is a complex and multifaceted construct, which whilst supposedly having no boundaries has actually polarised educational provision.

At the beginning of the 21st century we had a real opportunity to make inclusion happen in all of our early years settings, schools and colleges. Governments however have consistently failed to ensure that inclusive education has *actually* happened for every child or young person who wants it. They have allowed marketisation and accountability, as well as funding issues and the lack of effective teacher training (to name but a few issues), to get in the way of this important educational and social imperative. We now find ourselves in a position that despite numerous government interventions little has actually changed in relation to inclusive education since the 1980s. This is a real shame, especially when we consider the very real benefits inclusive education can bring for children and young people. This does make a recent education minister's statement seem rather ironic …

> This government won't shy away from seeking the best for every child, wherever they are … Children only get one childhood and one chance at their education, so there is a real urgency in our need to deliver … [we need to ensure] that vulnerable children are supported to succeed with opportunities as good as those for any other child. (Morgan, 2016: 3–4)

What we really need if inclusive education is to become a reality is old ideas, not new ones – the ideas promoted by early welfare pioneers and the disability community themselves. To be specific, the UPIAS (1976: 14) nearly fifty years ago stated that disabled peoples' groups should

> [work] as a political movement through which disabled people can gain expertise and take control over our own lives ... In this way, the problems of poverty, immobility, unemployment, etc., of physically impaired people would be increasingly integrated into the common problems of social life which also include these aspects and affect many other social groups.

It is also useful here to remind ourselves of UPIAS's statement referenced early in the book:

> In our view it is society which disables physically impaired people. Disability is something imposed on top of our impairments by the way we are unnecessarily isolated and excluded from full participation in society. (UPIAS, 1976: 3)

We must learn the lessons of history, not repeat its mistakes. Those who use education must drive education policies, i.e. children and young people with SEND and their families. The Children and Families Bill 2014 professed that it would listen to children and young people with SEND; however, early evaluations of its operations suggest that it is failing in this commitment. Inclusion I suggest, therefore, must be reframed within the principles of human rights, democracy, equity and social justice. Its ultimate aim must be to develop early years settings, schools and colleges where all children can participate equally, where they will be respected and have a right to be included at a social, intellectual and cultural level. My belief is that inclusive education must move beyond structures and policies towards strategies of empowerment. This world of inclusive education is still not beyond our grasp but *you* as the next generation of professionals working together with children and young people with SEND need to reach out and take it!

I leave you with a personal reflection upon my first days as a 'teacher of SEND'. This account draws out how as a practitioner I needed to reconceptualise special educational needs and disability.

In my employment as a one-to-one special needs tutor in further education I was tasked, on my first day, to support a student called Kenny. Kenny was in his forties, had cerebral palsy, and communicated with the world one letter at a time through a computer program he operated with a head pointer fashioned out of a metal coat hanger and a triangular rubber taken off a discarded pencil. When he did speak, it was virtually impossible to understand him, and involved being drenched in spittle and staring at his decaying and rotted teeth. In so many ways my first day was slow going.

At one level, Kenny was not contributing economically. Indeed, from one perspective he might be observed to be a burden on society. He was the epitome of a medical model approach to education that had failed. His mother had been advised to euthanise Kenny during pregnancy. He had been categorised as a child and shut away in a supposedly caring institution. He was denied education. However, in his thirties he pushed hard to be educated. So, his local authority placed him in a school nursery where he was only allowed to 'play' in the sand pit for hour after hour, and day after day. That was until his mother pushed him and his wheelchair two miles to the further education college.

I was there to support Kenny, but in reality he supported me. Over the next year, one letter at a time, I learnt so much from him about life, and how to live it to the full. Kenny encouraged me to visit the institution where he lived. I was shocked: I found him strapped to a chair and left to manipulate alphabet blocks, hour after hour and day after day. Kenny knew the effect this visit would have on my attitude and understanding of what we call SEND today. He was correct; from that moment forward, I knew that education had to change. It had to be inclusive; it had to respect and enable all people to fulfil their potential – whatever that might be.

Kenny eventually took an 'O' level in mathematics: his life's ambition. He started on the Monday, and four days, and hours of toil later, he finished. He was physically and emotionally drained. He had given everything of himself – it was his life's work. Later, we found out he had got an 'A' pass. The state education system had let him down; it had seen him as needing support and not able of achieving success. He had proved them all wrong. How he laughed and laughed!

To some people Kenny was a 'societal misfit', a person who had no place in an education system which prepared children to become economic units of production. He, and others I worked with in those early days, achieved success in their own ways. Not always the success of academic qualifications but success nonetheless. The lasting legacy of these few years was that I, as an educator, had to alter my attitude. I had to be re-educated as to the wonder and uniqueness of every individual. We have no need for more categorising in education, nor the continuance of definitions, nor ideologies and policies that exclude. What we need is to learn respect for all life and the pure awe-inspiring wonder it can bring to our early years settings, classrooms and colleges. Inclusion is not just a choice but also is a way of being. Moving forward, it must be observed as a basic human right – a right that is far too important to be left to the vagaries of politicians, ideology and models of disabilities.

I really hope that in your reading of this book you have appreciated that inclusion is a journey that we roll, walk, crawl and slide together. Every person can and does contribute to this journey. I hope in your life's work in education and beyond that your journey in this world they call SEND begins with a realisation that we must change ourselves before we try to change others. This for me is the key issue in special educational needs and inclusion.

FURTHER READING

Nutbrown, C., Clough, P. and Atherton, F. (2013) *Inclusion in the Early Years*. London: Sage. This book provides an overview of strategies to develop inclusive practice in the early years. It will offer you the opportunity to review and reflect upon issues related to inclusion and assist you in putting inclusive policies into practice.

Oliver, M. (1988) 'The Social and Political Context of Educational Policy: The Case of Special Needs'. In L. Barton (ed.), *The Politics of Special Educational Needs*. London: Falmer, pp. 13–31. This book offers a useful insight into the social and political context of SEND and inclusion. It will help in assisting you to contextualise evolving provision and how this has changed over many years.

Slee, R. (2018) *Inclusive Education isn't Dead, It Just Smells Funny*. London: Routledge. This text places inclusive education as the cornerstone of democracy, social equality and effective education. It argues that inclusive education is neither outdated nor unfit for purpose.

REFERENCES

Abberley, P. (1987) The concept of oppression and the development of a social theory of disability, *Disability, Handicap and Society*, 2(1): 5–19.

Ainscow, M. (1995) Education for all: making it happen, *Support for Learning*, 10(4): 147–54.

Ainscow, M., Booth, T. and Dyson, A. (2006) Inclusion and the standards agenda: negotiating policy pressures in England, *International Journal of Inclusive Education*,10 (4–5): 295–308.

Ainscow, M., Farrell, P. and Tweddle, D. (2010) Developing policies for inclusive education: a study of the role of local education authorities, *International Journal of Inclusive Education*, 4(3): 211–29.

Allan, J. (1999) *Actively Seeking Inclusion: Pupils with Special Needs in Mainstream Schools*. London: Falmer.

Allan, J. (2003) Productive pedagogies and the challenge of inclusion, *British Journal of Special Education*, 30(4): 175–79.

Allan, J. and Youdell, D. (2017) Ghostings, materialisations and flows in Britain's special educational needs and disability assemblage, *Discourse: Studies in the Cultural Politics of Education*, 38(1): 70–82.

Allen, N. (2005) *Making Sense of the Children Act 1989* (4th edn). London: Wiley-Blackwell.

Armstrong, A.C., Armstrong, D. and Spandagou, I. (2009) *Inclusive Education: International Policy & Practice*. London: Sage.

Armstrong, D., Armstrong, A.C. and Spandagou, I. (2011) Inclusion: by choice or by chance?, *International Journal of Inclusive Education*, 15(1): 29–39.

Armstrong, F. and Barton, L. (1999) *Disability, Human Rights and Education*. Buckingham: Open University Press.

Atkinson, M., Wilkin, A., Stott, A., Doherty, P. and Kinder, K. (2002) *Multi-agency Working: A Detailed Study*. London: National Foundation for Educational Research.

Bailey, J. (1998) 'Australia: Inclusion through Categorisation', in T. Booth and M. Ainscow (eds), *From Them to Us: An International Study of Inclusion in Education*. London: Routledge.

Baker, J. and Zigmond, N. (1995) The meaning and practice of inclusion for students with learning disabilities: themes and implications from five cases, *Journal of Special Education*, 29(2): 163–80.

Baran, J. and Winzer, M. (2017) Democratizing education: a case study of inclusive schooling for students with special needs in Poland, *Education and Society*, 35(2): 5–21.

Barnes, C. (1992) *Disabling Imagery and the Media*. Halifax: Ryburn/BCOCP.

Barnes, C. (1997) 'A Legacy of Oppression: A History of Disability in Western Culture'. In L. Barton and M. Oliver (eds), *Disability Studies: Past, Present and Future*. Leeds: Disability.

Barnes, C. and Mercer, G. (2003) *Disability*. Cambridge: Polity.

Barnes, C. and Mercer, G. (2010) *Exploring Disability* (2nd edn). Cambridge: Polity.

Barnes, C., Oliver, M. and Barton, L. (eds) (2002) *Disability Studies Today*. Cambridge: Polity.

Bartlett, S. and Burton, D. (2012) *Introduction to Education Studies* (3rd edn). London: Sage.

Bartlett, S. and Burton, D. (2016) *Introduction to Education Studies* (4th edn). London: Sage.

Bartolo, P.A. (2010) Why school psychology for diversity?, *School Psychology International*, 31(6): 567–80.

Barton, L. (1997) Inclusive education: romantic, subversive or realistic?, *International Journal of Inclusive Education*, 1(30): 231–42.

Barton, L. (2003) 'Inclusive education and teacher education: A basis for hope or a discourse of delusion?' Inaugural Professorial Lecture, London, London Institute of Education.

Batty, D. (2005) Children's Services: The Issue Explained, *Guardian*, 18 May.

BBC (n.d.) Available at: http://news.bbc.co.uk/local/lancashire/hi/people_and_places/newsid_8697000/8697441.stm

Beckett, A.E. (2014) Non-disabled children's ideas about disability and disabled people, *British Journal of Sociology of Education*, 36(6): 856–75.

Benning, T.B. (2015) Limitations of the biopsychosocial model in psychiatry, *Advances in Medical Education and Practice*, 6: 347–52.

Beveridge, S. (2004) *Children, Families and Schools: Developing Partnerships for Inclusive Education*. London: Routledge.

Bishop, R. (2001) *Designing for Special Educational Needs in Mainstream Schools*. London: Blackwell Synergy.

Block, M. and Obrusnikova, I. (2007) Inclusion in physical education: a review of the literature from 1995–2005, *Adapted Physical Activity Quarterly*, 24: 103–24.

Boesley, L. and Crane, L. (2018) 'Forget the Health and Care and just call them Education Plans': SENCos' perspectives on Education, Health and Care Plans', *JORSEN*. Available at: https://doi.org/10.1111/1471-3802.12416

Booth, T. (2000) 'Inclusion and Exclusion Policy in England: Who Controls the Agenda?' In F. Armstrong and D. Armstrong (eds), *Inclusive Education*. London: Fulton.

Borsay, A. (2005) *Disability and Social Policy in Britain since 1750*. Basingstoke: Palgrave Macmillan.

Bowen, P. (n.d.) *Human Rights: Transforming Services* (Institute for Social Care Excellence). Available at: www.scie.org.uk/news/events/previousevents/humanrights06/socialcare-bowen.pdf

Brainhe (2007) *Best Resources for Achievement and Intervention re Neurodiversity in Higher Education*. Available at: www.brainhe.com

Brown, J. (2014) 'Rights and Legislation'. In C. Cameron (ed.), *Disability: A Student's Guide*. London: Sage.

Burt, C. (1917) *The Distributions and Relations of Educational Abilities*. London: King & Son.

Burt, C. (1937) *The Backward Child*. London and Aylesbury: University of London Press.

Byrne, B. (2013) Hidden contradictions and conditionality: conceptualisations of inclusive education in international human rights law, *Disability & Society*, 28(2): 232–44.

Cabinet Office (2010) *The Coalition: Our Programme for Government*. London: Cabinet Office. Available at: www.gov.uk/government/publications/the-coalition-our-programme-for-government

Cairns, B. and McClatchey, K. (2013) Children's attitudes towards disability, *British Journal of Special Education*, 40(3): 124–29.

Cameron, C. (2013) 'The Affirmation Model'. In C. Cameron (ed.), *Disability Studies: A Student's Guide*. London: Sage.

Care Co-ordination Network United Kingdom (2004) Information sheet. Available at: www.york.ac.uk/inst/spru/pubs/rworks/jan2004-1.pdf

Care Quality Commission (CQC) and Office for Standards in Education (Ofsted) (2017) *Local Area SEND Inspections: One Year On*. Available at: www.gov.uk/government/publications/local-area-send-inspections-one-year-on

Carpenter, B., Ashdown, R. and Bovair, K. (2001a) *Enabling Access: Effective Teaching and Learning for Pupils with Learning Difficulties*. London: Fulton.

Carpenter, B., Stevens, C., Bovair, K. and Ashdown, A. (2001b) *Effective Teaching and Learning for Pupils with Learning Difficulties*. London: Fulton.

Carrier, J.G. (1986) Sociology and special education: differentiation and allocation in mass education, *American Journal of Education*, 94(3): 282–312.

Cavet, J. (n.d.) *Working in Partnership through Early Support: Distance Learning Text Best Practice in Key Working: What Do Research and Policy Have to Say?* London: Care Co-ordination Network UK. Available at: www.slideshare.net/gaz12000/best-practice-in-key-working1

Centre for Studies in Inclusive Education (CSIE) (2005) *Evidence to the UK Parliament's Inquiry into Special Educational Needs*. Available at: www.csie.org.uk/campaigns/2004-07.shtml

Charlton, J.I. (2000) *Nothing About Us Without Us: Disability Oppression and Empowerment*. Berkeley, CA: University of California Press.

Cheminais, R. (2009) *Effective Multi-Agency Partnerships: Putting Every Child Matters into Practice*. London: Sage.

Clough, P. and Corbett, P. (2000) *Theories of Inclusive Education: A Students' Guide*. London: Paul Chapman.

Clough, P. and Garner, G. (2003) 'Special Educational Needs and Inclusive Education: Origins and Current Issues'. In S. Bartlett and D. Burton (eds), *Education Studies: Essential Issues*. London: Sage.

COI (2001) *Images of Disability*. London: COI Communications and Department for Work and Pensions.

Coles, C. and Hancock, R. (2002) *The Inclusion Quality Mark*. Croyden: Creative Education.

Conservative Party Manifesto (2010) Available at: www.conservatives.com/~/media/Files/Manifesto2010

Contact (1991) No.70, Winter, pp.45–48 (available at www.leeds.ac.uk/disability-studies/archive/Barnes/Media.pdf).

Copeland, I.C. (2001) Integration versus segregation: the early struggle, *British Journal of Learning Disabilities*, 29(1): 5–11.

Corbett, J. (2001) *Supporting Inclusive Education: A Connective Pedagogy*. London: Routledge Falmer.

Corbett, J. and Norwich, B. (2005) 'Common or Specialised Pedagogy?' In M. Nind, J. Rix, K. Sleehy and K. Simmons (eds), *Curriculum and Pedagogy in Inclusive Education: Values into Practice*. Abingdon: RoutledgeFalmer.

Council for Disabled Children (2014) Available at: https://councilfordisabledchildren.org.uk

Coune, E. (2003) *The SENCo Handbook* (4th edn). London: Fulton.

Croll, P. and Moses, M. (2000) Ideologies and utopias: education professionals' views of inclusion, *European Journal of Special Needs Education*, 15(1): 1–12.

Crowther, N. (2007) Nothing without us or nothing about us?, *Disability & Society*, 22(7): 791–94.

Cumberbatch, G. and Negrine, R. (1992) *Images of Disability on Television*. London: Routledge.

Curran, H., Mortimore, T. and Riddell, R. (2017) Special Educational Needs reforms 2014: SENCos' perspectives of the first six months, *British Journal of Special Education*, 44(1): 44–64.

Ćwirynkało, K., Kisovar-Ivanda, T., Gregory, J.L., Żyta, A. and Arciszewska, A. (2017) 'Attitudes of Croatian and Polish elementary school teachers towards inclusive education of children with disabilities', *Hrvatska Revija za Rehabilitacijska Istrazivanja, suppl.*, 53: 252–64.

Czyż, A.K. (2018) Attitudes of Polish schools' teachers towards the idea of inclusive education for disabled people, *International Journal of Social Sciences*, 4(1): 542–54.

Daniel, P. (1997) Educating students with disabilities in the least restrictive environment: a slippery slope for educators, *Journal of Educational Administration*, 35(5): 397–410.

Das, A.K, Kuyini, A.B. and Desai, I. (2013) Inclusive education in India: are the teachers prepared?, *International Journal of Special Education*, 28(1): 27–36.

Davis, J.M. and Watson, D. (2001) Where are the children's experiences? Cultural and social exclusion in 'special' and 'mainstream' schools, *Disability & Society*, 16: 671–87.

Davis, K. (1996) 'Disability and Legislation: Right and Equality'. In G. Hales (ed.), *Beyond Disability: Towards an Enabling Society*. London: Sage.

Davis, T. (2000) *Moving from residential institutions to community based services in eastern Europe and the former Soviet Union* (accessed at www.worldbank/sp, Disability World Bank Publications).

Deal, M. (2003) Disabled people's attitudes toward other impairment groups: a hierarchy of impairments, *Disability & Society*, 18(7): 897–910.

de Boer, A., Pijl, S.J. and Minnaert, A. (2012) Students' attitudes towards peers with disabilities: a review of the literature, *International Journal of Disability, Development and Education*, 59(4): 379–92.

Department for Education (DfE) (2011) *Support and Aspiration: A New Approach to Special Educational Needs and Disability*. London: DfE.

Department for Education (DfE) (2013) *Teachers' Standards: Guidance for school leaders, school staff and governing bodies*. Available at: https://assets.publishing.service.gov.uk/government/uploads/system/uploads/attachment_data/file/665520/Teachers__Standards.pdf

Department for Education (DfE) (2014a) *Children and Families Act*. London: HMSO.

Department for Education (DfE) (2014b) *Special Needs Code of Practice*. London: HMSO.

Department for Education (DfE) (2014c) *The Equality Act 2010 and Schools Departmental Advice for School Leaders, School Staff, Governing Bodies and Local Authorities*. Available at: www.gov.uk/government/uploads/system/uploads/attachment_data/file/315587/Equality_Act_Advice_Final.pdf

Department for Education (DfE) (2014d) *The National Curriculum in England: Framework Document*. Available at: www.gov.uk/government/publications/national-curriculum-in-england-framework-for-key-stages-1-to-4/the-national-curriculum-in-england-framework-for-key-stages-1-to-4

Department for Education (DfE) (2018a) *Statements of SEN and EHC Plans: England 2018*. Available at: https://assets.publishing.service.gov.uk/government/uploads/system/uploads/attachment_data/file/709590/Statements_of_SEN_and_EHC_plans_England_2018_Main_Text.pdf

Department for Education (DfE) (2018b) *Special Educational Needs: An Analysis and Summary of Data Sources – May 2018*. Available at: https://assets.publishing.service.gov.uk/government/uploads/system/uploads/attachment_data/file/709496/Special_educational_needs_Publication_May18.pdf

Department for Education and Employment (DfEE) (1997) *Excellence for All Children Green Paper, 22 October*. London: HMSO.

Department for Education and Employment (DfEE) (1998) *Meeting Special Educational Needs: A Programme of Action*. London: HMSO.

Department for Education and Skills (DfES) (2001) *Special Educational Needs and Disability Act*. London: DfES.

Department for Education and Skills (DfES) (2003) *The Report of the Special Schools Working Group*. Annesty: DfES.

Department for Education and Skills (DfES) (2004a) *Removing Barriers to Achievement: The Government's Strategy for SEN*. London: DfES.

Department for Education and Skills (DfES) (2004b) *Children's Act*. London: HMSO.

Department for Education and Skills (DfES) (2005) *The Youth Matters Green Paper*. London: HMSO.

Department for Education and Skills/Qualification and Curriculum Authority (DFES/QCA) (1999) *The National Curriculum*. London: HMSO.

Department of Education (DoE) (1970) *The Education (Handicapped Act) 1970*. London: HMSO.

Department of Education (DoE) (1994) *Code of Practice on the Identification and Assessment of Special Educational Needs*. London: HMSO.

Department of Education (DoE) (2005) *Special Educational Needs and Disability Order 2005* [online]. Available at: www.opsi.gov.uk/si/si2005/20051117.htm

Department of Education and Science (DES) (1978) *Special Educational Needs: Report of the Committee of Enquiry into the Education of Handicapped Children and Young People (The Warnock Report)*. London: HMSO.

Department of Education and Science (DES) (1981) *The 1981 Education Act*. London: HMSO.

Dickinson, R. (2018) Parenting a child with disabilities: the intersection of education and cultural perceptions in Southern India, *Journal of Human Rights and Social Work*, 3(2): 72–80.

Disability Discrimination Act (DDA) (1995) Available at: www.opsi.gov.uk/acts/Acts1995/ukpga_19950050_en_1

Durham, C. and Ramcharan, R. (2018) *Insights into Acquired Brain Injury*. Singapore: Springer, pp. 31–51.

Dyson, A. and Millward, A. (2000) *Schools and Special Needs: Issues of Innovation and Inclusion*. London: Paul Chapman.

Dyson, A. and Slee, R. (2001) 'Special Needs Education from Warnock to Salamanca: The Triumph of Liberalism?' In R. Phillips and J. Firlong (eds), *Education Reform and the State: Twenty Five Years of Politics, Policy and Practice*. London: RoutledgeFalmer.

Edinburgh Review (1865) Idiot asylums, 121: 37–72.

Education and Skills Committee (2006) Available at: www.publications.parliament.uk. London: House of Commons.

Edwards, A., Daniels, D., Gallagher, T., Leadbetter, J. and Warmington, P. (2009) *Enhancing Interprofessional Collaborations in Children's Services: Multi-Agency Working for Children's Wellbeing* (Improving Learning Series). London: Routledge.

Elkins, D.N. (2009) The medical model in psychotherapy: its limitations and failures, *Journal of Humanistic Psychology*, 49: 66–84.

Equality and Human Rights Commission (EHRC) (2014) *Equality Act Codes of Practice and Technical Guidance*. Available at: www.equalityhumanrights.com/en/advice-and-guidance/equality-act-technical-guidance

Equality and Human Rights Commission (EHRC) (2017) *Being Disabled in Britain: A Journey Less Equal*. Available at: www.equalityhumanrights.com

Evans, J. (1995) 'Implementing the 1981 Education Act'. In I. Lunt, B. Norwich and V. Varma (eds), *Psychology and Education for Special Needs: Recent Developments and Future Directions*. Aldershot: Arena.

Evans, J. (1996) *Chairperson, European Network on Independent Living, Campaign for Civil Rights Legislation: The Direct Payments Act and the Disability Discrimination Act (DDA)*. Available at: www.independentliving.org/docs2/enilevans9610.html

Evans, J. and Lunt, I. (2005) 'Inclusive Education: Are there Limits?' In K. Topping and S. Maloney (eds), *The RoutledgeFalmer Reader in Inclusive Education*. London: RoutledgeFalmer.

Farrell, M. (2000) *Special Educational Needs: The Importance of Standards of Pupil Achievement*. London: Continuum.

Farrell, M. (2004) *Special Educational Needs: A Resource for Practitioners*. London: Paul Chapman.

Farrell, M. (2005) *Key Issues in Special Education: Raising Standards of Pupil Attainment and Achievement*. London: Routledge.

Finkelstein, V. (1980) *Attitudes and Disabled People*. New York: World Rehabilitation Fund.

Fisher, P. and Goodley, D. (2007) The linear medical model of disability: mothers of disabled babies resist with counter-narratives, *Sociology of Health and Illness*, 29(1): 66–81.

Florian, L. (2008) Special or inclusive education: future trends, *British Journal of Special Education*, 35(4): 201–20.

Foley, P. and Rixon, A. (eds) (2014) *Changing Children's Services: Working and Learning Together* (2nd edn). Bristol: Policy.

Frederickson, N. and Cline, T. (2002) *Special Educational Needs, Inclusion and Diversity*. Buckingham: OUP.

Frederickson, N. and Cline, T. (2009) *Special Educational Needs, Inclusion and Diversity* (2nd edn). Maidenhead: OUP.

Frederickson, N. and Cline, T. (2015) *Special Educational Needs, Inclusion and Diversity* (3rd edn). Maidenhead: OUP.

Gajda, M. (2008) *Dwuglos w Sprawie Edukacji*. Available at: www.niepelnosprawni.pl/ledge/x/27040

Gargiulo, R.M. and Kilgo, J.L. (2014) *An Introduction to Young Children with Special Needs: Birth Through Age Eight*. Belmont, CA: Wadsworth.

Gibb, N. (2015) 'The purpose of education'. Address to the Education Summit, 9 July. Available at: www.gov.uk/government/speeches/the-purpose-of-education

Gibson, S. and Blandford, S. (2005) *Managing Special Educational Needs: A Practical Guide for Primary and Secondary Schools*. London: Paul Chapman.

Glazzard, J. (2014) 'The standards agenda: reflections of a special educational needs co-ordinator', *Support for Learning*, 29(1): 39–53.

Gleeson, B.J. (1997) Disability Studies: a historical materialist view, *Disability & Society*, 12(2): 179–202.

Goering, S. (2010) Revisiting the relevance of the social model of disability, *American Journal of Bioethics*, 10(1): 54–55.

Goering, S. (2015) Rethinking disability: the social model of disability and chronic disease, *Current Reviews in Musculoskeletal Medicine*, 8(2): 134–38.

Goodey, C.F. and Rose, L.M. (2013) 'Mental States, Bodily Dispositions and Table Manners: A Guide to Reading Intellectual Disability from Homer to Late Antiquity'. In C. Laes, C. Goodey and L.M. Rose (eds), *Disabilities in Roman Antiquity: Disparate Bodies A Capite ad Calcem*. The Netherlands: Koninklijke Brill.

Goodley, D. (2011) *Disability Studies: An Interdisciplinary Introduction*. London: Sage.

Goodley, D. (2014) 'Who is Disabled? Exploring the Scope of the Social Model of Disability'. In J. Swain, S. French, C. Barnes and C. Thomas (eds), *Disabling Barriers – Enabling Environments* (3rd edn). London: Sage.

Gove, M. in Sellgren, K. (2011) *Gove: Tougher New Teacher Standards Needed*. Available at: www.bbc.co.uk/news/education-12717061

Graham, J. and Wright, J.A. (1999) What does 'inter-professional collaboration' mean to professionals working with pupils with physical disabilities?, *British Journal of Special Education*, 26(1): 37–41.

Grainger, T. and Todd, J. (2000) *Inclusive Educational Practice: Literacy*. London: Fulton.

Gray, D.E. (2002) 'Everybody just freezes. Everybody is just embarrassed': felt and enacted stigma among parents of children with high functioning autism, *Sociology of Health & Illness*, 24(6): 734–49.

The Guardian (2009) Children Act 2004, 19 January. Available at: www.theguardian.com/commentisfree/libertycentral/2009/jan/13/children-act

Gupta, Y., Singh, V. and Parween, S. (2018) Teacher attitude: a key factor for the inclusion of students with learning disabilities, *Journal of Disability Management & Special Education*, 1(1): 13–20.

Guralnick, M.J. (2002) Involvement with peers: comparisons between young children with and without Down's syndrome, *Journal of Intellectual Disability Research*, 46(5): 379–83.

Haffter, C. (1969) The changeling: history and the psychodynamics of attitudes to handicapped children, *European Folklore Journal of the History of Behavioural Sciences*, 4: 55–61.

Hanko, G. (2003) Towards an inclusive school culture – but what happened to Elton's affective curriculum?, *British Journal of Special Education*, 30(3): 125–31.

Harasymiw, S.J., Horne, M.D. and Lewis, S.C. (1976) A longitudinal study of disability group acceptance, *Rehabilitation Literature*, 37: 98–102.

Harpur, P. (2012) Embracing the new disability rights paradigm: the importance of the Convention on the Rights of Persons with Disabilities, *Disability & Society*, 27(1): 1–14.

Harris, N. (2018) *Autonomy, Rights and Children with Special Needs: A New Paradigm?* Working Paper 2. Manchester: University of Manchester. Available online at: www.docs.hss.ed.ac.uk/education/creid/Projects/39_ii_ESRC_SENChildren_WP_2.pdf

Haug, P. (2016) Understanding inclusive education: ideals and reality, *Scandinavian Journal of Disability Research*, 19(3): 206–17.

Henriques, G. (2011) *A New Unified Theory of Psychology*. London: Springer.

Henriques, G. (2015) *The Biopsychosocial Model and Its Limitations: Recognizing the Limitations of the Biopsychosocial Model*, Psychology Today. Available at: www.psychologytoday.com/gb/blog/theory-knowledge/201510/the-biopsychosocial-model-and-its-limitations

Hervey, D. (1992) *The Creatures Time Forgot: Photography and Disability Imagery*. London: Routledge.

Higginbotham, P. (2017) *Children's Homes: A History of Institutional Care for Britain's Young*. Barnsley: Pen & Sword Books.

Hills, G. (2011) *The Equality Act for Educational Professionals: A Simple Guide to Disability Inclusion in School*. London: David Fulton/Nasen.

Hindu Business Line (2007) Available at: www.thehindubusinessline.com/2007/04/16/26hdline.htm

Hodkinson, A. (2005) 'Conceptions and misconceptions of inclusive education: a critical examination of final year teacher trainees' knowledge and understanding of inclusion, *Research in Education*, 73: 15–29.

Hodkinson, A. (2006) Conceptions and misconceptions of inclusive education – one year on: a critical analysis of newly qualified teachers' knowledge and understanding of inclusion, *Research in Education*, 76: 43–55.

Hodkinson, A. (2007) Inclusive education and the cultural representation of disability and disabled people: a recipe for disaster or the catalyst for change? An examination of nondisabled primary school children's attitudes to children with a disability, *Research in Education*, 77: 56–76.

Hodkinson, A. (2009) Pre-service teacher training and special educational needs in England 1970–2008: is government learning the lessons of the past or is it experiencing a groundhog day? *European Journal of Special Needs Education*, 24(3): 277–89.

Hodkinson, A. (2010) Inclusive and Special Education within the English Education System: historical perspectives, recent developments and future challenges, *British Journal of Special Education*, 37(2): 61–67.

Hodkinson, A. (2011) Inclusion: a defining definition? *Power and Education*, 3(2): 179–85.

Hodkinson, A. (2012a) Inclusive education and the cultural representation of disability and disabled people within the English education system: the influence of electronic media in the primary school, *Journal of Research in Special Educational Needs*, 12(4): 252–62.

Hodkinson, A. (2012b) 'All present and correct?' Exclusionary inclusion within the English educational system, *Disability & Society*, 27(5): 675–88.

Hodkinson, A. (2017) Constructing impairment and disability in school reading schemes, *Education 3–13*, 45(3): 572–85.

Hodkinson, A. (2019) 'Pre-service Teacher Training and Special Educational Needs in England 1978–2018: Looking Back but Moving Forward?' In *Including Children and Young People with Special Educational Needs and Disabilities in Learning and Life: How Far Have We Come Since the Warnock Enquiry – And Where Do We Go Next?* London: Routledge.

Hodkinson, A. and Burch, L. (2017) The 2014 special educational needs and disability code of practice: old ideology into new policy contexts?, *Journal of Education Policy*. Available at: https://doi.org/10.1080/02680939.2017.1412501

Hodkinson, A. and Devarakonda, C. (2011) Conceptions of inclusion and inclusive education: a critical examination of the perspectives and practices of teachers in India, *Research in Education*, 82: 85–96.

Holland, J. and Pell, G. (2017) Parental perceptions of the 2014 SEND legislation, *Pastoral Care in Education*, 35(4): 293–311.

Hornby, G. (2001) 'Promoting Responsible Inclusion: Quality Education For All'. In T. O'Brien (ed.), *Enabling Inclusion: Blue Skies ... Dark Clouds?* London: HMSO.

Houston, E. (2017) 'The representation of disabled women in Anglo-American advertising: Examining how cultural disability tropes impact on the subjective wellbeing of disabled women'. PhD Thesis, Lancaster University.

Huckstadt, L.K. and Shutts, K. (2014) How young children evaluate people with and without disabilities, *Journal of Social Issues*, 70(1): 99–114.

Humphrey, N. and Symes, W. (2013) Inclusive education for pupils with autistic spectrum disorders in secondary mainstream schools: teacher attitudes, experience and knowledge, *International Journal of Inclusive Education*, 17(1): 32–46.

Hunt, V. (2013) *In Loco Parentis?* TES Connect. Available at: www.tes.com/news/loco-parentis

Hussain, H.D. and Brownhill, S. (2014) 'Integrated Working: From the Theory to the Practice'. In S. Brownhill (ed.), *Empowering the Children's and Young People's Workforce: Practice Based Knowledge, Skills and Understanding*. London: Routledge.

Huws, J.C. and Jones, R.S. (2010) Missing voices: representations of autism in British newspapers, 1999–2008, *British Journal of Learning Disabilities*, 39(2): 98–104.

infed.org (2007) *The Hadow Reports: An Introduction*. Available at: www.infed.org/schooling/hadow_reports.htm

Jackson, P. (1983) Principles and problems of participant observation, *Geografiska Annaler*, 65B: 39–46.

Jacques, N., Wilton, K. and Townsend, M. (1998) Cooperative learning and social acceptance of children with mild intellectual disability, *Journal of Intellectual Disability Research*, 42(1): 29–36.

Jahoda, A., Dagnan, D., Jarvie, P. and Kerr, W. (2006) Depression, social context and cognitive behavioural therapy for people who have intellectual disabilities, *Journal of Applied Research in Intellectual Disabilities*, 19(1): 81–89.

Jenkinson, J.C. (1997) *Mainstream or Special? Educating Students with Disabilities*. London: Routledge.

Johansson, S.T. (2014) A critical and contextual approach to inclusive education: perspectives from an Indian context, *International Journal of Inclusive Education*, 18(12): 1219–36.

Johnstone, D. (2001) *An Introduction to Disability Studies* (2nd edn). London: Fulton.

Jones, B. (2003) *Childhood Disability in a Multicultural Society*. Abingdon: Radcliffe Medical.

Jones, C.A. (2004) *Supporting Inclusion in the Early Years*. Maidenhead: OUP.

Joseph Rowntree Foundation (1999) *Disabled Children and the Children Act*. Available at: www.jrf.org.uk/sites/files/jrf/scr378.pdf

Judge, B. (2003) 'Inclusive Education: Principles and Practices'. In K. Crawford (ed.), *Contemporary Issues in Education*. Norfolk: Peter Francis.

Kaehne, A. (2014) *Multi-Agency Protocols as a Mechanism to Improve Partnerships in Public Services, Local Government Studies, 2014*. Available at: www.tandfonline.com/doi/abs/10.1080/03003930.201 3.861819#preview

Karppi, T. (2013) 'Change name to No One Like. People's status': Facebook trolling and managing online personas, *Fibreculture Journal*, 166: 278–300.

Kavale, K. (2000) History, rhetoric and reality, *Remedial and Special Education*, 21(5): 279–97.

Keers, J., Blaauwwiekel, E., Hania, M., Bouma, J., Scholten-Jaegers, S., Sanderman, R. and Links, T. (2004) Diabetes rehabilitation: development and first results of a multidisciplinary intensive education programme for patients with prolonged self-management difficulties, *Patient Education and Counselling*, 52(2): 151–57.

Keil, S., Miller, O. and Cobb, R. (2006) Special education needs and disability, *British Journal of Special Education*, 33(4): 168–72.

Kenworthy, J. and Whittaker, J. (2000) Anything to declare? The struggle for inclusive education and children's rights, *Disability and Society*, 15(2): 219–31.

Kirby, M. (2016) Implicit assumptions in special education policy: promoting full inclusion for students with learning disabilities, *Child and Youth Care Forum*, 2: 175–91.

Kirk, S. and Glendinning, C. (1999) *Supporting Parents Caring for a Technology-Dependent Child*. Manchester: National Primary Care Research and Development Centre, University of Manchester.

Kitzel, M.E. (2017) Creating a Deaf place: the development of the Asylum for Deaf and Dumb Poor Children in the early nineteenth century, *Journal of Cultural Geography*, 34(2): 149–69.

Koller, D., Le Pouesard, M. and Rummen, J.A. (2018) Defining social inclusion for children with disabilities: a critical literature review, *Children & Society*, 32: 1–13.

Kristensen, K. (2002) Can the Scandinavian perspective on inclusive education be implemented in developing countries?, *African Journal of Special Needs Education*, 7(2): 104–14.

Laat, S., Freiksen, E. and Vervloed, M.P.J. (2013) Attitudes of children and adolescents toward persons who are deaf, blind, paralyzed or intellectually disabled, *Research in Developmental Disabilities*, 34(2): 855–63.

Lacey, P. and Ouvry, C. (eds) (2000) *People with Profound and Multiple Learning Disabilities: A Collaborative Approach to Meeting Complex Needs*. London: Fulton.

Laes, C., Goodey, C.F. and Rose, M.L. (2013) 'Approaching Disabilities A Capite ad Calcem: Hidden Themes in Roman Antiquity'. In C. Laes, C. Goodey and L.M. Rose (eds), *Disabilities in Roman Antiquity: Disparate Bodies A Capite ad Calcem*. The Netherlands: Koninklijke Brill.

Lees, C. and Ralph, S. (2004) Charitable provision for blind and deaf people in the late nineteenth century London, *Journal of Research in Special Educational Needs*, 4(3): 148–60.

Lendrum, A. (2014) Developing positive school–home relationships through structured conversations with parents of learners with special educational needs and disabilities (SEN), *Journal of Research in Special Educational Needs*. Available at: doi: 10.1111/1471-3802.12023

Lenney, M. and Sercombe, H. (2002) 'Did you see that guy in the wheelchair down the pub?' Interactions across difference in a public place, *Disability & Society*, 17(1): 5–18.

Lewis, A. (1991) Changing views of special educational needs, *Education 3–13*, 27(3): 45–50.

Lloyd, C. (2012) 'Special Educational Needs'. In L. Gearon (ed.), *Education in the United Kingdom: Structures and Organisation*. London: Fulton.

Lockewood, G., Henderson, C. and Thornicroft, G. (2012) The Equality Act 2010 and mental health, *British Journal of Psychiatry*, 200:182–83.

Long, P. (2018) *Special Education Needs Support in England, Briefing Paper 07020, 20th April 2018*. Available at: https://researchbriefings.parliament.uk/ResearchBriefing/Summary/SN07020 #fullreport

Longmore, P.K. (1987) 'Screening Sterotypes: Images of Disabled People in Television and Motion Pictures'. In A. Gartner and T. Joe (eds), *Images of the Disabled, Disabling Images*. New York: Praeger.

Low, C. (1997) 'Is inclusivism possible?', *European Journal of Special Needs Education*, 12(1): 71–79.

Luke, C. (1996) *Feminisms and Pedagogies of Everyday Life*. Albany: State University of New York Press.

Machingura, F. and Museka, G. (2018) '"We are not asexual": The Bible, Disability and Pentecostal Spirituality'. In F. Machingura, L. Togarasei and E. Chitando (eds), *Pentecostalism and Human Rights in Contemporary Zimbabwe* (pp. 159–74). Newcastle: Cambridge Scholars.

MacLeod, F. (2001) Towards inclusion – our shared responsibility for disaffected students, *British Journal of Special Education*, 28(4): 191–94.

Madan, A. and Sharma, N. (2013) Inclusive education for children with disabilities: preparing schools to meet the challenge, *Electronic Journal for Inclusive Education*, 3(1).

Manion, M.L. and Bersani, H.A. (1987) Mental retardation as a western sociological construct: a cross-cultural analysis, *Disability, Handicap & Society*, 2(3): 231–41.

Manni (2000) *A manual for planning and implementation of inclusive education in SSA*, MHRD [Ministry of Human Resource Development] (2003). Available at http://ssa.nic.in/manual.asp

Marchbanks, P. (2006) From caricature to character: the intellectually disabled in Dickens's novels (Part One), *Dickens Quarterly*, 1–13. Available at: http://digitalcommons.calpoly.edu/cgi/viewcontent.cgi?article=1021&context=engl_fac

Martlew, M. and Hodson, J. (1991) Children with mild learning difficulties in an integrated and in a special school: comparisons of behaviour, teasing and teacher attitudes, *British Journal of Educational Psychology*, 61(3): 355–72.

Mencap (2007) Press release, available at mencap.org.uk (accessed 12 November 2007).

Mencap (2016) *First In-depth Research on Public Attitudes Towards Learning Disability for 30 Years Reveals Confusion, Support Yet Small Group of Negative Attitudes*. Available at: www.mencap.org.uk/press-release/first-depth-research-public-attitudes-towards-learning-disability-30-years-reveals

Miles, S. and Singal, N. (2010) The Education for All and inclusive education debate: conflict, contradiction or opportunity?, *International Journal of Inclusive Education*, 14(1): 1–15.

Mind (2005) *Mental Capacity Act 2005: A brief legal guide to the Mental Capacity Act, including details of where you can go for further information or support*. Available at: www.mind.org.uk/information-support/legal-rights/mental-capacity-act-2005/

Mittler, P. and Daunt, P. (eds) (1995) *Teacher Education for Special Needs in Europe*. London: Cassell.

Morgan, H. (2012) The social model of disability as a threshold concept: troublesome knowledge and liminal spaces in social work education, *Social Work Education*, 31(2): 215–26.

Morgan, N. (2016) *DfE Strategy 2015–2020: World-class Education and Care*. London: DfE.

Morina Diez, A. (2010) School memories of young people with disabilities: an analysis of barriers and aids to inclusion, *Disability & Society*, 33(2): 163–75.

Morris, J. (1991) *Pride Against Prejudice: Transforming Attitudes to Disability*. London: Women's Press.

Morris, J. (2005) *Citizenship and Disabled People – A scoping paper prepared for the Disability Rights Commission*. London: Disability Rights Commission.

National Association for Special Educational Needs (Nasen) (n.d.) *Draft Special Educational Needs (SEN) code of practice: Summary*. Available at: www.nasen.org.uk/uploads/publications/284.pdf

National Association for Special Educational Needs (Nasen) (2014) *Preparing for Change: New SEN Legislation and What This Means for the Strategic Management of Schools and Front Line Teaching Staff*. Available at: www.rnlcom.com/wp-content/uploads/2014/.../Jane-Friswell-PPoint.pptx

National Autistic Society (2016) *School Report 2016*. Available at: www.autism.org.uk/school report2016

National Center for Education Statistics (NCES) (2014) Available at: http://nces.ed.gov/fastfacts/display. asp?id=372

National Council of Educational Research and Training (NCERT) (2000) *The National Curriculum Framework for School Education*. New Delhi: NCERT.

National Parent Partnership Network (NPP) (2013) *Parent Partnership Services in England Survey on the Extent to which PPS Meet the Exemplifications of the Minimum Standards and Additional National Data Collection 2013*. Available at: www.bathnes.gov.uk/sites/default/files/nppn_benchmarking_2013.pdf

National Union of Teachers (NUT) (2004) *Special Educational Needs Study*. London: National Union of Teachers.

National Union of Teachers (NUT) (2013) *Education, The Law and You*. Available at: www.teachers.org. uk/files/the-law-and-you--8251-.pdf

Nind, M. (2005) 'Introduction-models and Practice in Inclusive Curricula'. In M. Nind, J. Rix, K. Sheeh and K. Simmons (eds), *Curriculum and Pedagogy in Inclusive Education: Values into Practice*. Abingdon: RoutledgeFalmer.

Nind, M., Sheehy, K. and Simmons, K. (eds) (2003) *Inclusive Education: Learners and Learning Contexts*. London: Fulton.

Norden, M. (1994) *The Cinema of Isolation: A History of Disability in the Movies*. New Brunswick, NJ: Rutgers University Press.

Norwich, B. (2000) 'Inclusion in Education: From Concepts, Values and Critique to Practice'. In H. Daniels (ed.), *Special Education Reformed Beyond the Rhetoric*. London: Falmer.

Norwich, B. (2002) Education, inclusion and individual differences: recognising and resolving dilemmas, *British Journal of Education Studies*, 50(4): 482–502.

Norwich, B. (2007) SEN Policy Options Group Special Schools in the new era: how do we go beyond generalities? Policy Paper 2, 6th Series, *Journal of Research in Special Educational Needs*, 7(2): 71–89.

Norwich, B. (2010) Can we envisage the end of special educational needs? Has special educational needs outlived its usefulness?, *Psychology of Education Review*, 34: 13–21.

Norwich, B. (2014) How does the capability approach address current issues in special educational needs, disability and inclusive education field?, *Journal of Research in Special Educational Needs*, 14(1): 16–21.

Norwich, B. (2016) Conceptualizing special educational needs using a biopsychosocial model in England: the prospects and challenges of using the International Classification of Functioning Framework, *Frontiers in Education*. Available at: https://doi.org/10.3389/feduc.2016.00005

Norwich, B. and Kelly, N. (2004) Pupils' views on inclusion: moderate learning difficulties and bullying in mainstream and special schools, *British Educational Research Journal*, 30(1): 43–64.

Nowicki, E.A. and Sandieson, R. (2002) A meta-analysis of school-age children's attitudes towards person with physical or intellectual disabilities, *International Journal of Disability, Development, and Education*, 49: 243–65.

Ofsted (2000) *Evaluating Educational Inclusion: Guidance for Inspectors and Schools*. London: Office for Standards in Education.

O'Hanlon, C. (1995) *Inclusive Education in Europe*. London: Fulton.

Oliver, M. (1988) 'The Social and Political Context of Educational Policy: The Case of Special Needs'. In L. Barton (ed.), *The Politics of Special Educational Needs*. London: Falmer.

Oliver, M. (1990a) *The Politics of Disablement*. Basingstoke: Macmillan.

Oliver, M. (1990b) 'The individual and social models of disability'. Paper presented at the Joint Workshop of the Luing Options Group, 23 July.

Oliver, M. (1996) 'Defining Impairment and Disability: Issues at Stake'. In C. Barnes and G. Mercer (eds), *Exploring the Divide: Illness and Disability*. Leeds: Disability.

Oliver, M. (2013) The social model of disability: thirty years on, *Disability & Society*, 28(7): 1024–26.

Oliver, M. and Barnes, C. (1998) *Disabled People and Social Policy: From Exclusion to Inclusion*. Harlow: Addison Wesley Longman.

Orbe, M.P. (2013) 'The Reality of Media Effects'. In A. Kurylo (ed.), *Inter/Cultural Communication: Representations and Constructions of Culture*. London: Sage.

Pajak-Wazna, E. (2013) Teachers' intercultural competence and teacher education: a case of Poland, *European Scientific Journal*, 2. Available at: http://eujournal.org/index.php/esj/article/view/1343

Palikara, O., Castro, S., Gaona, C. and Eirinaki, V. (2018) Professionals' views on the new policy for special educational needs in England: ideology versus implementation, *European Journal of Special Needs Education*. Available at: https://doi.org/10.1080/08856257.2018.1451310

Panda, P. (2005) 'Responsiveness of Pre-service Teacher Education in India: Appraisal of Curricular Dimensions and Practices'. Paper presented at ISEC Conference, Glasgow, August.

Park, J. and Hodkinson, A. (2017) 'Telling Tales': an investigation into the representation of disability in classic children's fairy tales, *Educational Futures*, 8(2): 48–68.

Parry, M. (2013) 'From Monsters to Patients: A History of Disability'. Unpublished PhD, Arizona State University. Available at: http://repository.asu.edu/attachments/110533/content/Parry_asu_0010E_12951.pdf

Parton, N. (2011) 'The increasing length and complexity of central government guidance about child abuse in England: 1974–2010'. Discussion paper, University of Huddersfield, Huddersfield (unpublished). Available at http://eprints.hud.ac.uk/9906/

Payler, J. and Georgeson, J. (2013) Multiagency working in the early years: confidence, competence and context, *Early Years: An International Research Journal*, 33(4): 380–97.

Pearson, C. and Watson, N. (2007) Tackling disability discrimination in the United Kingdom: the British Disability Discrimination Act, *Washington University Journal of Law and Policy*, 23(95): 95–120.

Pearson, S., Mitchell, R. and Rapti, M. (2014) 'I will be "fighting" even more for pupils with SEN': SENCOs' role predictions in the changing English policy context, *Jorsen*, I: 1–9.

Perry, J. (2014a) England: SEN measures-implementation, *British Journal of Special Education*, 41(3). Available at http://onlinelibrary.wiley.com/doi/10.1111/1467-8578.12075/pdf

Perry, J. (2014b) England: Children and Families Act, *British Journal of Special Education*, 41(2). Available at: http://onlinelibrary.wiley.com/doi/10.1111/bjsp.2014.41.issue-2/issuetoc

Pijl, S., Meijer, C. and Hegarty, S. (eds) (1997) *Inclusive Education: A Global Agenda*. London: Routledge.

Porter, J., Daniels, H., Feiler, A. and Georgeson, J. (2011) Recognising the needs of every disabled child: the development of tools for a disability census, *British Journal of Special Education*, 38(3): 120–25.

Postlethwaite, K. and Hackney, A. (1989) *Organising a School's Response: Special Needs in Mainstream Schools*. London: Macmillan.

Pritchard, D.G. (1963) *Education of the Handicapped, 1760–1960*. London: Routledge & Kegan Paul.

Raghavan, N.S. (2014) Inclusion of Students with Disabilities: A Case Study of a Private, Primary School in an Urban City in Southern India. Unpublished PHD, University of Texas at Austin.

Reid, K. (2005) The implications of Every Child Matters and the Children Act for schools, *Pastoral Care in Education*, 23(1): 12–18.

Reynolds, M.C. (1989) An historical perspective: the delivery of special education to mildly disabled and at-risk students, *Remedial and Special Education*, 10(6): 11.

Rieser, R. (2014) *Disability Equality: Medical Model/ Social Model*. Available at: www.worldofinclusion. com/medical_social_model.htm

Roberts, A. (2007) *Mental Health History Timeline*. Available at: www.mdx.ac.ukWWW/STUDYIMHHTIM. HTM

Robinson, D., Moore, N. and Hooley, T. (2018) Ensuring an independent future for young people with special educational needs and disabilities (SEND): a critical examination of the impact of education, health and care plans in England, *British Journal of Guidance & Counselling*, 46(4): 479–91.

Roche, J. and Tucker, S. (2007) Every Child Matters: 'tinkering' or 'reforming' – an analysis of the development of the Children Act (2004) from an educational perspective, *Education 3–13*, 35: 213–23.

Rose, R. (2001) Primary school teacher perceptions of the conditions required to include pupils with special educational needs, *Educational Review*, 53(2): 147–57.

Rose, R. (2003) *Strategies to Promote Inclusive Practice*. London: RoutledgeFalmer: pp. 182–202.

Rose, R. and Howley, M. (2007) *The Practical Guide to Special Education Needs in Inclusive Primary Classrooms*. London: Paul Chapman.

Rouse, M. (2017) 'A Role for Teachers and Teacher Education in Developing Inclusive Practice'. In M. Etherington (ed.), *What Teachers Need to Know: Topics in Diversity and Inclusion*. Eugene, OR: Wipf & Stock.

Runswick-Cole, K. (2011) 'Time to end the bias towards inclusive education?', *British Journal of Special Education*, 38(3): 112–19.

Ryan, J. with Thomas, F. (1980) *The Politics of Mental Handicap*. Harmondsworth: Penguin.

Safford, L. and Safford, J. (1996) *A History of Childhood and Disability*. New York: Teachers College Press.

Sawhney, S. (2015) Unpacking the nature and practices of inclusive education: the case of two schools in Hyderabad, India, *International Journal of Inclusive Education*, 19(9): 887–907.

Sayers, D. (2018) 'Rights Not Needs: Changing the Legal Model for Special Educational Needs (SEN)'. In K. Runswick-Cole, T. Curran and K. Liddiard (eds), *The Palgrave Handbook of Disabled Children's Childhood Studies* (pp. 617–42). London: Palgrave Macmillan.

Seligman, M. and Darling, R.B. (2017) *Ordinary Families, Special Children: A Systems Approach to Disability* (3rd edn). London: Guilford Press.

Sen, A.S. (2018) How the school-choice paradigm subverts equal education for students with disabilities, *New York University Public Law and Legal Theory Working Papers*, 593. Available at: http://lsr.nellco. org/nyu_plltwp/593

Sen, R. and Broadhurst, K. (2011) Contact between children in out-of-home placements and their family and friends networks: a research review, *Child & Family Social Work*, 16(2): 298–309.

Shakespeare, T. (1994) Cultural representation of disabled people: dustbins for disavowal?, *Disability & Society*, 9(3): 283–99.

Shakespeare, T. (2006) *Disability Rights and Wrongs*. London: RoutledgeFalmer.

Shama, K. (2002) Attitudinal changes: breaking the psycho-social barriers, *Journal of Indian Education*, 27(4): 85–89.

Sharma, U. and Deppeler, J. (2005) Integrated education in India: challenges and prospects, *Disability Studies Quarterly*, 25(1). Available at: www.dsq-sds.org/article/view/524/701

Sheligevich-Urban, D. (2011) *Integration of Disabled Child in a Social Environment*. Available at: http:// archive.kharkiv.org/View/26556/

Singal, N. (2005) Mapping the field of inclusive education: a review of the Indian literature, *International Journal of Inclusive Education*, 9(4): 331–50.

Singal, N. (2006a) Inclusive education in India: international concept, national interpretation, *International Journal of Disability, Development and Education*, 53(3): 351–69.

Singal, N. (2006b) Adopting an ecosystemic approach for understanding inclusive education: an Indian case study, *European Journal of Psychology of Education: Special Issue*, 'Inclusive Education ten years after Salamanca', 21(3): 239–52.

Singal, N. and Rouse, M. (2003) 'We do inclusion': practitioner perspectives in some 'Inclusive Schools' in India, *Perspectives in Education [Special Issue: The Inclusion/Exclusion Debate in South Africa and Developing Countries]*, 21(3): 85–98.

Singh, Y.P. and Agarwal, A. (2015) *Problems and Prospects of Inclusive Education in India*. Proceeding of the 3rd Global Summit on Education GSE 2015 (e-ISBN 978-967-0792-01-1), 9–10 March, Kuala Lumpur, Malaysia.

Siperstein, G.N. and Gottlieb, J. (1997) Physical stigma and academic performance as factors affecting children's first impressions of handicapped peers, *American Journal of Mental Deficiency*, 81: 455–62.

Skarstad, K. and Stein, A. (2017) Mainstreaming disability in the United Nations treaty bodies, *Journal of Human Rights*, 17(1): 1–24.

Skidmore, D. (1996) Towards an integrated theoretical framework for research in special educational needs, *European Journal of Special Needs Education*, 11(1): 33–42.

Slee, R. (1998) 'The Politics of Theorising Special Education'. In C. Clarke, A. Dyson and A. Millward (eds), *Theorising Special Education* (2nd edn). London: Routledge.

Slee, R. and Allan, J. (2005) 'Excluding the Included'. In J. Rix, K. Simmons, M. Nind and K. Sheehy (eds), *Policy and Power in Inclusive Education: Values into Practice*. London: RoutledgeFalmer.

Slonje, R., Smith, P.K. and Frisén, A. (2013) The nature of cyberbullying, and strategies for prevention, *Computers in Human Behavior*, 29: 26–32.

Sloper, P. (2004) 'Facilitators and barriers for co-ordinated multi-agency services', *Child Care, Health and Development*, 30(6): 571–580.

Smith, A. and Thomas, N. (2006) Including pupils with special educational needs and disabilities in National Curriculum Physical Education: a brief review, *European Journal of Special Needs in Education*, 21(1): 69–83.

Smith, M. (2006) 'Teachers Urge Rethink on Inclusion Policy', cited in A. Smith, *Education Guardian.co.uk*, 13 July.

Snyder, L., Garriot, P. and Aylor, M. (2001) Inclusion confusion: putting the pieces together, *Teacher Education and Special Education*, 24 (3): 198–207.

Soan, S. (2005) *Primary Special Educational Needs*. Exeter: Learning Matters.

Spaling, E. (2002) Social acceptance at senior high school, *International Journal of Special Education*, 17(1): 91–100.

Spikins, P. (2014) *The Stone Age Origins of Autism*. Available at: www.intechopen.com/books/recent-advances-in-autism-spectrum-disorders-volume-ii/the-stone-age-origins-of-autism

Srivastava, M., De Boer, A. and Pijl, S.P. (2013) *Inclusive Education in Developing Countries: A Closer Look at its Implementation in the Last 10 Years*. E Danuta Sheligevich: Urban.

Starczewska, A., Hodkinson, A. and Adams, G. (2012) Conceptions of inclusion and inclusive education: a critical examination of the perspectives and practices of teachers in Poland, *Journal of Research in Special Educational Needs*, 12(3): 162–69.

Starczewska, A., Hodkinson, A. and Adams, G. (2014) 'Special Education in Poland'. In C.R. Reynolds, K.J. Vannest and E. Fletcher-Janzen (eds), *Encyclopaedia of Special Education: A Reference for the Education of Children, Adolescents, and Adults with Disabilities and Other Exceptional Individuals* (4th edn). Hoboken, NJ: Wiley.

Stone, B. and Foley, P. (2014) 'Towards Integrated Working'. In P. Foley and A. Rixon (eds), *Changing Children's Services: Working and Learning Together* (2nd edn). Bristol: Policy Press.

Stothers, G. (2008) 'I hate Tiny Tim'. Available at: http://mainstream-mag.com/tinytim.html

Strogilos, V. and Tragoulia, E. (2013) Inclusive and collaborative practices in co-taught classrooms: roles and responsibilities for teachers and parents, *Teaching and Teacher Education*, 35: 81–91.

Sturt, G. (2007) *Special Educational Needs*. Available at: www.garysturt.free-online.eo.uk/Special%20 Educational%20Needs.htm

Subramanian, M. (2014) *Bullying: The Ultimate Teen Guide*. Plymouth: Rowman and Littlefield.

Swain, J. and French, S. (2000) Towards an affirmation model of disability, *Disability & Society*, 15(4): 569–82.

Swain, J. and French, S. (2004) 'Whose Tragedy? Towards a Personal Non-tragedy View of Disability'. In J. Swain, S. French, C. Barnes and C. Thomas (eds), *Disabling Barriers: Enabling Environments*. London: Sage.

Tar, J. (2014) 'Education'. In J. Thomas, K. Pollard and D. Sellman (eds), *Interprofessional Working in Health and Social Care: Professional Perspectives*. London: Palgrave Macmillan.

Terzi, L. (2005) Beyond the dilemma of difference: the capability approach to disability and special educational needs, *Journal of Philosophy of Education*, 19(3): 443–59.

Terzi, L. (2010) *Justice and Equality in Education: A Capability Perspective on Disability and Special Educational Needs*. London: Continuum.

Thomas, G. (1996) *Teaching Students with Mental Retardation: A Life Goals Planning Curriculum*. Englewood Cliffs, NJ: Merril.

Thomas, G. and Loxley, A. (2001) *Deconstructing Special Education and Constructing Inclusion*. Buckingham: OUP.

Thomas, G. and Loxley, A. (2007) *Deconstructing Special Education and Constructing Inclusion* (2nd edn). Buckingham: OUP.

Thomas, G., Walker, D. and Webb, J. (2005) 'Inclusive Education'. In K. Topping and S. Maloney (eds), *The Routledge Falmer Reader in Inclusive Education*. London: RoutledgeFalmer.

Thomazet, S. (2009) From integration to inclusive education: does changing the terms improve practice?, *International Journal of Inclusive Education*, 13(6): 553–63.

Timmons, V. (2002) International perspectives on inclusion: concluding thoughts, *Exceptionality Education*, 12(2): 187–92.

Tiwari, A., Das, A. and Sharma, M. (2015) Inclusive education a 'rhetoric' or 'reality'? Teachers' perspectives and beliefs, *Teaching and Teacher Education*, 52: 128–36.

Tod, J. (2002) 'Enabling Inclusion for Individuals'. In T. O'Brien (ed.), *Enabling Inclusion: Blue Skies ... Dark Clouds*. London: Optimus.

Townsen, M.A.R., Wilton, K.M. and Vakilirad, T. (1993) Children's attitudes towards peers with intellectual disability, *Disability & Society*, 37: 405–11.

Townsley, R. and Robinson, C. (2000) *Food for Thought: Effective Support for Families Caring for a Child who is Tube Fed*. Bristol: Norah Fry Research Centre.

Troung, Y. and Ellam, H. (2013) *Educational Workforce Survey 2013*. Available at: http://dera.ioe. ac.uk/19840/

United Nations (2006) *Convention on the Rights of Persons with Disabilities*. Available at: www.un.org/ disabilities/defau It.asp?id=259

United Nations Children's Fund (UNICEF) (2003) *Examples of Inclusive Education: India*. Regional Office for South Asia. Kathmandu, Nepal: UNICEF.

United Nations Children's Fund (UNICEF) (2007) *Human Rights-Based Approach to Education for All: A Framework for the Realization of Children's Right to Education and Rights Within Education*. New York: UNESCO.

United Nations Educational Scientific and Cultural Organization (UNESCO) (1994) *The Salamanca Statement and Framework for Action on Special Needs Education*. Available at: www.unesco.org/ education/pdf/SALAMA_E.PDF

United Nations Educational Scientific and Cultural Organisation (UNESCO) (2004) Available at: http://portal. unesco.org/education/en/ev.php-URL_ID=28705&URL_DO=DO_TOPIC&URL_SECTION= 201.html

United States Department of Education (2005) *Twenty-Fifth Annual Report to Congress on the Implementation of the Individuals with Disabilities Education Act*. Available at: www.ed.gov/about/ reports/annual/osep/2003/index.html

Union of the Physically Impaired Against Segregation (UPIAS) (1976) *Fundamental Principles of Disability*. London: UPIAS.

US Census Bureau (2014) *State and Other Areas Excluding the USE Minor Outlying Islands*. Available at: http://www.census.gov/en.html

Vanhala, L. (2010) *Making Rights a Reality? Disability Rights Activists and Legal Mobilisation*. Cambridge: Cambridge University Press.

Vickerman, P. (2007) *Including Children with Special Educational Needs in Physical Education*. London: Routledge.

Wade, D.T. and Halligan, P.W. (2017) The biopsychosocial model of illness: a model whose time has come, *Clinical Rehabilitation*, 31(8): 995–1004.

Wadham, J., Ruebain, D., Robinson, A. and Uppal, S. (eds) (2012) *Blackstone's Guide to the Equality Act 2010*. Oxford: Oxford University Press.

Wapiennik, E. (2005) *Rights of People with Intellectual Disabilities: Access to Education and Employment*. Warszawa, Poland: Open Society Institute.

Warnock, M. (1999) 'If Only We had Known Then', *Times Educational Supplement*, 31 December.

Warnock, M. (2005) *Special Educational Needs: A New Look*. London: Philosophy of Education Society of Great Britain.

Watson, D., Townsley, R., Abbott, D. and Latham, P. (2002) *Working Together? Multi-agency Working in Services to Disabled Children with Complex Health Care Needs and their Families: A Literature Review*. Birmingham: Handsel Trust.

Wearmouth, J. (2001) 'Introduction'. In J. Wearmouth (ed.), *Special Educational Provision in the Context of Inclusion: Policy and Practice in Schools*. London: Fulton.

Wearmouth, J. (2017) *Special Educational Needs and Disabilities in Schools: A Critical Introduction*. London: Bloomsbury.

Weinberg, N. (1978) Preschool children's perceptions of orthopedic disability, *Rehabilitation Counselling Bulletin*, 21(3): 183–89.

Weiserbs, B. and Gottlieb, J. (2000) The effect of perceived duration of physical disability on attitudes of schoolchildren towards friendship and helping, *Journal of Psychology*, 134: 343–45.

Welsh Assembly Government (2006) *Children and Young People: Rights to Action Safeguarding Children: Working Together Under the Children Act 2004*. Available at: www.conwy.gov.uk/upload/ public/attachments/328/safeguarding_children__english.pdf

Whittaker, K.A., Cox, P., Thomas, N. and Cocker, K. (2014) A qualitative study of parents' experiences using family support services: applying the concept of surface and depth, *Health & Social Care in the Community*, 22(5): 479–87.

Wilde, A. (2018) *Film, Comedy, and Disability: Understanding Humour and Genre in Cinematic Constructions of Impairment and Disability*. London: Routledge.

Williams, C. (2005) Old Liverpool. Available at: www.old liverpool.co.uk/Blind.html (accessed 16 February 2008).

Williams-Findlay, R. (2013) 'The Representation of Disabled People in the News Media'. In J. Swain, S. French, C. Barnes and C. Thomas (eds), *Disabling Barriers, Enabling Environments* (3rd edn). London: Sage.

Wilson, M.C. and Scior, K. (2014) Attitudes towards individuals with disabilities as measured by the Implicit Association Test: a literature review, *Research in Developmental Disabilities*, 35(2): 294–321.

Winnick, J. (ed.) (2005) *Adapted Physical Education and Sport* (4th edn). Champaign, IL: Human Kinetics.

Wood, K. (2004) *International Perspectives: The USA and the Pacific Rim*. Self-assessment of relationships with peers in children with intellectual disability, *Journal of Intellectual Disability Research*, 45(3): 202–11.

Wood, P. (1980) (WHO) *International Classification of Impairments, Disability and Handicaps*. Geneva: World Health Organization.

Wright-Southwell, W. (2013) 'Past Perspectives: What Can Archaeology Offer Disability Studies?' In M. Wappett and K. Arndt (eds), *Emerging Perspectives on Disability Studies*. London: Palgrave Macmillan.

Zic, S. and Igri, L. (2001) Self-assessment of relationships with peers in children with intellectual disability, *Journal of Intellectual Disability Research*, 45(3): 202–11.

INDEX